Liberating Conscience

Liberating Conscience

FEMINIST EXPLORATIONS
IN CATHOLIC MORAL THEOLOGY

ANNE E. PATRICK

Continuum • New York

1997
The Continuum Publishing Company
370 Lexington Avenue, New York, NY 10017

Printed in the United States of America

Library of Congress Cataloging-in-Publication Data

Patrick, Anne E.
    Liberating conscience : feminist explorations in Catholic moral
    theology / Anne E. Patrick.
        p.   cm.
    Includes bibliographical references and index.
    ISBN 0-8264-1051-0 pbk
    1. Christian ethics — Catholic authors. 2. Feminist ethics.
    3. Conscience. I. Title.
    BJ1249.P325   1996
    241'.042'082—dc20   96-6125
                                                              CIP

To my parents,
Estelle Flynn Patrick
and
William Davis Patrick

Who celebrated the blessings
of a family of six daughters
and taught us the meaning of
love that seeks justice.

Contents

Preface

By the time these explorations have reached the reader, a millennial renewal may have swept the Catholic landscape and rendered them obsolete. The wisdom of magisterial teachings on race, peace, and economic justice may have been taken to heart by the faithful. The crusading absolutism associated with late-twentieth-century opposition to abortion and euthanasia may have modulated into more effective forms of leadership on behalf of suffering and endangered persons. The moral energy of Catholics may at last have burst open the casing of dutiful individualism and blossomed into a socially conscious responsibility that is transforming unjust patterns and systems on a global scale.

If this were the case, how would we know? Can we imagine what such a renewal might mean for our world? For a moment, let us dream:

Through the eyes of the imagination we can see promising developments everywhere. Not only are abortion rates dramatically lower, but so are instances of rape, domestic violence, and urban homicide. Infant mortality statistics have never been so low, and they are expected to be equal across the globe within the decade. No child has died for want of food or routine vaccinations since the mid-1990s. These improvements in health, together with economic growth in the developing world, have led to the stabilization of the world's population at six billion. New uses have been found for tobacco and coca leaves, and instances of lung cancer and drug addiction have become so rare that medical students rely on video tapes to observe their symptoms.

A mysterious and transforming hope for the future has taken hold among the world's peoples, and energies formerly devoted to militarism are now focused on care of the earth and its creatures. The ozone layer is replenished, the rain forests are replacing themselves, and air quality in Mexico City is as fine today as it was two centuries ago. Drinking water is as pure in São Paulo and Lagos as it is in Stockholm and Palm Springs.

There remain illness, instances of greed and violence, and other reminders that human beings are finite and morally fragile, but even the most skeptical recognize that a corner has been turned in the way we are managing our situation. Some credit the serious ecumenical and interfaith respect that took root after the atrocities of World War II. Others thank the secular leaders who transcended nationalism and inspired new ways of ordering economic activity more equitably and with a much lighter ecological footprint. Still others thank the women's movement for changing the way so many issues were approached. And many see in these and other influences for good the power of God's Spirit alive in our hearts, renewing the face of the earth.

* * * * *

If Catholics are to help make this futuristic vision a reality, we must grow to new levels of confidence and competence as moral agents. Our consciences must be freed from all that inhibits a generous response to the ethical challenges we face. Our moral tradition offers many resources for the conversion that is required, but this tradition itself still needs to integrate theological affirmations of women's full human dignity into its official moral teachings and ecclesiastical practices.

This book is offered as a contribution toward closing the gap between present realities and a hoped-for future of justice, peace, and ecological responsibility. It has been written with much support and assistance from others. I thank especially the Patrick and Flynn clans and the Sisters of the Holy Names, who have provided nurturing contexts for my life and work. Faculty development grants and sabbatical leaves from Carleton College, along with encouragement from students and colleagues, have supported my research and writing. This writing has been facilitated also by time spent at several very special places: the Studium of the Benedictine women's community in St. Joseph, Minnesota; Norcroft, a writing retreat on the north shore of Lake Superior supported by the Harmony Women's Fund; Mount Saint Agnes Theological Center for Women in Baltimore, Maryland; and the Institute for Ecumenical and Cultural Research in Collegeville, Minnesota. A semester as Warren Professor at the University of Tulsa in 1989 provided the occasion for launching this project, as well as for receiving invaluable advice and encouragement from the late John Carmody and his spouse, Denise Lardner Carmody. My editor, Frank Oveis, formerly with Crossroad and now Publishing Director of the Continuum Group, has been a steady source of support over these several years, as has friend and systematic theologian Anne E. Carr, whose careful reading of the chapters as they developed led to significant improvements of substance and style. More recently, Russell B. Connors has read the entire manuscript and made helpful suggestions from the perspective of moral theology.

It is impossible to list by name all the others who read portions of this work and offered advice and encouragement, but a number of persons were involved to an outstanding degree: Avis Allmaras, Lucy Arimond, Mary Bertoli, Mara Faulkner, Ed Flahavan, Clare S. Foley, Mike Foley, Ranae Hanan, Nancy Hynes, Ephrem Hollermann, Theresa King, Mary Kaye Medinger, Rick Mertz, Maureen O'Connor, Anita Pampusch, Virginia Pharr, Clare Rossini, Carol A. Tauer, Joan Timmerman, and Janet R. Walton. In addition, several of the individuals whose positions are discussed read early drafts of relevant sections and provided helpful responses, particularly Lisa Sowle Cahill, M. Shawn Copeland, Charles E. Curran, Margaret A. Farley, Ada María Isasi-Díaz, Bryan Massingale, Judith A. Vaughn, and Ann Patrick Ware. My debt of gratitude to them and to all who assisted in any way remains substantial.

Along with this great debt of gratitude there is also a debt of justice I want to acknowledge here. Justice is owed to the Dakota people, who in the early 1860s suffered starvation, war, and exile from the southern Minnesota lands near or including those that eventually became available to the Congregationalists who founded Carleton College in Rice County in 1866, and to my immigrant ancestors of the Flynn and Farrell families, who settled in Murray County in the 1870s. Justice is owed to the enslaved African peoples whose suffering and labor on the eastern seaboard contributed to the economic climate entered by my Patrick and Corbin ancestors when they crossed the Atlantic more than two centuries ago. And justice is owed to many others, living and dead.

Introduction:
The Nakedness of Noah

To begin these feminist explorations in Catholic moral theology, consider one of the earliest images of patriarchy supplied by the tradition. The image is from a narrative in the ninth chapter of Genesis, immediately after the story of the Great Flood and God's covenant with Noah. In the *New American Bible* the episode is called "Noah and His Sons":

> Now Noah, a man of the soil, was the first to plant a vineyard. When he drank some of the wine, he became drunk and lay naked inside his tent. Ham, the father of Canaan, saw his father's nakedness, and he told his two brothers outside about it. Shem and Japheth, however, took a robe, and holding it on their backs, they walked backward and covered their father's nakedness; since their faces were turned the other way, they did not see their father's nakedness. When Noah woke up from his drunkenness and learned what his youngest son had done to him, he said: "Cursed be Canaan! The lowest of slaves shall he be to his brothers." He also said: "Blessed be the LORD, the God of Shem! Let Canaan be his slave. May God expand Japheth, so that he dwells among the tents of Shem; and let Canaan be his slave." (Genesis 9:18–27)

The text carries overtones of violence—not the bloody violence of the earlier "man of the soil," Cain, but the *violencia blanca* of domination. Drunken, raging, cursing, controlling . . . hardly the patriarch's finest hour. Nor does the learned footnote cautioning readers not to take this story literally undo the harm it has legitimated in Christian history. The footnote reads:

> This story seems to be a composite of two earlier accounts; in the one, Ham was guilty, whereas in the other, it was Canaan. One purpose of the story is to justify the Israelites' enslavement of the Canaanites because of certain indecent sexual practices in the Canaanite religion. Obviously the story offers no justifi-

cation for enslaving African Negroes, even though Canaan is presented as a "son" of Ham because the land of Canaan belonged to Hamitic Egypt at the time of the Israelite invasion.[1]

"Obviously to whom?" is the first question the note suggests to me. Not to those colonizers of the sixteenth through nineteenth centuries, who used such biblical stories to rationalize mistreatment of Native American and African peoples, among others. Not to contemporary racists and homophobes, who still believe there is biblical warrant for discriminating against groups presumed to have been cursed by God.

At the very least this story invites reinterpretation. For one thing, the tale omits entirely the perspective of the nameless one who bore Ham and Shem and Japheth, who may well have been down at the stream washing Noah's robe at the time of the incident. Can we imagine her reaction to Noah's pique about who has seen his nakedness? Does the question even occur to us? It is not accidental that Catholics have rarely asked such questions of biblical stories, for a worldview that regards male experience as normative has conditioned the way we interpret our tradition.

Noah's spouse is absent from this story, as she was from the earlier story of the covenant. It is impossible to regain her perspective at this late date, but we can honor her memory by bringing contemporary wisdom to bear on the classical text. We can note, for example, that the narrative establishing the rainbow as a sign of God's fidelity also sets the tone for much of the biblical understanding of moral responsibility, particularly where violence and sexuality are concerned. Genesis 9:6 has been used to justify war and capital punishment: "If anyone sheds the blood of man, by man shall his blood be shed." And verse 7 has reinforced a procreationist emphasis in sexual ethics and legitimated a certain lack of respect for the earth that people today have cause to question: "Be fertile, then, and multiply; abound on earth and subdue it."

My point here is not to dismiss the biblical and classical Christian traditions for being limited in ways we have only lately begun to notice. Much less is it to imply that Christianity has superseded Judaism on these matters, which is clearly not the case. Instead, I seek to go beyond the critical stage and invite this text to speak some of the truth it has for us today, approaching its symbolism with the sort of attitude the contemporary hermeneutical philosopher Paul Ricoeur has termed "second naïveté."[2] Long before Ricoeur, of

---

1. *The New American Bible* (New York: Benziger, 1970), p. 14. Unless otherwise noted, subsequent biblical passages in this volume are from the 1991 edition of the NAB.

2. Paul Ricoeur, *The Symbolism of Evil* (Boston: Beacon, 1967), p. 351.

course, thinkers such as Origen and Augustine also encouraged symbolic readings of such stories. Although I differ profoundly with some aspects of their thought, I see myself in continuity with these ancient Christian thinkers as I let the story of "The Nakedness of Noah" play across the field of my late-twentieth-century consciousness. To me the story is above all about the unjust system of domination and subordination I have learned to name "patriarchy." Patriarchy literally means "father-rule"; here I am using the term in a more specialized ethical sense to designate social patterns and structures of domination and subordination, especially (but not exclusively) those flowing from and contributing to attitudes that do not respect the full humanity of females.[3] Among the other patterns of domination and subordination associated with patriarchy are racism and classism, both of which compound the injustices suffered by many women.

In this reading, Noah symbolizes male authoritarianism, indeed male addiction to the power of dominating others. "Inebriated with power," is a phrase that says it well. The nakedness here represents the ordinary, limited, and messy embodiedness, and especially the vulnerable sexuality, of the patriarchal authority figure, which must be covered up and denied at all costs. And the angry response to being seen in his finitude typifies the ethic of control

---

3. Various feminist theorists distinguish "patriarchy" and other key terms in slightly different ways, but there is basic agreement that bias against females has both social-systemic and intellectual-attitudinal components. For example, historian Gerda Lerner places central emphasis on the concept of "patriarchy" in *The Creation of Patriarchy* (New York: Oxford University Press, 1986) and *The Creation of Feminist Consciousness* (New York: Oxford University Press, 1993). In the latter work she observes that patriarchy depends on mistaken assumptions about gender, which "constructed the male as the norm and the female as deviant; the male as whole and powerful; the female as unfinished, physically mutilated and emotionally dependent" (p. 3). Theologian Elizabeth A. Johnson, by contrast, places central attention on the category of "sexism" in *She Who Is* (New York: Crossroad, 1992) and *Women, Earth, and Creator Spirit* (New York: Paulist, 1993). In *She Who Is* Johnson characterizes sexism as a "social sin that has debilitating effects on women both socially and psychologically, and interlocks with other forms of oppression to shape a violent and dehumanized world." Its "twin faces" are "patriarchy" and "androcentrism" (p. 22). Her 1993 book stresses that sexism and its social and intellectual manifestations are all rooted in hierarchical dualistic thinking. The emphasis of these two authors is slightly different, but their analyses are both convincing and compatible. More recently Elisabeth Schüssler Fiorenza has proposed that "kyriarchy" (related to the German *Herr-schaft*) replace "patriarchy" for analysis of injustice in Western contexts, because this term is less likely to be limited to associations with gender injustice, and thus has more potential to be understood as inclusive of racism and classism. See her *Jesus: Miriam's Child, Sophia's Prophet* (New York: Continuum, 1994), p. 14.

that patriarchy identifies with moral responsibility.[4] "How dare you see what is there to be seen? How dare you talk honestly with your brothers about my weakness and limitations? If you want to enjoy power like mine, you will respect my absolute authority by denying what you see and feel."

Now imagine the voice of Ham's mother, whom I shall call Ruah, interrupting the curse in mid-sentence. "Noah, be still. Remember the God who gave us our lives and the lives of all our children, including the daughters you so easily forget. God saw both of us naked in this tent, and blessed our love with delight and with children—children, with eyes to see and tongues to tell. Who are you to punish them for being themselves? If you feel offended by Ham, a word from you will earn an apology for the harm he did not intend, and you will both feel better for the embrace you need from each other. Call him, and when you've talked, join me in the stream for a while. When we're done your robe will be dry and you can enjoy yourself tonight when we host the children and grandchildren for dinner. And why don't we save what's left of the wine for another occasion? It's meant to gladden the heart, not deaden the pain or drown out the truth. A little now and then goes a long way, but not on top of a hangover. Well, here comes Ham now. I'll leave you two alone. But don't be long. I'll be waiting for you in the stream!"

* * * * *

No meditation exhausts a powerful text, and before leaving the image of Noah's embarrassment I believe something more should be said. The alternative ending of my midrash (or symbolic retelling of the biblical story) represents a goal of fuller honesty and mutuality in human relationships, which is worth striving for in the Catholic Church and in the world beyond the church. This being the case, I must also add that the "happy ending" cannot happen if the *causes* of the original ending are not both probed and remedied. It is not enough for the contemporary feminist to identify the problem as the patriarch's behavior being "drunken, raging, cursing, and controlling." For one thing, it would be a mistake to leave the impression that any woman married to Noah would have offered the sort of wisdom that my imaginary character did on this occasion. There is nothing in "women's nature" to prevent us from being drunken, raging, cursing, and controlling ourselves, though manifestations of these behaviors may vary according to the sorts of power we

4. Sharon D. Welch develops this point in *A Feminist Ethic of Risk* (Minneapolis: Fortress, 1990).

enjoy. Nor is there anything in "men's nature" to prevent them from thinking and acting like Ruah. To put matters directly: Noah's maleness did not cause his behavior, nor did her femaleness cause Ruah's. Of course, socially constructed gender does influence behavior, but human beings created in God's image have some freedom to decide how we will think and behave, a fact that has given rise to the realm called ethics or morality in the first place.

Recognizing that maleness itself is not the problem, nor femaleness itself the solution, we must press further in our analysis. Why did Noah behave as he did? The original drunkenness seems not to have been deliberate, for the story suggests the patriarch was simply enjoying the fruits of his first grape harvest. He is, after all, the one who saved this family from destruction in the flood; he's earned their gratitude and respect; let's not judge one instance of unintentional drunkenness too harshly. Instead, let's try to imagine how such a responsible patriarch would feel upon waking up naked with a hangover. My sense is that two feelings would predominate: shame for having let things get so out of hand and fear of what else might happen if he does not regain control immediately. These are not pleasant feelings, nor are they easy to articulate if one is a patriarch in a patriarchal culture. This is why we see so much raging, cursing, and controlling. But the Ruahs among us, male and female alike, are on to a different possibility. They believe that a better response to finding ourselves in a mess partly of our own making is to acknowledge what we see and feel, and trust that our experience has something good to teach us. Divine mercy is always ahead of our limitations, ready to clothe us again and again in fresh garments.

* * * * *

The present book seeks to do some of the theological work that is required for a happier version of the Noah story to become more widely experienced in the Catholic Church. Both my midrash and my allegorical interpretation are, of course, limited by my own angle of vision, as will be the case also with the less poetic material that follows. My hope in offering this work is that readers will test what is said in light of their own knowledge and experience, and carry the reflection on *Liberating Conscience* to a stage beyond that which I have reached.

In the following pages, I shall focus on the concept of "conscience," a term that has fascinated me for decades. The intriguing questions include the following: From what and for what does conscience need liberating? What would it mean to have a conscience that contributes to the gospel-inspired movements for liberation and justice of our time? My use of the concept of liberation refers to the deeply relational freedom of the daughters and sons of God and not to the isolated autonomy of secular liberalism. I understand this project to be part of a complex, collaborative effort to reinterpret the Christian faith and its implications for life that goes by the designation "theologies of liberation." Within this large category, my work reflects the feminist-liberationist perspective, and has been conducted with increasing awareness of my participation in entrenched systems of injustice, particularly the racial and economic injustices that have allowed me as a white North American woman to have much greater access to educational and material advantages than most women of my generation.

Many authors have discussed the connections between feminist theology and other forms of liberation theology. Early and influential examples of Catholic arguments for an explicitly liberationist feminism were Rosemary Radford Ruether's 1972 volume *Liberation Theology* and Elisabeth Schüssler Fiorenza's 1975 article "Feminist Theology as a Critical Theology of Liberation."[5] In 1988 Anne E. Carr described the task of feminist theology in terms of an effort "to correlate the central and liberating themes of biblical and Christian tradition with the experience of women in the contemporary situation."[6] A recurrent theme in this literature, one voiced increasingly in recent years, is that of the complexity and diversity of women's experience. This recognition has led some thinkers to prefer to speak in the plural of "feminist theologies."

Moreover, to offset the dominance of European and European-American women theologians, women of other backgrounds have in many cases come to call their theological efforts by names other than "feminist," including "womanist" (African-American), "*mujerista*" (Hispanic), and "*minjung*" (Korean).[7] At the same time, others have retained the term "feminist" because

---

5. Rosemary Radford Ruether, *Liberation Theology* (New York: Paulist, 1972); Elisabeth Schüssler Fiorenza, "Feminist Theology as a Critical Theology of Liberation," *Theological Studies* 36 (1975): 605–26. Ruether analyzes several types of secular and religious feminism in *Sexism and God Talk* (Boston: Beacon, 1983), where she also develops her own anti-dualistic, liberationist ideas on various topics in systematic theology.

6. Anne E. Carr, *Transforming Grace: Christian Tradition and Women's Experience* (San Francisco: Harper, 1988), p. 9.

7. For influential examples of these approaches, see Delores S. Williams, *Sisters in the Wilderness: The Challenge of Womanist God-Talk* (Maryknoll, N.Y.: Orbis, 1993); Ada María Isasi-Díaz and Yolanda Tarango, *Hispanic Women: Prophetic Voice in the Church* (San Francisco:

it is still used more generally by theologians outside the United States as well as by scholars in other disciplines both here and abroad. The diversification reflects the value of self-assertion (as theologian Ada María Isasi-Díaz has observed, "To name oneself is one of the most powerful acts that any human person can do") as well as a judgment that white women's feminism has yet to transcend its historic racism and live up to the ideals of inclusive justice its more thoughtful advocates have been articulating in the last few decades.[8] The diversification has on the whole increased the visibility of theological contributions by women of color, despite some continuing risk of marginalization.

However they are catalogued, these contributions have taught me much about the limits of my experience as a white U.S. woman. They have also deepened my desire to strive toward a form of "feminism" (perhaps yet to be named) that would be authentically pluralistic. The philosopher María C. Lugones has demonstrated that disclaimers about one's background and generalizations about "difference" do not suffice for reaching authentic pluralism; what is needed is commitment to genuinely interactive theorizing, which requires openness to continual learning and change.[9] At present the feminist-womanist-*mujerista* discussion among Catholic theologians is at a very early stage; I hope this volume will advance it to some degree, for the benefit of all the communities involved.

"Feminist" is indeed a term with many meanings; I use it here in a broad sense to indicate a position that involves (1) a solid conviction of the equality of women and men, and (2) a commitment to reform society so that the full equality of women is respected, which requires also reforming the thought systems that legitimate the present unjust social order. I hope it is clear that my analysis does not see males as such as "the problem." On the contrary, I presume that men and women both suffer under the injustices of patriarchy, although in different ways and to different degrees. The goal of the feminism I support has been stated well by theologian Elizabeth Johnson:

Harper & Row, 1988); and Hyun Kyung Chung, *Struggle to be Sun Again: Introducing Asian Women's Theology* (Maryknoll, N.Y.: Orbis, 1990).

8. Ada María Isasi-Díaz, "*Mujeristas:* A Name of Our Own," in *Yearning to Breathe Free: Liberation Theologies in the U.S.,* ed. Mar Peter-Raoul, Linda Rennie Forcey, and Robert Frederick Hunter, Jr. (Maryknoll, N.Y.: Orbis, 1990), p. 121.

9. María C. Lugones, "On the Logic of Pluralist Feminism," in *Feminist Ethics,* ed. Claudia Card (Lawrence: University Press of Kansas, 1991), pp. 35–44. See also Elizabeth V. Spelman, *Inessential Woman: Problems of Exclusion in Feminist Thought* (Boston: Beacon, 1988).

What Christian feminism hopes for is a transformed community. Cooperating with the Spirit of life, feminism hopes so to change unjust structures and distorted symbol systems that a new community in church and society becomes possible, a liberating community of all women and men characterized by mutuality with each other, care for the weakest and least powerful among them, and harmony with the earth.[10]

I would like to see increasing numbers of both sexes claim this ethical stance, for not to do so is to be complicit with its opposite, namely, sexism.[11]

Because of this commitment to an ideal of freedom-in-justice and mutuality, my book seeks to connect two things that many people regard as unrelated: *conscience and community.* The stereotype about conscience is that it is personal and private. When conscience is exercised it seems to be a matter of the rugged individual facing into the prevailing winds of conventional opinion and standing up for what one thinks (all by oneself) is good and right—enduring the loneliness of the long-distance moral runner, we might say.

There is some truth in the stereotype. When we think of conscience we think of "conscientious objectors," of people who follow their personal sense of obligation when no one else seems to understand why they are doing it. We

10. Elizabeth A. Johnson, "Feminism and Sharing the Faith: A Catholic Dilemma" (Tulsa: University of Tulsa Warren Center for Catholic Studies, 1994), p. 6. There are many definitions and types of feminism, with considerable overlapping among them, not to mention controversy about the meanings and normative implications of the various types. One crucial distinction should be noted: some definitions emphasize the participation of women as *subjects* of their own liberative process against the injustice of sexism, while others emphasize the fact that human beings of both sexes are capable of recognizing and seeking to remedy it. The definition I use here is of the latter sort, which can be called "inclusive feminism." An example of the former, which I designate "women-centered feminism," is Gerda Lerner's definition of feminist consciousness as "the awareness of women that they belong to a subordinate group; that they have suffered wrongs as a group; that their condition of subordination is not natural, but is societally determined; that they must join with other women to remedy these wrongs; and finally, that they must and can provide an alternate vision of social organization in which women as well as men will enjoy autonomy and self-determination" (*Creation of Feminist Consciousness,* p. 14). I do not believe Lerner means by this definition to exclude men from sharing in the alternate vision or working toward its social realization, but her definition recognizes that there is indeed a difference between being the *subject* of a liberative process and participating empathetically in such a movement when one does not suffer the precise injustice oneself.

11. For a succinct discussion of the dialectical relationship between "sexism" and "feminism," see Patricia Beattie Jung, "Give Her Justice," *America* 150 (April 14, 1984): 276–78. Feminists, of course, differ widely in their analyses of injustice, levels of commitment to liberating action, degrees of explicitness of commitment, and opinions regarding specific problems and their solutions.

recall St. Thomas More, who was executed because he refused to take an oath that others in sixteenth-century England thought reasonable enough. Or, closer to our own times, we remember Franz Jägerstätter, the Austrian farmer who died rather than serve in Hitler's army during World War II. The words playwright Robert Bolt attributes to More in *A Man for All Seasons* seem applicable to both of these martyrs of conscience and to countless others who have paid a great price for holding to their convictions: "In matters of conscience, the loyal subject is more bounden to be loyal to his conscience than to any other thing."[12] These words ring true, although the masculine pronoun, which must be forgiven a sixteenth-century saint, clinks a bit at the close of this millennium. And the clinking yields a question: Where are the *women* of moral innovation and courage in our tradition? When will we honor and learn from females whose ethical judgments differed from those of most of their contemporaries, including priests and bishops? Is there a hidden tradition of moral wisdom that has yet to be made available, perhaps because its conclusions have seemed too abhorrent to the males who defined good actions and good traits of character in the official literature of moral theology?

But there is St. Joan of Arc to consider, is there not? Wasn't she cut from the same brave cloth as More and Jägerstätter? Wasn't she a martyr of conscience too? Maybe so, although we would not know this from the stories we have heard. A crucial difference between Joan and the male martyrs is that her human powers of thought and judgment are replaced in the popular imagination with the divine influence of her "voices and visions." Whatever the nature of her mystical experiences, the dominant interpretation of Joan has made her essentially into one more outstanding example of obedience; the innovations of her life are credited to God, not to her human decisions. In this respect she is premodern and mythical, in contrast to the modern and historical male saints of conscience. Joan is remembered for obeying unusual expressions of "God's will," and not for the intelligence, imagination, love, and courage she brought to the choices of her life.

A recent study by Anne Llewellyn Barstow, *Joan of Arc: Heretic, Mystic, Shaman,* complicates this picture, however. Barstow, a social historian, cuts through the legendary interpretations and looks at this woman in the context

---

12. Robert Bolt, *A Man for All Seasons* (New York: Vintage Books, 1962), p. 89. See also Donald J. Moore, "The Contemporary Witness of Franz Jägerstätter," *America* (October 30, 1982): 247–50; idem, "Franz Jägerstätter and the Dilemma of the Austrian Church," *America* (October 11, 1986): 187–90, 196. For a full-length study of Jägerstätter, see Gordon Zahn, *In Solitary Witness* (Toronto: Holt Rinehart & Winston of Canada, Ltd., 1964).

of Celtic-influenced late medieval France. Her conclusion suggests that although Joan-the-legend may not model moral authenticity for us, Joan-the-woman is another matter: "Joan's lesson for women is first to follow her example in taking themselves seriously and finding their own truth, in searching for their authentic voice, free of the definitions of male authority." But, she continues, Joan's execution by male authorities in 1431 brings a balancing lesson of realism: "women must not assume that their truth is acceptable in the world of male values."[13] Barstow's reminder that Joan was executed for heresy and witchcraft is indeed sobering. It would seem, in fact, that the early-twentieth-century canonization of Joan (which Barstow views as a concession to the French Right) is tied to the mythical version of her significance as an obedient vessel of God's will, which obscures the human complexities of her life.

What I would add to this analysis is that Joan, a woman of her society and times, can be an example for men as well as for women. Her willingness to cross rigid gender boundaries in response to the sense of vocation received in her mystical experiences is as instructive for males as it is for females. The point is not that one should imitate the details of Joan's choices but that one should be true to the spiritual vision one receives. Such has always been a requirement for authentic Christian living, regardless of gender. Although I would thus extend the application of Joan's example beyond Barstow's emphasis on women, I concur with this historian that Joan's insistence on "the authenticity of her voices is not only valuable evidence about mystical experience but is also a witness to individual conscience, rare in any time." In other words, Joan of Arc deserves to be ranked with More and Jägerstätter after all.[14] Moreover, our appreciation of all three martyrs of conscience can benefit from the insight that guided Barstow's illuminating study of Joan, namely, that although mystical experience is privately received, it is at the

---

13. Anne Llewellyn Barstow, *Joan of Arc: Heretic, Mystic, Shaman* (Lewiston: Edwin Mellen, 1986), p. 131.

14. Also supporting the idea of Joan as a martyr of conscience is the brief analysis of her life in Bruno Chenu et al., *The Book of Christian Martyrs* (New York: Crossroad, 1990), where historian Claude Prud'homme places her at the dawn of an age of martyrdom remarkable for persons sacrificing their lives "in faithfulness to their convictions" (p. 97). Significantly, Prud'homme observes that she "does not appear among the Catholic saints as a martyr but as a virgin," adding that "with Joan, the mediaeval tradition of the prophetic woman confronts the claim of the clergy and doctors to monopolize the public work pronounced in the name of God. Joan forcefully reminds her judges that ecclesiastical power is in the service of holiness, and not the contrary" (pp. 98–99).

same time a thoroughly social matter. As the anthropologist I. M. Lewis, whom Barstow quotes at the outset of her book, has noted, mystical experience "'is grounded in and must relate to the environment in which it is achieved. It thus inevitably bears the stamp of the culture and society in which it arises.'"[15]

Such is also the case with conscience, I maintain. Although the social dimension of conscience has not been stressed in most ethical discussions of the concept, it is important to recognize that the consciences of Joan of Arc, Thomas More, and Franz Jägerstätter were not nearly so isolated as the stereotype of the long-distance moral runner would have it. Yes, conscience is indeed quite personal, and there is a sense in which the self is alone (before God) in the conscience experience. Nevertheless, the experience is a thoroughly social one. The paradox is that we are alone and not alone at the same time in this experience. The responsibility for our choices is ours, and no one else's. But others are bound up in our moral feelings and decisions—in their causes, their motivation, their effects. How this is the case and why it is important to recognize the connection between conscience and community is a principal theme of this study, which will recur frequently as I explore some of the challenges confronting Catholic moral theology today.

Moral theology, that branch of theology concerned with the practical implications of Christian faith for ideals, values, and behavior, was identified by the Second Vatican Council as in particular need of renewal. As the conciliar "Decree on Priestly Formation," *Optatem Totius* (#16), states:

> Special attention needs to be given to the development of moral theology. Its scientific exposition should be more thoroughly nourished by scriptural teaching. It should show the nobility of the Christian vocation of the faithful, and their obligation to bring forth fruit in charity for the life of the world.[16]

The criterion of fruitfulness, or practical benefit to the world, suggests that past emphasis in moral theology had been too otherworldly, too preoccupied with the future state of believers' souls, to take sufficient notice of its effects on the present well-being of persons within and beyond the Catholic community. Today, some decades after the conciliar observation, I believe the call for the

---

15. Barstow, *Joan of Arc*, p. xvi. The source of the quotation is Lewis's volume *Ecstatic Religion: An Anthropological Study of Spirit Possession and Shamanism* (Baltimore: Penguin, 1971).

16. Quoted here from Walter M. Abbott, ed., *The Documents of Vatican II* (New York: The America Press, 1966), p. 452. Subsequent references to conciliar documents are from this edition.

renewal of moral theology still stands in need of fulfillment. Considerable progress has been made, but the discipline is not yet sufficiently integrated with biblical spirituality, nor is it fully adequate to the needs of today's world. And just as Barstow's feminist angle of vision enabled her to add significantly to our knowledge of Joan of Arc, medieval Catholicism, and mysticism, so too will such an approach prove productive for contemporary moral theology.

As I have indicated above, I employ the term "feminist" to describe a position that recognizes the full humanity and dignity of women and is committed to reforming structures of religious thought and practice in light of this relatively modern insight that women are equal to men as human beings. This approach assumes that asking the question, What about women's moral agency and women's moral experience? can yield beneficial results for everyone—women, men, children, other creatures, and the earth itself.[17] Surely other questions are also necessary, and other issues besides injustice to women require attention, but this angle of inquiry is essential if moral theology is to become more relatively adequate to the needs of our world.

I believe the challenges to the discipline are deeply religious and moral ones. Moral theology is being called, on the one hand, to foster a more radical trust in God and, on the other, to develop a more radical and thoroughgoing ethic of justice. These challenges are being leveled from several quarters, including such "signs of the times" as postmodern intellectual developments and contemporary liberation, peace, and ecology movements. In addition, the discipline is being challenged from places quite close to home, including the biblical tradition, the hierarchical magisterium, and believers of all sorts, especially those who have appropriated the new learnings and moral insights of the late twentieth century. The cultural diversity of all Catholics is increasingly being recognized today, and this is bound to affect the way the church

17. There has developed in the last two decades a burgeoning literature in Christian feminist ethics (the more inclusive term) and moral theology (the term more specific to Catholicism). Ethicists whose work has especially influenced my thought include Barbara Hilkert Andolsen, Lisa Sowle Cahill, Katie Geneva Cannon, Margaret A. Farley, Christine Gudorf, Beverly Wildung Harrison, Mary Hunt, Ada María Isasi-Díaz, Patricia Beattie Jung, Karen Lebacqz, Carol A. Tauer, and Sharon Welch. Cahill has surveyed this rapidly developing field in "Feminist Ethics," *Theological Studies* 51 (1990): 49–62, and discussed some of its implications in her presidential address to the Catholic Theological Society of America, "Feminist Ethics and the Challenge of Cultures," *CTSA Proceedings* 48 (1993): 65–83. See also Lois K. Daly, ed., *Feminist Theological Ethics: A Reader* (Louisville: Westminster John Knox Press, 1994); and Andolsen, ed., "Professional Resources: Selected Topics in Feminist and Womanist Ethics," *The Annual of the Society of Christian Ethics* (1994): 255–305.

regards ethical questions. The demands placed on church leaders during the present upheaval are considerable, and the international hierarchy is by no means monolithic in its understanding of what fidelity to tradition and openness to the signs of the times require, although in their efforts to promote unity and stability church authorities sometimes deny the pluralism that exists among themselves as well as among other Catholics.

To my reading the situation calls for change more fundamental than anything we have yet seen in this century; we need no less than a revolution of Catholic consciousness. What is required is a profound conversion, a shift of attention, a turning from certain questions and preoccupations to new topics and new ways of regarding old ones. In the chapters that follow I do not propose a full program for this conversion, but instead offer analyses of topics where work has begun and needs to go forward. I see this book as analogous to the surveying that must be done before architectural designs can be prepared for a large building project. In this respect I go somewhat further than the Brazilian thinkers Antonio Moser and Bernardino Leers, who argue in *Moral Theology: Dead Ends and Alternatives* that a substantial remodeling of the edifice we have known as "moral theology" is sufficient for our situation.[18] Instead, I think the time has come for the pilgrim people of God to move out of heavy, dark, romanesque living structures into something more spacious. We must plan for better access to light and warmth, and, thanks to techniques and materials that were not available when medieval buildings were constructed, we are able to do so. It will of course be desirable to make use of as many of the old materials that remain functional and beautiful as we can, and it will be crucial to plan the new dwelling well and execute the move with great care.

Architectural designs will need to be done later. For the present, basic investigative work in preparation for future construction is required. As I pursued this project, I found it important to acknowledge the ways in which moral theology itself has been complicit in systemic injustice, unintentionally clouding the vision of believers to the ambiguities of our own moral strivings and the realities of evil in our world. At the same time, it has seemed important to acknowledge that on the whole the tradition has served us well, indeed has brought us to this moment when it is possible to accept an invitation to significant and ongoing conversion. Our heritage has valued conscience for centuries; it is my hope that probing this reality from a feminist angle will

---

18. Antonio Moser and Bernardino Leers, *Moral Theology: Dead Ends and Alternatives,* trans. Paul Burns (1987; Maryknoll, N.Y.: Orbis, 1990), pp. 2–3.

enable us to trust yet more deeply in the presence and power of God's Spirit at work in the hearts of women and men who are sincerely seeking to discern God's intentions for their lives.

In chapter 1, "Conscience and Community: Catholic Moral Theology Today," I explore some of the tensions in moral theology that follow from developments since the Second Vatican Council. I suggest that believers today exemplify two contrasting styles of faith and ethics, namely, Catholic Fundamentalism and Catholic Revisionism. I also sketch a theory of conscience that seeks to do justice to the social dimensions of this phenomenon.

One aspect of cultural change that is particularly important for moral theology is the challenge from secular wisdom. Developments in philosophy, history, and the social and natural sciences have profoundly impacted the thought structures upon which pre–Vatican II moral theology was based. In chapter 2, "Conscience at the Crossroads: Invitation to Radical Conversion," I probe some of the implications for Catholic morality of new knowledge and changed historical circumstances.

Much discussion of Catholic moral theology today focuses on the morality of *actions*. We are well aware of debates concerning the rightness or wrongness of decisions regarding medicine, sexuality, capital punishment, the nuclear deterrent, and so forth. Whatever side one takes on these questions, they all have to do with the dimension of the moral life that has been dominant in modern ethics, namely, judgments about the morality of particular acts. In recent years, however, a growing movement in philosophical and religious ethics insists that issues of character and virtue also require attention. This insight, which has been developed by such philosophers as Iris Murdoch and Alasdair MacIntyre and by such religious ethicists as James Laney and Stanley Hauerwas, has greatly influenced several chapters of the present book.[19] In chapter 3, "Changing Paradigms of Virtue: The Good Life Reconsidered," I indicate that contemporary debates in Catholicism can be understood in terms of a tension between two competing models of virtue: a

---

19. See, for example, Iris Murdoch, "Vision and Choice in Morality," in *Christian Ethics and Contemporary Philosophy*, ed. Ian Ramsey (New York: Macmillan, 1966), pp. 195–218; idem, *The Sovereignty of Good* (New York: Schocken Books, 1971); Alasdair MacIntyre, *After Virtue: A Study in Moral Theory* (Notre Dame: University of Notre Dame Press, 1981); James T. Laney, "Characterization and Moral Judgments," *Journal of Religion* 55 (October 1975): 405–14; and various books by Stanley Hauerwas, particularly *Vision and Virtue: Essays in Christian Ethical Reflection* (Notre Dame: Fides/Claretian, 1974), and *A Community of Character* (Notre Dame: University of Notre Dames Press, 1981).

patriarchal paradigm that has long held sway and an emerging egalitarian-feminist paradigm that is now inspiring many. The next two chapters illustrate the significance of this controversy over virtue. In chapter 4, "Contested Authority: The Cases of Charles Curran and the Vatican 24," I discuss the 1986 dismissal of an eminent moral theologian from a tenured position at the Catholic University of America and also analyze the controversy over twenty-four nuns who signed a newspaper advertisement concerning the abortion issue in the heat of the 1984 U.S. presidential election. The analysis of both cases is deepened in chapter 5, "Seeking Truth in a Complex World," which also examines the 1993 encyclical of Pope John Paul II on moral theology, *Veritatis Splendor.*

Chapter 6, "Toward Liberating Conscience: Spirituality and Moral Responsibility," probes the relationship between spirituality and ethics, invites reconsideration of the meaning of moral responsibility, and discusses the importance of living in solidarity with victims of injustice. Finally, chapter 7, "Conscience as Process: Choosing Our Common Good," indicates the need to bring a self-critical perspective to the doing of ethics and also offers a model for moral discernment.

A major inadequacy of unrenewed moral theology has been the way it reduces the mystery of Christian living to a matter of obeying rules that earlier generations developed as they strove to live as faithful disciples of Jesus in times and circumstances different from our own.[20] Given this inadequacy, the need today is twofold. First, the universal call to holiness, which was so rightly stressed by the Second Vatican Council, must be seen to entail that *all* believers bear responsibility for discerning the moral obligations of our lives. Second, moral theology should provide leadership in helping Catholics become more confident and competent as ethical decision-makers. These ideas are hardly novel; classical teaching on conscience has in fact contained similar notions, but such teaching has not yet been integrated into the moral education of Catholics in a large-scale, practical way.[21] Rather the message

20. Here I develop a point emphasized by John Mahoney in *The Making of Moral Theology: A Study of the Roman Catholic Tradition* (Oxford: Clarendon Press, 1987). Moral theology, he claims, needs to recover a sense of religious mystery about its task, since "[i]t is the mystery of God which earths all theology and at the same time makes theological pluralism unavoidable" (p. 337).

21. Much valuable work in this area has already been contributed by moral theologians. For example, Daniel Maguire's *The Moral Choice* (Garden City, N.Y.: Doubleday, 1978) has gone through several editions and been widely studied in colleges and universities. But the practical

has been: Here is the behavior you must do or avoid under pain of serious sin; of course, you have a duty to obey your conscience, but if your conscience is a good one it will virtually always agree with magisterial teaching. The net effect is to advocate either blind obedience or ethical intuitionism, neither of which does justice to the moral resources of individuals or the Catholic tradition. In this volume, then, I attempt to illustrate what "liberating conscience," can mean: freeing persons from whatever inhibits a full response to the divine invitation to love God, neighbor, and self in ways that are recognizably good. The goal of moral discernment, after all, should be deeds that "bring forth fruit in charity for the life of the world." Our consciences will be functioning as they should, it seems to me, when those who suffer most from oppression and injustice experience our lives and deeds as expressions of God's liberating love for us all.

* * * * *

Those who hold hierarchical office in today's church have a particularly important role to play in contributing to the renewal of moral theology. Catholic institutions have many strengths, but they also have the limitations and vulnerability that accompany the enjoyment of power. The dangers of inebriation and denial seem to go with the territory of being a worldwide church. Let Noah in the story in Genesis 9 be an image of institutional Catholicism—not of any particular leader but rather of the sinful-yet-redeemed human organization gifted with a treasure of wisdom it can never fully understand or practice. Its moments of embarrassment are by no means the whole story of its life and worth. On the contrary, they are relatively rare. But when they happen they must be faced and dealt with honestly. These embarrassments are like ciphers on church organs, defects that cause the pipes to sound without the keys being played. A single cipher is enough to ruin an

---

methods of revisionist moral theologians have not in my judgment been sufficiently promoted among the Catholic population because many church authorities have been protecting an authoritarian vision of the moral life, especially where questions of personal morality are concerned. This authoritarianism has provoked a reaction of anti-authoritarianism on the part of many Catholics, which tragically undermines the inspirational power of prophetic papal and episcopal statements on matters of peace and justice. Richard A. McCormick's *The Critical Calling: Reflections on Moral Dilemmas Since Vatican II* (Washington, D.C.: Georgetown University Press, 1989) includes an impressive critique of ecclesiastical authoritarianism, at the same time displaying the value of an approach to morality that stresses personal responsibility and ethical discernment in light of basic Christian principles.

entire musical experience, no matter how splendid the composition or accomplished the organist. A droning note ought not to be endured. Someone must say, "Stop the music. No one can follow the melody on racial and economic justice, no one can hear the harmonies of peace and respect for life until this cipher on women and sexuality is repaired."

In the sixteenth century, Catholic practices around indulgences were the cipher that had to be dealt with, and the price of denial and delay was steep. Closer to our own times, the cipher of Catholic complicity with industry's exploitation of workers and even with systems of chattel slavery was allowed to keep sounding for a scandalous length of time. Surely the embarrassment that needs attention now is the nexus of issues involving women, sexuality, and patriarchal authoritarianism. The *Humanae Vitae* crisis was the first tip of this iceberg to surface. The clergy sexual misconduct scandals are part of the same problem, as is the institutional church's injustice toward women. Noah, in this reading, stands for official Catholicism's patriarchal mentality and social system. Since this is our institutional reality at this point in history, the responsibility for change lies especially with those men who occupy positions analogous to Noah's favored sons. There are many more than ten just bishops in today's church. Some of them are already facing the reality of patriarchy's problems and are onto the idea that the ecclesiastical tent and the wider world are entrusted as much to Ruah's care as to Noah's. These contemporary "sons of Ham" are willing to risk their privileged status for the values of truth and justice. It is perhaps better not to mention their names here. But the daughters and sons of the poor will one day rise up and call them blessed.

CHAPTER ONE

Conscience and Community: Catholic Moral Theology Today

> When I was young . . . there never was any question of right and wrong. We knew our catechism, and that was enough. We learned our creed and our duty. Every respectable church person had the same opinions.

Any number of Catholics might have uttered such words, especially since the 1960s, when ethical differences among us have received so much attention in the press. But actually this lament for the good old days when catechism knowledge settled every question of right and wrong, when believers all held the same "correct" opinion, does not date from the Second Vatican Council, nor was it voiced by a Roman Catholic. Rather this quotation comes from a novel about religion and social change in England nearly two centuries ago—George Eliot's masterpiece *Middlemarch*.[1] Eliot, who took pride in being realistic in her fiction, judged that nostalgia for moral certainty might well be voiced by an elderly Anglican woman in 1830.

My point is threefold: first, nostalgia for the good old days of moral certainty is by no means a recent phenomenon; second, Roman Catholics are by no means the only Christians who have to deal with nostalgia for the simplicity of catechism or biblical answers to questions of right and wrong; and finally, twentieth-century ethical disputes among church people are best understood as part of the post-Enlightenment problem of how to balance new knowledge and changed historical circumstances with traditional religious authority. There is, however, a special tonality to the way Roman

---

1. George Eliot, *Middlemarch* (1871–72; Harmondsworth: Penguin, 1976), pp. 199–200. The story is set in rural England just prior to the Reform Bill of 1832.

Catholics experience the longing for certitude and the tensions between tradition and modernity. As the great German theologian Karl Rahner once noted, Catholicism in the twentieth century has begun to emerge from nearly two millennia of European cultural dominance and is on its way to becoming a truly world church, instead of a European church with missionary influence around the globe.[2] What this entails for Catholic morality is that a plurality of views on ethical questions is bound to develop, precisely because cultural differences are beginning to be recognized and respected. This will require, of course, that we come to see that unity is not the same thing as uniformity; indeed, real unity can accommodate a great deal of diversity because of the conviction that God loves and supports the human community in our efforts to discern what goodness requires. In the area of ethics, unity requires consensus on basic values and principles and allows for some differences in applying principles to specific circumstances.

In the last thirty years Catholics have experienced an enormous amount of change. This change is the result not only of causes within the church such as the Second Vatican Council but also of factors in the wider culture such as political and technological developments. Our tradition has survived a number of critical episodes in previous centuries, and there are many resources within Catholicism to help us negotiate the present one. Among these resources is the wisdom that particular groups of believers have developed in their struggles to be faithful to God in difficult historical circumstances. African-American Catholics, for example, have much to contribute in the present crisis, particularly their painfully won knowledge that biblical interpretation and ecclesiastical pronouncement are far from sufficient for solving ethical problems. Not to put too fine a point on the matter: There is no getting around the fact that the ordinary magisterium of the Catholic church was *wrong* in what it taught about race and about slavery—by word, deed, and especially by omission—during some crucial centuries of Western history. Moreover, the fact that millions of African-Americans are devout Catholics today testifies to something very important, namely, that people of faith can absorb a good deal more change in official Catholic teaching than some high-ranking churchmen believe possible where certain contemporary issues are concerned. Clearly a *development of moral doctrine,* indeed an about-face in moral teaching, had to occur in order for Catholics of European ancestry—be they bishops, moral theologians, priests, religious, or layfolk—to repudiate

2. Karl Rahner, "Towards a Fundamental Theological Interpretation of Vatican II," *Theological Studies* 40 (1979): 716–27.

slavery as an immoral system and racism as a serious sin.[3] Furthermore, if the gifts and experiences of black Catholics had been taken seriously by church authorities in earlier centuries, the necessary development of doctrine would have occurred much sooner than it did. Bartolome de Las Casas was onto something in the sixteenth century when he observed, "If we were Indian we should see things differently," but he failed, at least initially, to extend the insight to Africans enslaved to labor for the conquering Europeans.[4]

Something parallel is going on in our day with respect to justice for women. Having published prophetic pastoral letters on nuclear weapons (1983) and the American economy (1986), the U.S. bishops concluded in 1992 that a decade-long effort to compose a pastoral letter on "women's concerns" was best abandoned. After four drafts and significant Vatican intervention, they were unable to reach a consensus on the proposed document and instead agreed to publish the fourth draft as simply a committee report. Although all the drafts have serious limitations, they are commendable for a number of reasons, especially for the forthright way they name sexism as morally evil. In 1994 the bishops noted in a brief pastoral reflection, "Strengthening the Bonds of Peace," that "sexism, defined as 'unjust discrimination based on sex,' is still present in some members of the church." They went on to declare: "We reject sexism and pledge renewed efforts to guard against it in church teaching and practice."[5]

3. See John Francis Maxwell, *Slavery and the Catholic Church* (London: Barry Rose Publishers, 1975); and Cyprian Davis, *The History of Black Catholics in the United States* (New York: Crossroad, 1990).

4. Las Casas's words are cited here from Gustavo Gutiérrez, "Towards the Fifth Centenary," in *1492–1992: The Voice of the Victims*, ed. Leonardo Boff and Virgil Elizondo (Philadelphia: Trinity Press International, 1990), p. 3. Helen Rand Parish, author of *Las Casas: The Untold Story* (Berkeley: University of California Press, 1993) explains that in 1518 Las Casas had suggested bringing "a few white and black slaves" from Spain to the islands, thinking of them as skilled laborers who had been captured in battles against Muslim invaders. As soon as he learned the true nature of the Portuguese slave trade in 1522, he objected to it. According to Parish, "Las Casas was, as far as we know, the only voice in his century to denounce this inhumanity" (quoted by James S. Torrens, "Las Casas: Defender of the Indians—An Interview with Helen Rand Parish," *America* [July 25, 1992]: 34).

5. *Origins* 24 (December 1, 1994): 421. This statement was issued in the wake of Pope John Paul II's "Apostolic Letter on Ordination and Women" (*Origins* [June 9, 1994]: 49ff.), which insisted that the priesthood of women is against the divine plan, and also in the wake of a Vatican reversal of the bishops' decision to employ inclusive language in the U.S. editions of the *Catechism of the Catholic Church*. "Strengthening the Bonds of Peace" makes general affirmations of women's leadership and equality, while recognizing a diversity of gifts. It urges that

To acknowledge the sin of sexism is a new insight for many Catholics, and drawing out its implications is no easy task in a religious culture that has to some extent been shaped by the very sin it now wants to repudiate. Much of the difficulty stems from the fact that the two main expressions of revelation, scripture and tradition, have not really addressed something called sexism. Indeed, although there are some important exceptions, on balance both scripture and tradition have tended to reinforce a widely held opinion that the male form of humanity has a primary role and special worth in God's eyes, while the female belongs in a secondary and subordinate place. Things are not put so baldly in the late twentieth century, of course. On the contrary, official Catholic teaching has progressed to the point where women's full human dignity is affirmed in ways that would astound the ancient and medieval church fathers, who excluded women from holy orders precisely because of age-old assumptions about their alleged inferiority and their sup- posedly more carnal and less rational nature than men's.[6] So we have today a long-standing policy against celebrating and ordering women's ministries sacramentally that is based on discarded anthropological assumptions. And since 1976 the Vatican has been defending this policy with arguments people find less and less convincing.[7]

"catechetical and religious materials, and hymnals as well as our daily language and prayer, honor the concerns which shape a more inclusive language, while taking care to ensure that they do not become a source of division, anger and hurt" (p. 421). For a review of the bishops' earlier efforts, see Thomas J. Reese, "Women's Pastoral Fails," *America* (December 5, 1992): 443–44. The several drafts were published as "Partners in the Mystery of Redemption: A Pas- toral Response to Women's Concerns for Church and Society," *Origins* 17 (April 21, 1988): 763–64; "One in Christ Jesus," *Origins* 19 (April 5, 1990): 717–40; "Called to be One in Christ Jesus," *Origins* 21 (April 23, 1992): 761–76; and "One in Christ Jesus," *Origins* 22 (September 10, 1992): 221–40. The "Final Report by the U.S. Bishops' Ad Hoc Committee for a Pastoral Response to Women's Concerns" was published in *Origins* 22 (December 31, 1992): 491ff.

  6. See Ida Raming, *The Exclusion of Women from the Priesthood: Divine Law or Sex Discrim- ination? A Historical Investigation of the Juridical and Doctrinal Foundations of the Code of Canon Law, Canon 968, Section 1*, trans. Norman R. Adams (Metuchen, N.J.: Scarecrow Press, 1976).

  7. See Leonard Swidler and Arlene Swidler, eds., *Women Priests: A Catholic Commentary on the Vatican Declaration* (New York: Paulist, 1977); Sara Butler, ed., *CTSA Research Report: Women in Church and Society* (Bronx, N.Y.: Catholic Theological Society of America, 1978); and Anne E. Carr, *Transforming Grace: Christian Tradition and Women's Experience* (San Francisco: Harper & Row, 1988). Pope John Paul II's letter *Ordinatio Sacerdotalis* (May 30, 1994) reiterated the offi- cial ban on ordaining women that had been articulated in *Inter Insigniores* in 1976, the year after the first meeting of the Women's Ordination Conference in Detroit. According to an article by

What I have been suggesting is that significant change has occurred in Catholic moral teaching in the past, and we may expect even more change in the future. Meanwhile we are experiencing a great deal of tension within the church between two opposing views of the nature and task of Catholic moral theology. This controversy is the result of a seismic shift in Catholic religious sensibility, which began on a large scale with the Second Vatican Council and is now meeting resistance from important quarters. Below I shall sketch the lines of the debate where moral theology is concerned. My own position is that the debate itself is a healthy thing and that thinkers who responsibly dissent from Vatican positions are supporting the hierarchical teaching authority rather than subverting it. Indeed, such theologians are helping to prepare the Catholic community for a day when central church leaders will be more trusting of the Spirit of God present in the faithful than current Vatican officials appear to be. When I think of "responsibly dissenting moral theologians," I have in mind, for example, Bernard Häring, now retired from a distinguished teaching career in Rome, who in 1989 called for the pope to set up a worldwide consultation of bishops, theologians, and laity to study anew the question of birth control.[8] I am thinking also of a number of Americans, including Charles Curran, who in 1986 was removed from his tenured professorship on the theology faculty of the Catholic University of America because of his unwillingness to deny the conclusions of his scholarly research on certain questions in sexual ethics.[9] It is precisely because such thinkers recognize the importance of the papal ministry as a focus of church unity and a source of moral leadership that they are voicing their differences with a relatively small number of papal teachings. With this background in view, I shall

---

Bill Cole in the *National Catholic Reporter* for June 17, 1994, Gallup polls indicate that "support for women's ordination has climbed steadily among Catholics in the United States." A 1993 survey "showed that 64 percent of Catholics agreed with the statement in favor of women's ordination" (p. 7). For discussions of the moral dimensions of this issue, see Richard A. McCormick, *Notes on Moral Theology 1965 Through 1980* (Washington, D.C.: University Press of America, 1981), pp. 735–36; and Margaret Farley, "Moral Imperatives for the Ordination of Women," in *Women and Catholic Priesthood,* ed. Anne Marie Gardiner (New York: Paulist, 1976), pp. 35–51.

8. Häring's proposal was published January 15, 1989, in the Italian Catholic magazine *Il Regno.* An English translation appears under the title "Does God Condemn Contraception? A Question for the Whole Church" in *Commonweal* (February 10, 1989): 69–71. See also Häring, *My Witness for the Church,* trans. Leonard Swidler (New York: Paulist, 1992).

9. Curran's case is presented, along with official Vatican correspondence and related documents, in *Faithful Dissent* (Kansas City: Sheed & Ward, 1986). Also informative is William W. May, ed., *Vatican Authority and American Catholic Dissent: The Curran Case and Its Consequences* (New York: Crossroad, 1987).

next discuss the nature and task of moral theology and connect the current tensions in this field with two contrasting styles of Catholic faith, designated Catholic Fundamentalism on the one hand, and Catholic Revisionism on the other. I shall then conclude the chapter by exploring the relationship between individual conscience and the larger community that Catholic moral theology at its best enhances and supports.

THE NATURE AND TASK OF MORAL THEOLOGY

Moral theology, we must admit, is not everyone's favorite subject. The laugh that humorist Garrison Keillor evokes when he refers to the Catholic church in his mythical town of Lake Wobegon, Minnesota, as "Our Lady of Perpetual Responsibility" says much about moral theology as American Catholics knew it in the past, and this past continues to influence our feelings about the discipline.[10] Moral theology has provided more than one generation with sweaty brows and clammy palms as they examined their consciences and worked up the courage to confess hard-to-name sins in confessional boxes around the country. Moral theology, in short, has supplied the peculiarly Catholic variety of guilt so prominent in the literature of parochial school nostalgia. It is no wonder that veterans of catechism education find themselves drawn much more readily to discussions of prayer and spirituality than to books and conferences on morality. The phrase "moral burnout" may not be too strong to describe a syndrome suffered by devout persons who identified all the opinions published in official Catholic books or uttered by religious authority figures as clearly and certainly God's opinion too and then tried to live in their God-given bodies in the real world.

Nor is it surprising that such Catholics came to admire the novels of Graham Greene. This author had the good sense to press the crucial distinction between the church's opinion and God's opinion, a distinction that tends at times to be obscured by persons in the pews as well as by members of the hierarchy. Many took heart from the words spoken by Father Rank to the widow of Major Scobie at the end of Greene's novel from 1948, *The Heart of the Matter:* "The Church knows all the rules. But it doesn't know what goes on in a single human heart."[11] There is wisdom in what Father Rank says, though in his effort to console a woman whose husband has committed sui-

---

10. See Garrison Keillor, *Lake Wobegon Days* (New York: Viking, 1985).
11. Graham Greene, *The Heart of the Matter* (1948; rev. ed.; Harmondsworth: Penguin, 1971), p. 272.

cide the priest overstates his case. But surely his main insight is correct, indeed biblically grounded: "For who has known the mind of the Lord? Or who has been his counselor?" (Rom. 11:34). Who can be a Christian, a follower of Jesus, and doubt that God's tender mercies are above all God's works? Still, although Father Rank was correct to challenge a Catholicism that so stressed rules and rituals that God's mercy at times seemed hamstrung by spiritual bureaucracy, he went too far when he implied that the church's moral tradition lacks knowledge of the human heart. On the contrary, traditional Catholic moral teaching contains a wealth of wisdom about human life and the human heart, though Rank is right to imply that none of us can judge another's state of soul. We need, in sum, to appreciate the ambiguity of our ethical heritage as Catholics. Ours is an amazingly rich moral tradition that deserves to be celebrated and made use of. But it is not a perfect, fully finished system in no need of improvement.

The great debate in Catholic moral theology today revolves around the question of how much development is possible in Catholic moral teaching and who is entitled to contribute to this development. On the one side is "Catholic Fundamentalism," which sees moral theology as a static heritage containing all truths necessary for solving ethical problems. This view would keep any change in traditional teaching to a minimum, holding that to question a past teaching is to undermine the very authority of the tradition. It sees the role of professionally trained moral theologians as that of explaining and applying "what the church has always taught" to new cases as they come up. From this perspective, scholars may have their private quibbles, but they must never voice dissent in public, even from magisterial doctrine that defines itself as "non-infallible," a curious provision in view of the fact that "non-infallible" is a convoluted way of saying "capable of being wrong."

Opposed to Catholic Fundamentalism is the position known as "Catholic Revisionism." This stance insists on the classic Catholic view that faith and reason are compatible, and therefore it is willing to reinterpret and develop traditional teaching in a way that takes contemporary experience adequately into account, which includes respecting the discoveries of modern philosophy, history, and the natural and social sciences. Instead of viewing past teaching as a static set of truths, this theological stance looks to the actual history of the tradition and observes that crisis, change, and reinterpretation of doctrine have been a continual feature of the church's life in its pilgrimage through time.[12] Although the scholars who take this position currently object

---

12. As with all typologies, the categories "Catholic Fundamentalist" and "Catholic Revi-

to the authoritarianism of fundamentalist-leaning Vatican officials, I believe most of their number are solidly orthodox in their respect for scripture, tradition, and church authority. Moreover, these theologians, some of whom have been forced out of Catholic institutions of higher learning, will in time be appreciated for their good pastoral sense in putting the needs of the faithful above personal concern for approval and job security.

The tensions between Catholic Fundamentalism and Catholic Revisionism should not be surprising in view of the dramatic changes that have taken place since the 1960s, especially where moral theology is concerned. For much of the period between the sixteenth-century Council of Trent and the Second Vatican Council, moral theology was basically a discipline taught in seminaries for the purpose of training future priests to hear confessions. These seminarians studied manuals written in Latin, which provided categories for judging the gravity of sins but were not designed to help the clergy educate the faithful in mature ethical discernment.[13] The emphasis during this era was legalistic and individualistic, particularly in the immigrant American church, where, as John P. Boyle has observed, for most of its history

---

sionist" are abstract heuristic terms that can facilitate our grasp of a reality that is far more complex than the model itself. John A. Coleman analyzes contemporary Catholic Fundamentalism in "Who Are the Catholic 'Fundamentalists'?" *Commonweal* (January 27, 1989): 42–47, and Richard A. McCormick discusses its manifestations in moral theology in *Notes on Moral Theology 1981 Through 1984* (Lanham, Md.: University Press of America, 1984), pp. 81–86. I employ "Catholic Revisionism" in the rich and positive sense of "seeing anew" in a manner faithful to both the inherited wisdom of the tradition and the truth that emerges from intelligent scrutiny of contemporary experience. I am influenced here particularly by David Tracy's discussion of theology's task in *Blessed Rage for Order* (New York: Seabury, 1975) and Anne E. Carr's feminist development of Tracy's ideas in *Transforming Grace,* where she writes of the need for "revisioning Christian categories" (p. 8). A "Catholic Revisionist" perspective is expressed in the works of many contemporary moral theologians, including, for example, John P. Boyle, "The American Experience in Moral Theology," *CTSA Proceedings* 41 (1986): 23–46; and Richard A. McCormick, *The Critical Calling: Moral Dilemmas Since Vatican II* (Washington, D.C.: Georgetown University Press, 1989).

13. See James M. Gustafson, *Protestant and Roman Catholic Ethics* (Chicago: University of Chicago Press, 1978); John P. Mahoney, *The Making of Moral Theology: A Study of the Roman Catholic Tradition* (New York: Oxford University Press, 1988); and John P. Gallagher, *Time Past, Time Future: An Historical Study of Catholic Moral Theology* (New York: Paulist, 1990). Although I disagree with Gallagher's assertion that "moral theology" is a term that ought to be reserved for a particular genre of Christian ethical writing (that of the "Neo-Thomist manualists" who dominated the scene for three centuries prior to the Second Vatican Council), I find his historical analysis immensely helpful.

moral theology tended to see itself as "a relatively fixed object against a changing cultural background."[14] It is this outdated understanding of moral theology that some adherents of Catholic Fundamentalism are attempting to preserve. However, much has changed in the last thirty years, and an alternative understanding of the discipline and its role in the church has resulted from various changes in moral theology's setting as well as in its practitioners. If the story of moral theology could once be filmed in clerical black and white, with a dash of episcopal purple now and then, it presently is a much more colorful operation that involves women and men from various family and community backgrounds. Moral theology continues to be taught in seminaries, but the textbooks are now written in modern languages. Unlike the manuals of former days, contemporary texts do not just argue deductively from established Catholic sources; they also reflect new knowledge from history, philosophy, and the sciences. Moreover, moral theologians now teach in colleges and universities as well as in seminaries, and they understand their field in much broader and less individualistic ways than was typical before the Second Vatican Council.

Yale Divinity School theologian Margaret A. Farley, for example, defines *theology* as the effort of the Christian community to understand its faith, and *ethics* as the parallel effort of the Christian community to understand and articulate how this faith should be lived.[15] Two aspects of this Catholic thinker's definition are significant. First, ethics is the *community's* task, which means that everyone has a share in the work. It cannot be left entirely to the hierarchy or the professionally trained theologians, though clearly their roles are special and important. Second, the idea that *effort* is required as the faithful seek to understand how they should live is crucial; moral theology is not a matter of merely conforming to rules or automatically applying principles to cases. It cannot, in other words, be done by computer, even with the most elegant Vatican software. Instead, Christian decision making requires *discernment,* which is neither automatic nor unthinking. As the Dominican scholar Thomas O'Meara has observed, it is a mistake to think of the Bible and the pope as "answering machines."[16] Instead, Christian ethics involves faith and reason working together at the task that Protestant ethicist James M.

14. Boyle, "The American Experience in Moral Theology," p. 52.

15. Margaret A. Farley, "New Patterns of Relationship: Beginnings of a Moral Revolution," *Theological Studies* 36 (1975): 629.

16. Thomas F. O'Meara, "Bible and Pope: The Search for Authority" (Tulsa: University of Tulsa Warren Center for Catholic Studies, 1988), pp. 4–5.

Gustafson has described as discerning "what God is enabling and requiring us to be and to do."[17]

STYLES OF FAITH AND ETHICS

Ah yes, God. But where does the church come in? Doesn't the church, or at least the pope, speak for God? Now we are truly at the heart of the matter, for Catholics have long understood that divine authority is expressed in a human institution and through human leaders, much the way all Christians have believed that God's word has been expressed in a humanly composed and humanly edited collection of writings that is the Bible. But *how* is divine authority expressed in these human ways? Do the Bible and the pope speak *directly* for God, or are the moral teachings found in the various books of the Bible, the voluminous writings of the popes, and the documents of the ecumenical councils better understood as human responses to an ongoing process of divine revelation, that is, as human efforts to *interpret* what God is enabling and requiring of God's people?[18] Faithful Christians differ on how they answer these questions, and this is what leads me to say we are currently experiencing a collision of faith-worlds, or styles of Catholic faith and ethics, which I have termed Catholic Fundamentalism and Catholic Revisionism. When matters such as the Curran case are understood in this context, we see that the present troubles of moral theologians are the "second act" in a Catholic drama about religious authority in the modern world, the "first act" of which caused such harm to Catholic biblical scholarship at the dawn of the twentieth century.

It is no accident that of the two theologians in the history of the Catholic University of America ever to lose their teaching positions because of dissent from the ordinary magisterium, one was a biblical scholar and the other a moral theologian. Henry Poels, who early in this century became convinced of the then revolutionary notion that Moses did not write all the books of the Pentatuch, was removed from his university post in 1910 after a series of events that Jesuit historian Gerald Fogarty calls "as complicated as a bad script for a soap opera."[19] And seventy-six years later we saw the dismissal of

17. James M. Gustafson, *Can Ethics Be Christian?* (Chicago: University of Chicago Press, 1975), p. 179.

18. For a "Catholic Revisionist" interpretation of "Revelation," see Richard P. McBrien, *Catholicism* (Minneapolis: Winston Press, 1980), pp. 201–43.

19. Gerald Fogarty, "Dissent at Catholic University: The Case of Henry Poels," *America* (October 11, 1986): 181.

Charles Curran, who went on to press his civil case against the university in court for the sake of the intellectual credibility of American Catholic higher education.[20] What Poels and Curran have in common is that their scholarship was perceived as a threat to religious authority. It was not until 1943 that Pope Pius XII's encyclical *Divino Afflante Spiritu* cautiously accepted modern critical biblical scholarship and implicitly vindicated Father Poels; we should hope that the truth in Father Curran's insights will more quickly be incorporated into papal teaching, for although the biblical case was eventually well resolved, its immediate effects were tragic. As Fogarty puts it, the Vatican's intransigence on this matter in 1910 "virtually destroyed biblical scholarship in the United States for the next generation."[21] The evidence today suggests that Vatican intransigence on sexual teaching is destroying much more than scholarship.

It was not only the *intellectual* discoveries of historical scholarship and literary criticism that put pressure on fundamentalist ways of understanding biblical authority in the nineteenth and early twentieth centuries; *moral* concern over racism and slavery also challenged scriptural fundamentalism. Similarly today, moral concern about women and sexual justice is combining with the intellectual forces challenging Catholic Fundamentalism, which tends to be more ecclesiastical than biblical. Just as the questions of racism and slavery put pressure on the ways Christians had understood the Bible to be revelatory, which led many to a more critical appreciation of biblical authority, so now the questions of sexism and sexual injustice are putting

20. The March 10, 1989, issue of *National Catholic Reporter* stated that District of Columbia Superior Court Judge Frederick Weisberg ruled February 28 that "Curran's contract did not give him the right to teach Catholic theology at [Catholic University of America] in the face of a definitive judgment by the Holy See that he was ineligible to do so." Curran subsequently announced that he did not plan to appeal this decision. In a press release commenting on the decision, John P. Boyle, President of the Catholic Theological Society of America, observed: "The refusal of the court to enter into the substance of a dispute over issues of doctrine and governance at the Catholic University can be read as a welcome reaffirmation of the American constitutional tradition of separation of church and state. But that refusal also puts upon the church itself full responsibility for preserving and nurturing that 'lawful freedom of inquiry' for scholars, both clerics and lay persons, which was proclaimed by the Second Vatican Council (*Gaudium et Spes*, n. 62; cf. 1983 *Code of Canon Law*, canon 218). Bishops and scholars who value as highly as the fathers of the council did the indispensable contribution of theology and related scholarly disciplines to the life of the church today need to reaffirm that lawful freedom promptly" (*Origins* 18 [March 16, 1989]: 673). The court decision is published in the same issue of *Origins*, pp. 664–72.

21. Fogarty, "Dissent," p. 183.

pressure on Catholics to rethink what it means to affirm the revelatory dimension of tradition and ecclesiastical authority. It is too soon to know what will result from this reconsideration, but we may hope that a more critical and mature appreciation of papal and episcopal authority will eventually carry the day. It was no small task for Christians in the past to deal with the Pauline injunction "slaves, be obedient to your human masters" (Eph. 6:5), and even today there remain Christians who continue to hold racist views as well as to regard biblical texts as unmediated expressions of God's opinion. In the present era this problem is reduced, but it is by no means eliminated.

Biblical authors and saintly popes have been mistaken in certain things they have said about women and sexuality. Can one recognize this and still be a Catholic believer, someone who affirms the doctrines of scriptural inerrancy and papal infallibility? Would it be more honest for people who think this way to admit they have lost the faith, have stepped outside the fold and are no longer true Catholics? There are many who feel this way, and the picture is complicated by the fact that the present pontiff, John Paul II, at times appears to be among them. During his 1987 address to the American bishops in Los Angeles, the pope declared that those who claim that dissent from the magisterium is compatible with being a good Catholic are guilty of "a grave error that challenges the teaching office of the bishops of the United States and elsewhere."[22] He implied that Catholics who hold this opinion should refrain from receiving the sacraments. So the stakes are indeed high. There are, however, many theologians and a number of bishops who do not share this theory of religious authority. Some of them regard the classic doctrines of scriptural inerrancy and papal infallibility as parallel affirmations about God's faithfulness to God's people. These affirmations offer assurance that the truth needed for salvation is available in sacred scripture and the church; they do not mean there is a one-to-one correspondence between God's opinion and every opinion expressed by biblical authors or popes, bishops, and Vatican officials. Thus, to say that the Bible is inerrant is not to claim there are no mistakes of historical or scientific fact, or questionable statements of value or obligation in biblical texts. It took centuries, but eventually American Christians came to understand that the injunction "slaves, be obedient to your human masters" cannot have been an expression of God's will for Africans abducted into chattel slavery in the Americas. And many, though not all, have come to realize that scriptural inerrancy is not so much a doctrine about the words on the biblical page as it is a claim about the fidelity of God to God's people.

22. Quoted by Joseph Berger, *New York Times,* September 17, 1987.

The theological concept of infallibility should be allowed to function in a similar way, namely, as a way of affirming that God graces the church with freedom from error in fundamental matters of faith and morals. Until quite recently this gift has generally been understood to be exercised by the pope or an ecumenical council only under certain very limited circumstances. But there is now in the air something called "creeping infallibilism," which is promoted by Catholic Fundamentalism and opposed by Catholic Revisionism.[23] The tension surrounding this difference is illustrated in the report of a general chapter meeting of Franciscans in Assisi published in the *National Catholic Reporter* for July 25, 1985, which observed that the friars were troubled by "some of the actions and statements of Archbishop Vincenzo Fagiolo, the pope's delegate at the chapter. Fagiolo [had] asked the friars to meditate on a letter from John Paul II, adding that there 'was no substantial difference between the word of God and the word of the pope.'" But can Fagiolo's opinion be sustained without risking confusion of Ultimate Reality with legitimate human authority? Would St. Paul have written this of the apostle Peter? Would St. Peter have allowed something like this to be said about himself? In my view, this opinion represents an ecclesiastical fundamentalism that betrays the wisdom of both Vatican ecumenical councils and promotes an idolatrous form of faith, in which the devout are encouraged to place their trust in the supposed certainty of human words rather than in the God who inspires them. In fact, as more and more Christians have come to realize, it is a serious mistake to place one's faith in the supposed certitude that biblical or ecclesial fundamentalism purports to guarantee, for this misguided quest for certitude deflects faith from its only proper object, namely, Divine Reality itself.

It should by now be apparent that I favor Catholic Revisionism and hope that the resurgence of Catholic Fundamentalism we are experiencing today is not a sign that Catholicism as a whole will return to the insular and triumphalistic attitudes of the period before the Second Vatican Council. But I believe it is important to appreciate where the energy of Catholic Fundamentalism is coming from and to understand that it holds a real attraction for many people. To convey this, I recall a song popular in my youth, which could well serve as a theme song for Catholic Fundamentalism. This is Father Daniel A. Lord's hymn "For Christ the King." Note the feeling of certainty and purpose it conveys, the sense of being part of a glorious campaign for good:

23. Charles E. Curran discusses this in *Tensions in Moral Theology* (Notre Dame: University of Notre Dame Press, 1988), p. 82.

> An army of youth
> Flying the standards of truth,
> We're fighting for Christ the Lord.
> Heads lifted high,
> Catholic Action our cry,
> And the cross our only sword.
> On earth's battlefield,
> Never a vantage we'll yield
> As dauntlessly on we swing.
> Comrades true, dare and do
> 'Neath the Queen's white and blue,
> For our flag, for our faith,
> For Christ the King.[24]

This song had everything: religious conviction, possession of ultimate truth, solidarity in a valiant cause, even patriotism. And we who think it is too simplistic, too rigid and militaristic have to recognize that some of its values, particularly the feeling of solidarity in a struggle for good, deserve to be retained, if only the uncritical notions of truth and righteousness can be appropriately complicated. But I am not sorry this song has fallen into disuse among Catholics or that a new song is now popular, one that fits much better with the values of Catholic Revisionism:

> Though the mountains may fall
> And the hills turn to dust,
> Yet the love of the Lord will stand
> As a shelter for all who will call on [God's] name,
> Sing the praise and the glory of God.[25]

It is good to hear so many Catholics singing this around the country. But do we realize what we are singing? We may have suffered droughts, but our hills have hardly turned to dust, and even those who have witnessed earthquakes have not seen a mountain fall. Such natural disasters are metaphors originally supplied by the prophet Isaiah to express the extremities that can be sustained when God's love and mercy are the context within which we interpret our

24. Daniel A. Lord, ed., *The Sodality Manual* (St. Louis: The Queen's Work, 1945), pp. 416–17.
25. Copyright Daniel L. Schutte, North American Liturgy Resources. The text is based on Isaiah 54:6–10; 49:15; 40:31–32.

lives. Isaiah is talking about what happens when finite objects, realities that seemed solid and dependable, suddenly prove otherwise.

"Though the mountains may fall and the hills turn to dust." Seemingly indestructible things will not last forever, but God's love does last forever. Christians have been through this before. First there was the law of Moses. More recently there have been the supposed literal truth of the Bible and, for Catholics, the supposed literal truth of papal teachings. These are all finite realities. Even if to some extent they are transcended in history, the God who inspired them remains, and their value—though never absolute or on a par with the divine—also remains. "Though the mountains may fall . . ."— though the pope should revise the teaching on artificial contraception and reverse the policy on women's ordination. "And the hills turn to dust . . ."— though the American bishops should decide to use the same methodology on the abortion question that they did on the use of nuclear weapons, stating their beliefs in the strongest possible terms but recognizing that they do not see all the factors in every situation and thus that a conscientious person might not share quite their same sense of obligation.[26] Though these and other earth-shaking things might happen, this will not mean that God has abandoned the people.

The danger is that while the contest goes on among scholars and church officials, the ordinary faithful may be left too much to their own resources. This may not be a bad thing if the situation does not continue indefinitely, for after such a long time in which Catholicism operated as if people were only capable of a passive style of morality involving obedience to rules set by others, there was undoubtedly need for a period of seeming chaos in order for us to assume more personal responsibility for our lives and decisions. But it troubles me that the human tendency to seek certitude in places short of God

26. See National Conference of Catholic Bishops, *The Challenge of Peace: God's Promise and Our Response* (Washington, D.C.: United States Catholic Conference, 1983). In the summary of this document the bishops declare: "At times we state universally binding moral principles found in the teaching of the Church; at other times the pastoral letter makes specific applications, observations and recommendations which allow for diversity of opinion on the part of those who assess the factual data of situations differently. However, we expect Catholics to give our moral judgments serious consideration when they are forming their own views on specific problems" (pp. i–ii). In the text itself the bishops declare in paragraph #153: "we judge resort to nuclear weapons to counter a conventional attack to be morally unjustifiable," and add the following footnote: "Our conclusions and judgments in this area although based on careful study and reflection of the application of moral principles do not have, of course, the same force as the principles themselves and therefore allow for different opinions, as the Summary makes clear" (note #69, p. 48).

may unwisely displace the notion of infallibility to something that cannot begin to bear its weight, namely, the individual conscience.

CONSCIENCE AND COMMUNITY

Conscience is a highly valued item in our culture, and something we rightly treasure. Few would disagree with St. Thomas Aquinas's judgment that "anyone upon whom the ecclesiastical authority, in ignorance of true facts, imposes a demand that offends against his clear conscience, should perish in excommunication rather than violate his conscience."[27] We resonate also with John Henry Newman's observation with respect to papal infallibility in a famous letter to the Duke of Norfolk: "Certainly, if I am obliged to bring religion into after-dinner toasts, (which indeed does not seem quite the thing) I shall drink,—to the Pope, if you please,—still, to Conscience first, and to the Pope afterwards."[28]

But this is not all that needs to be said. For although conscience is a deservedly valued item, it is also a problematic one. Mark Twain illustrates this brilliantly in his novel *Huckleberry Finn,* when he describes Huck's debate with himself about whether or not to turn in his friend Jim as a runaway slave. The narrator depicts Huck saying to himself: "Conscience says to me, 'What had poor Miss Watson done to you that you could see her nigger go off right under your eyes and never say one single word? What did that poor woman do to you that you could treat her so mean?'" Commenting on this incident, philosopher Alan Donagan points out that Huck's "conscience," which today we would recognize as erroneous, was "not merely sincere but was an instructed conscience in a professedly Christian society."[29] His elders might have described it as a "properly formed" conscience, for it reflected both civil law and church teaching.

Well, did Huck do wrong by acting directly against what he called his "conscience"? He certainly felt *guilty* about his choice not to betray his friend Jim. As Twain narrates in Huck's voice: "'Goodbye, sir,' says I; 'I won't let no

---

27. Quoted from *IV Sentences,* dist. 38, a.4, in McBrien, *Catholicism,* p. 1003.

28. Quoted in John T. Ford, "'Dancing on the Tight Rope': Newman's View of Theology," *CTSA Proceedings* 40 (1985): 133.

29. Alan Donagan, *The Theory of Morality* (Chicago: University of Chicago Press, 1977), p. 131. Quotations from *Huckleberry Finn* are taken from Donagan's discussion of conscience, which concludes with mention of the famous aphorism from Newman (p. 142).

runaway niggers get by me if I can help it.' They went off and I got aboard the raft, feeling bad and low, because I knowed very well I had done wrong." Is Huck right that he acted wrongly? Most would agree with Donagan that Huck's *action* was right and his *analysis* of his own behavior mistaken. As Donagan writes, Huck's "belief that the runaway was not a being to whom he owed respect," despite its sincerity, "was false to his deepest consciousness."[30]

This case of confusion of conscience shows how problematic the notion can be. Yet we continue to use it uncritically, often for the sake of avoiding ethical arguments, as if to say: "You follow your conscience, I'll follow mine; let a thousand consciences bloom." But surely we know of many instances where conscience is clear but behavior questionable or evil. Marquette University theologian Daniel Maguire is wise to insist: "To the general statement that one should always follow one's conscience should be added that one should always question one's conscience. The autonomy of conscience is not absolute."[31]

Certainly the popular use of this term has some problems. In the first place, perhaps because the reality of conscience has been expressed in so many metaphors—as an inner light, a guide, a still small voice within—we have gotten the mistaken impression that conscience is a sort of thing, on the order of moral radar equipment that automatically homes in on the right deed like a plane landing in a fog. Actually, these metaphors, as well as the once-popular language of conscience as a "faculty" of the soul, are quite limited and often misleading. Instead of regarding "conscience" as moral radar equipment, we do better to understand it as an aspect of the self, perhaps on a par with "intelligence." We all have some of it, but degrees vary greatly, and even a lot of it is no guarantee we'll always be right. Conscience is simply a *dimension of the self*, one central to our experience of moral agency.[32] I define it as personal moral awareness, experienced in the course of anticipating future situations and making moral decisions, as well as in the process of reflecting on one's past decisions and the quality of one's character, that is, the sort of person one is becoming.

Another thing that is problematic about popular notions of conscience is the tendency to regard it individualistically, whereas in reality conscience is a

30. Ibid., p. 139.

31. Daniel C. Maguire, *The Moral Choice* (Garden City, N.Y.: Doubleday, 1978), p. 379.

32. This view of conscience is similar to that discussed by Walter E. Conn in his interdisciplinary study *Conscience: Development and Self-Transcendence* (Birmingham, Ala.: Religious Education Press, 1981). I concur with Conn's judgment that "the term 'conscience' does not refer to any power or faculty, but is rather a metaphor pointing to the specifically moral dimension of the human person, to the personal subject as sensitive and responsive to value" (pp. 1–2).

very social phenomenon. This is so because the individual is always a self-in-relation to others, and our awareness of moral obligation is intimately bound up with our experiences of others who are significant in our lives. At one level the fact that conscience is a social phenomenon should be obvious. If we are at all aware of our experience, we are using language to think about it, and language comes from the linguistic community (or communities) in which we have been shaped as human selves. Moreover, what constitutes us as moral agents is our ability to care about other persons. We would not even be the persons we are if it were not for our relationships with others, whether living or dead, whether real or imaginary. As the social psychologist George Herbert Mead has expressed it, we are "constitutively social" beings.[33] We carry our relationships with us whether we attend to them or not, and we are influenced by them especially when we confront a difficult decision. The very brain cells we use to weigh the pros and cons of a course of action are affected by the persons we have known and loved, and whom we carry in these cells or, to use the more traditional metaphor, in our hearts. For this reason theologian H. Richard Niebuhr described the experience of conscience as a sort of "conversation" between the self and the others who matter to it.[34] George Eliot expressed the same insight even more poetically in the novel *Middle-march:* "'The theatre of all my actions is fallen,' said an antique personage when his chief friend was dead; and they are fortunate who get a theatre where the audience demands their best."[35]

This social dimension of conscience has been powerfully rendered in an early novel by the Nobel laureate Elie Wiesel. *Dawn* is a story about a fictitious survivor of the Holocaust who settled in British-ruled Palestine after World War II. There he joined the Zionist movement and fought against the British. The novel's plot revolves around whether or not Elisha will obey an order to execute a British officer, whom movement leaders have declared must die because the British have killed a captured Zionist. In this novel Wiesel dramatizes the conscience experience in terms of conversations between Elisha and "visitors" from his past in Europe, which take place in his imagination during the night before the scheduled execution of Captain John Dawson:

33. This theory of the social constitution of the self is presented in George Herbert Mead, *Mind, Self, and Society,* ed. Charles W. Morris (Chicago: University of Chicago Press, 1934).

34. H. Richard Niebuhr, "The Ego-Alter Dialectic and the Conscience," *Journal of Philosophy* 42 (1945): 352–59. Niebuhr's social (and historical) approach to moral agency is also discussed in *The Responsible Self* (New York: Harper & Row, 1963).

35. George Eliot, *Middlemarch,* p. 274.

The room was small, far too small to receive so many visitors at one time. Ever since midnight the visitors had been pouring in. Among them were people I had known, people I had hated, admired, forgotten. As I let my eyes wander about the room I realized that all of those who had contributed to my formation, to the formation of my permanent identity, were there.[36]

The young man's father and mother, his teacher, brothers, friends, comrades, and even his child-self are all present as Elisha considers whether he will become a murderer in the morning. The decision to obey the order to execute Dawson is an agonizing one because, on the one hand, the action seems necessary for Jewish survival and, on the other, it seems a betrayal of the slain victims of the Holocaust. Paradoxically, Elisha is both terribly alone and intensely aware of his relatedness as he comes to accept an identity he loathes out of a sense of duty to the Zionist cause. In the morning he ends the life of a man he knows does not deserve to die, and he endures the reproach of "the dead" who had "trooped in" to the cell with him: "My father and mother were there too, and the grizzled master, and Yerachmiel. Their silence stared at me."[37] Readers of *Dawn* complete the book with a felt understanding of a truth that psychologist Sidney Callahan has stated in the following terms: "[T]he inner self-self moral dialogue is to a great extent based upon past experiences of interpersonal dialogues."[38]

How a decision to follow through on one's personal sense of obligation is reached and held in the *presence* of one's community of accountability is evident also in Robert Bolt's play about St. Thomas More, *A Man for All Seasons*. In this drama we see what pain a person feels when those one loves do not understand a decision, pain stemming precisely from the fact that one cares about these others. Bolt's script conveys this anguish in the farewell scene between More and his family, in which More tells his daughter how deeply his decision is bound up with his sense of who he is in himself and in relation to her: "When a man takes an oath, Meg, he's holding his own self in his own hands. Like water. . . . And if he opens his fingers *then*—he needn't hope to find himself again. Some men are capable of this, but I'd be loathe to think your father one of them." Meg is not persuaded, nor is Alice, More's spouse, to whom he declares, "I am faint when I think of the worst that they may do

36. Elie Wiesel, *Dawn* (1960; trans. Frances Frenaya 1961; New York: Avon Books, 1970), p. 75.

37. Ibid., pp. 124–25.

38. Sidney Callahan, *In Good Conscience: Reason and Emotion in Moral Decision Making* (San Francisco: HarperCollins, 1991), p. 20.

to me. But worse than that would be to go with you not understanding why I go." Clearly More sees his obligation differently from his family members and friends at court; but his difficult choice is reached and maintained with them in mind. Nor does More consider only his family; he also voices concern for the king who will execute him: "I do none harm, I say none harm, I think none harm. . . . [M]y poor body is at the King's pleasure. Would God my death might do him some good." He is even aware of the situation of the man who will carry out the King's order, and he says to the headsman with kindness: "Friend, Be not afraid of your office. You send me to God."[39]

This same paradox of loneliness and relatedness in the living out of a conscientious choice is evident in the story of Franz Jägerstätter. Summoned to enlist in Hitler's army during World War II, he felt it was wrong to do so because the regime was evil. Not to serve, however, meant certain death in post-*Anschluss* Austria. Franz sought counsel from various advisors, and everyone, including his spouse, his pastor, and his bishop, declared it was his duty to preserve his life for the sake of his family. He was told that serving in the army did not necessarily imply an endorsement of Nazism; after all, millions of other Catholics experienced no great conflict of conscience in yielding to conscription under the circumstances. Franz considered this advice carefully, but still sensed God was asking something else of him. His letters from prison reveal a great love for his three young daughters and for the spouse who did not understand his decision. He was executed August 9, 1943. It has taken decades for people to appreciate his unsupported decision for the prophetic act it was, and today we are inclined to regret that there were not more like him. But even his lonely course was not taken in isolation from community. There has been a time lag in community appreciation, but not in community involvement.[40]

From these several examples, then, we see that conscience has important connections with our social worlds, and especially with those others whose ideals we admire, whose presence we care about, and whose esteem we want to deserve. And this is where the church can function so positively in our moral lives. The church does not supply the perfect answer to all our moral questions, but it gives us a community where faithful moral reasoning can go on, always with attention to the values Jesus cherished and with confidence in his continued presence in our midst. In addition, the church gives us saints to inspire us, friends to support us, spiritual guides to assist us, and teachers to

39. Bolt, *A Man for All Seasons*, pp. 81–94.
40. For literature on Franz Jägerstätter, see above, introduction, n. 12.

challenge and instruct us. Properly understood and exercised, the church's teaching authority is a marvelous gift for our moral and spiritual development, for it offers the wisdom gained from centuries of experience with the human heart to individuals who might otherwise have to reinvent the ethical wheel for themselves. Such an understanding of the relationship between authority and conscience is expressed in the *Declaration on Religious Freedom* of the Second Vatican Council: "In the formation of their consciences the faithful ought carefully to attend to [*diligenter attendere debent*] the sacred and certain doctrine of the Church" (*Dignitatis Humanae* #14). Giving diligent attention to official teaching is expected of Catholics, but this does not mean abdicating their own judgment and responsibility.[41]

In summary, the current tensions in Catholic moral theology are indicative of a crisis of growth; as a church we are groping for a more mature form of faith and ethics, one that has things properly in balance: authoritative teachers who convince by their wisdom instead of coercing by their punishments, and responsible believers whose faith is focused on God, not fixated on human books or authority figures. For however holy or close to God these may be, they are not themselves to be confused with the Divine Mystery that grounds our existence, who asks only one thing of us: "to do justice, and to love kindness, and to walk humbly with your God" (Micah 6:8 NRSV).

A prime challenge facing Catholic moral theology today is to understand and articulate what this biblical ideal means for our world, a world that has moved beyond modernity to a condition termed "postmodernity" by contemporary thinkers. Whether or not we have analyzed this shift in much depth, we al feel the effects of this condition. For this reason I shall next probe some of the major philosophical developments of the twentieth century and discuss their implications for the spiritual and moral lives of Catholics.

---

41. As Richard M. Gula notes in *Reason Informed by Faith: Foundations of Catholic Morality* (New York: Paulist, 1989), the conciliar fathers decided against a more restrictive formulation of this passage, which would have enjoined the faithful to "form their consciences *according to* the teaching of the church" (emphasis added). Instead, the language of "ought carefully to attend to" was chosen to respect the complexity of moral decision making. As Gula observes, "The less restrictive reading means that while Catholics must pay attention to the teaching of the church and give it presumptive authority, the magisterial teaching alone cannot settle a concrete case of conflicting values. Other circumstantial and personal factors also must be considered in trying to resolve a conflict of values" (p. 159).

CHAPTER TWO

Conscience at the Crossroads: Invitation to Radical Conversion

All conversion implies a break. . . . Our conversion process is affected by the socio-economic, political, cultural, and human environment in which it occurs. Without a change in these structures, there is no authentic conversion. We have to break with our mental categories, with the way we relate to others, with our way of identifying with the Lord, with our cultural milieu, with our social class, in other words, with all that can stand in the way of a real, profound solidarity with those who suffer, in the first place, from misery and injustice.

—Gustavo Gutiérrez, *A Theology of Liberation*[1]

In the last chapter we saw how differences between Catholic Fundamentalist and Catholic Revisionist approaches to faith and ethics account for certain tensions in the church. We also probed the experience of conscience as both an individual and a social phenomenon. It is time now to ask a question about the final part of that chapter, which introduced several examples to illustrate ideas about conscience. Is it merely coincidence that all of these examples (Huck Finn, Elisha, St. Thomas More, and Franz Jägerstätter) were from male experience? Why is it that the moral struggles that came so readily to mind all happened to involve boys and men wrestling with difficult choices in the world beyond their homes? Several reasons suggest themselves. In the past, moral theology and philosophy were written by men, which led to a "natural" preoccupation with male experience, a presumption that the "interesting" moral problems are those boys and men encounter in "their" spheres of action. We simply have a great deal more literature about males

---

1. Gustavo Gutiérrez, *A Theology of Liberation*, trans. Caridad Inda and John Eagleson (1973; rev. ed. Maryknoll, N.Y.: Orbis, 1988), p. 118.

struggling with moral decisions than about females. Moreover, Catholic authorities have tended to see women as divinely intended for "special" functions within a restricted sphere of activity, usually the home, where the moral life is seen to center on the duties of motherhood. When we add to this the fact that Catholic theology has traditionally presumed that the magisterium has a level of certainty on matters related to the domestic sphere (particularly sex and reproduction) that contrasts markedly with a tolerance for ambiguity on matters associated with the wider world (such as war and economics), it is easy to understand why women's moral experience has not been central to the literature of conscience.

But a feminist perspective by definition challenges these assumptions of patriarchal ethical tradition. It takes inspiration from such thinkers as Sarah Grimké, the abolitionist who responded to an 1837 pastoral letter from the General Association of Congregational Ministers of Massachusetts with words that remain true today: "Our [women's] powers of mind have been crushed, as far as man could do it, our sense of morality has been impaired by his interpretation of our duties, but nowhere does God say that he made any distinction between us, as moral and intelligent beings."[2]

Not only does a feminist perspective object to the presumption that women are moral minors, whose only task is to observe the norms set by men; it also questions the neat division of life spheres according to gender, and it disputes the claim that sexual and reproductive ethics are absolute, clear, and certain, whereas other sorts of human decisions are clouded with ambiguity. Thus, while the examples of conscience from chapter 1 retain their validity and are instructive for women as well as men, both groups can also learn from instances where women struggled to reach moral decisions, particularly on matters that male religious authorities presumed were "settled." Perhaps St. Joan of Arc's moral conflicts are too remote from our lives for her to be a practical model of conscience for us, but is there not a contemporary Joan, or two or three, whose experiences could enhance our grasp of the issues?

CONTEMPORARY WOMEN AND DILEMMAS OF CONSCIENCE

Take Joan X, for example, a thirty-eight-year-old teacher of physically impaired preschoolers. Her husband, George, is also employed, and the family income, while modest, is relatively secure. They have two teenage sons and

---

2. Sarah Grimké, quoted in Elizabeth Clark and Herbert Richardson, eds., *Women and Religion* (New York: Harper & Row, 1977), p. 212.

an eight-year-old daughter when Joan becomes aware of her fourth pregnancy, which surprises the couple because they had considered their family
complete and were using barrier methods to prevent conception. But they
accept the surprise and prepare to welcome a fourth child into the family.
Then the question arises: What about the next several years of fertility?
Should Joan be open to a fifth pregnancy? A sixth? Official Catholic teaching
insists there is an absolute obligation on Joan's part to do so or else to abstain
from sexual intercourse altogether.[3]

But Joan's sense of obligation is different. Some years ago she had concluded that her duty was to use artificial means of contraception, for several
reasons: the judgment that three children were "about right" for a family in
their circumstances, the sense that sexual spontaneity was important to her
marriage and that "natural" family planning was less helpful than "artificial"
alternatives, the perception that health risks to mother and child increase
with the age of a pregnant woman, the need to provide good educations for
the existing children, and the belief that justice for everyone in a limited
global economy is better served when couples in wealthy, high-consumption
countries do not have "large" families. If she felt this way before the fourth
pregnancy, she feels all the more so now, and she is particularly worried about
the health-risk factor in view of her increasing age. These concerns, and the
failure of the contraceptive measures the couple has taken, lead Joan to
believe that she ought to undergo a tubal ligation after their fourth child is
born.[4] This sense of obligation, however, conflicts markedly with official
Catholic teaching against sterilization for contraceptive purposes, which is
reinforced by a stringent policy against such procedures in all Catholic hospitals.[5] Is Joan simply being sinful and selfish in reaching the conclusion she

3. This teaching is expressed by Pope Paul VI in *Humanae Vitae:* "each and every marriage
act (*quilibet matrimonii usus*) must remain open to the transmission of life." The pontiff goes
on to condemn all "directly willed and procured abortion, even if for therapeutic reasons," and
adds: "Equally to be excluded, as the teaching authority of the Church has frequently declared,
is direct sterilization, whether perpetual or temporary, whether of the man or of the woman"
(Boston: St. Paul Editions, 1968), pp. 10–11 (##11, 14).

4. These judgments also concern George, whose conscience is not the focus of consideration here. Fortunately he and Joan have been able to discuss the issues and agree on the decisions together. George has long shared her sense of obligation to limit the family's size in light
of various needs, and he has even expressed a willingness to undergo a vasectomy to spare Joan
the more intrusive surgery. But he also sees Joan's point about the clarity of her felt obligation
not to become pregnant in her forties, even should unforeseen tragedy alter their circumstances, whereas his reproductive capacity is not so greatly affected by aging.

5. "Formal cooperation in the grave evil of contraceptive sterilization, either by approving

does, or is her situation in some way analogous to that of Franz Jägerstätter, who also received a clear message from religious authorities that differed from his sense of what God was asking of him?

Or we might take the case of Joan Y, a woman in circumstances even more difficult than our first example. This twenty-four-year-old is poor, unmarried, and already the mother of three young children, the eldest of whom suffers long-term effects from complications of a very premature birth. Joan wants to turn her life around and take responsibility for providing as well as she can for herself and her children, and she is discussing marriage with Robert, the father of her youngest child. Neither parent has the skills or education to hope for a well-paying job, but Catholic Charities has helped them find employment. Joan and Robert believe they can succeed as a family if no more children come along. Joan knows her earlier entanglements were not good, but she has a sense of hope about the present relationship, and she believes a tubal ligation is essential to keep the economic demands that will always be a pressure on this marriage from getting too difficult to bear.

Also worth considering is Sister Joan Z, who administers the only hospital serving the town where the other Joans live. More thoroughly educated in Catholic theology than these women, she is aware of the tradition's injustice toward females in general and of moral theology's inconsistent patterns of tolerance and rigidity in particular. It troubles her that the Catholic ethical tradition has accepted ambiguity in areas that have mainly involved men's experience of value tensions, such as politics and war, but has insisted on perfection in areas where women have been keenly aware of value conflicts and human limitations, especially decisions around reproduction.[6]

Indeed, to Sister Joan both women's decisions to undergo tubal ligation seem responsible, if ambiguous; and she regrets being required to enforce a

---

or tolerating it for medical reasons, is forbidden and totally alien to the mission entrusted by the church to Catholic health-care facilities. . . . In the unlikely and extraordinary situation in which the principle of material cooperation seems to be justified, consultation with the bishop or his delegate is required" (National Conference of Catholic Bishops, "Statement on Tubal Ligation," *Origins* 10 [August 28, 1980]: 175).

6. For a detailed discussion of methodological differences between official Catholic social and sexual teachings, see Charles E. Curran, *Tensions in Moral Theology* (Notre Dame: University of Notre Dame Press, 1988), pp. 87–109; and Richard A. McCormick, "Human Sexuality: Toward a Consistent Ethical Method," in *One Hundred Years of Catholic Social Thought*, ed. John A. Coleman (Maryknoll, N.Y.: Orbis, 1991), pp. 189–97. McCormick calls for a thorough renewal of Catholic sexual teaching and declares that such teaching must become personalist, collaborative, ecumenical, compassionate, and feminist, among other characteristics.

policy she finds unreasonable. Their situations are less extreme than those of other women she has known, who, despite heart or kidney ailments serious enough to make pregnancy a life-threatening danger, cannot receive tubal ligations in Catholic hospitals that observe the official guidelines. From history she knows that women's genetic role in reproduction was not understood before the invention of the microscope and that the procedure of tubal ligation could not even have been imagined by the theologians who originally declared sterilization to be "intrinsically evil."[7] She has reason to think they had castration in mind when making this judgment, and she believes that modern forms of sterilization need to be assessed in light of changed historical circumstances as well as traditional values and principles. She recognizes that there is loss of human good in all decisions to limit reproductive capacity, including the choice of evangelical celibacy, and she believes that sometimes the sacrifice of this capacity is warranted for the sake of other values. In terms of the cases of Joans X and Y, Joan Z is particularly troubled to know that the middle-class woman denied a tubal ligation because of Catholic hospital policy can obtain one elsewhere but the woman who cannot afford to travel so far from her children will need to risk further pregnancies, sacrifice marital relations, or else undergo a hysterectomy, a much more serious form of surgery than tubal ligation.

Sister Joan knows that this third option is not likely today, since medical requirements for hysterectomy are much stricter now than in the past, but she recalls the reasoning that led to some surgeries she heard discussed a number of years ago. According to the classical moral calculus, a physician could declare a woman's uterus to be diseased (for example, pre-cancerous due to a fibroid condition) and recommend its excision for medical rather than contraceptive reasons. If the uterus was judged to be a diseased organ, a hysterectomy could be performed on grounds acceptable to a Catholic hospital, despite the fact that patient and physician might have been aware that the immediate need was to prevent pregnancy and the risk of cancer was relatively remote. This way of proceeding took advantage of an established exception in Catholic moral reasoning, which prohibits "direct" sterilization (that is, surgery done for the purpose of rendering someone infertile) but tolerates "indirect" sterilization (that is, surgery done for the purpose of curing a disease, which merely causes infertility as a side effect). To Joan Z the idea of a

---

7. For a lucid presentation of historical background and theological and moral issues concerning sterilization, see John P. Boyle, *The Sterilization Controversy: A New Crisis for the Catholic Hospital?* (New York: Paulist, 1977).

woman's having a hysterectomy because it falls under the category of "indirect," when the safer, less costly procedure of tubal ligation would suffice, is hypocritical. Nor does she think much of the "solution" practiced in some urban settings of wheeling a woman from the delivery room of a Catholic hospital to an adjacent non-Catholic facility for a tubal ligation and then wheeling her back to recover in the original building, all for the sake of keeping to the letter of mandated policy on sterilizations. Sister Joan would prefer a more honest approach to the ambiguities involved, and it saddens her to see patients and staff suffering from an unreasonable church policy, as well as to know that some former members of her religious community cited Vatican attitudes toward women and women's moral agency as one of the factors in their own decisions to leave the community.

THE CONTINUING CONTROVERSY OVER STERILIZATION

All of my Joans are fictitious, but the dilemmas portrayed are very real. Such cases have not been widely considered in the literature of conscience, however, in part because their resolutions have seemed so obvious to dominant theorists, albeit for divergent reasons. On the one hand, official Catholic teaching has assumed that all three women are *objectively* wrong in their moral judgments, though perhaps excusable to some degree on subjective grounds. On the other hand, secular approaches tend to see the decisions as basically unproblematic. As long as a woman gives "informed consent," what else is there to say about tubal ligation? There is an important group in the middle, of course, but the discussion has been dominated by the extremes, and to many Catholic and non-Catholic thinkers the ban on tubal ligation seems more an instance of religious authoritarianism than the result of a persuasive moral argument. Perhaps if there could be a serious ethical discussion of tubal ligation among Catholic theologians and health professionals, the middle ground they share could be explored to everyone's advantage.

But this is precisely what is lacking in today's church. The painful truth is that sustained public discussion about contraceptive ("direct") sterilization is not acceptable in Catholic settings. Indeed, when the sponsors of one of the largest private healthcare systems in the United States, the Sisters of Mercy of the Union, attempted in 1980 to initiate discussion about the possibility of a policy change, Vatican officials intervened to prevent reconsideration of the policy prohibiting tubal ligations, even in cases involving serious medical conditions. Had the discourse the women sought taken place, our literature on conscience and reproductive ethics alike might have been enriched by consideration of cases in which Catholics struggled with the value conflicts involved. But, as the eminent Jesuit thinker Richard A. McCormick has noted, hierarchical interference with the process of moral reflection sought by the Mercy administrators has put Catholic hospitals in a very difficult position and undermined magisterial authority as well. During tense exchanges between church officials and Mercy leaders in 1980–1982, the substantive issue of sterilization never received attention. Instead the matter was reduced to the question of whether or not the Sisters of Mercy would obey Vatican authorities. McCormick, who as a consultant to the Mercy leaders had recommended that tubal ligations be permitted only when pregnancy would be medically irresponsible, has discussed the harmful results of Vatican use of juridical power to stifle a much-needed ethical conversation in several articles published in the 1980s.[8] Another consultant, Margaret A. Farley, herself a member of the Sisters of Mercy, has analyzed the decision of the Mercy leadership team to yield to Vatican pressure in a highly informative case study. Speaking at the 1982 convention of the Catholic Theological Society of America, Farley provides the following account of why the leaders of her religious community withdrew the invitation they had sent hospital administrators to discuss policy on tubal ligation:

> The decision to forgo a public position of dissent was not made because of a new belief in the teaching of the magisterium (on the issue of tubal ligation) or out of religious obedience to a disciplinary command. This does not mean that the Sisters of Mercy accept no fundamental authority in the Church, or that they see themselves in regard to their life and ministry as only autonomous agents in the Church, not subject to the Church and its legitimate authority in an important sense. It does mean that in this case they could not find the teaching of the magisterium persuasive and, in fact, interpreted the demands of the

---

8. Richard A. McCormick, *Notes on Moral Theology 1981 Through 1984* (Lanham, Md.: University Press of America, 1984), pp. 83–86, 187–92; idem, "Sterilization: The Dilemma of Catholic Hospitals," in *The Critical Calling: Reflections on Moral Dilemmas Since Vatican II* (Washington, D.C.: Georgetown University Press, 1989), pp. 273–87. An earlier essay by this same title appeared in *America* 143 (1980): 222–25. McCormick's comments on this publication are instructive: "In 1980 I coauthored (with bioethicist Corrine Bayley, CSJ) an article in *America* arguing that some sterilizations were morally defensible. A bishop friend of mine remarked to me, 'I can name you at least one hundred bishops who agree with you—but none who will say so publicly.' That is, of course, profoundly saddening for anyone who treasures the free flow of information in the Church." These words are found in McCormick, *Health and Medicine in the Catholic Tradition* (New York: Crossroad, 1984), pp. 103–4.

magisterium as an attempt to use juridical power to settle a question of truth. Perhaps even more importantly, they perceived the demand for continuation of a policy which they were convinced was unjustly injurious to other persons (patients in their hospitals) as contradictory to the overall obligation of the Sisters of Mercy (in fidelity and obedience to God and the Church) to carry on a ministry of healing. In other words, without special further justification, these specific demands by church officials entailed doing evil.[9]

Why then did these women decline to take a public position in opposition to the magisterium? After attending to three competing values at stake in the controversy—community, ministry, and truth—they judged that in this instance truth (and its potential to render the healthcare system more just) must be sacrificed. Silence and submission seemed necessary to preserve the religious community and its ministry, for a public confrontation with the Vatican could well have led to a split within the religious congregation that would have had a devastating impact on its institutional operations of all types. Therefore, employing language reminiscent of the sterilization discussion itself, Farley explains that the Mercy leadership accepted the evil entailed in "material cooperation" with a problematic Vatican directive and hoped that their decision would lead ultimately to greater good for the church. Farley describes the decision in terms of a relatively adequate choice that must continue to be scrutinized:

> The decision of the Sisters of Mercy must still be reviewed and critiqued by those within the Community and without. The answer to the question, "Why did this group of women agree to be silenced?" seems to me to be this: "In order that theirs and other voices may ultimately prevail." The danger, of course, is that the silence will grow, and that power in the Church will be more and more isolated, especially from the experience of women. But this story is unfinished.[10]

How did Catholicism get to the point where priests and sisters would object as strongly to magisterial teaching and Vatican policy as McCormick and Farley have done, not to mention other scholars who have published on the issues of sterilization and authoritarianism?[11] What has led to such

---

9. Margaret A. Farley, "Power and Powerlessness: A Case in Point," *CTSA Proceedings* 37 (1982): 117.

10. Ibid., p. 119.

11. For a European instance, see Johannes Gründel, "Zur Problematik de operativen Sterilisation in katholischen Krankenhäusern," *Stimmen der Zeit* 199 (1981): 671–77, which is discussed in McCormick, *Notes on Moral Theology 1981 through 1984*, pp. 83–85.

sharply divided opinions on right behavior for Catholics and church authorities? In this controversy we have a vivid instance of the tensions between the two approaches to faith and ethics that were discussed in the last chapter. Official positions and actions tend to reflect the approach of Catholic Fundamentalism, whereas the writings of McCormick and Farley reflect the approach of Catholic Revisionism, especially in its willingness to tolerate change and ambiguity in moral teachings that were once considered absolute. The impasse over tubal ligation has resulted from several factors, including twentieth-century advances in medicine and communications, the worldwide movement to respect the equality and dignity of women, and intellectual developments associated with twentieth-century philosophical attention to language and its uses.

THE SIGNIFICANCE OF TWENTIETH-CENTURY LINGUISTIC PHILOSOPHY FOR MORAL THEOLOGY

The importance of linguistic philosophy to church concerns may not be apparent until we notice how much the impasse over tubal ligation centers on words. Other items are also at stake, including lives and livelihoods, but the fact is that the Mercy sisters were asked to retract the words they had written to hospital administrators, McCormick has been calling for national guidelines for Catholic hospitals that reflect beliefs and practices more accurately than present statements of policy, and Vatican authorities have been insisting on classical formulas about what constitutes good and evil behavior. Clearly this controversy has everything to do with language and the way it is understood and employed. Since this question of language has been the focus of intense philosophical scrutiny in our time, it will be helpful here to probe some of the findings of twentieth-century philosophy's fascination with language.

This fascination has proved so revolutionary in outcome that it has come to be known as "the linguistic turn," a designation that calls to mind previous intellectual "turning points" such as "the Copernican turn" in sixteenth-century science and Immanuel Kant's "turn to the subject" in eighteenth-century philosophy. This metaphor of turning invites us to think of knowledge in terms of a progression in space and time. We are on a journey, and at times we need to shift direction both to correct the distortions that have accompanied our progress and to respect the new terrain we have reached. The image is a rich one, and it resonates well with the biblical view that life entails a series of conversions, or corrections of course, as people seek to follow the way of God more faithfully. The image also resonates well with one of the principal themes of the Second Vatican Council, that of the church as the pilgrim people of God. Moreover, this image of turning can help us appreciate why there are such deeply felt concerns on both sides of Catholic disputes in moral theology. Catholic Revisionism sees around the bend, as it were, and fears disaster if the turn is not made soon enough. Catholic Fundamentalism, by contrast, fears the whole caravan may go into a catastrophic skid if the turn is made too sharply, or even attempted at all. In this regard the example of the earlier "Copernican turn" is especially instructive. We know that a striking conceptual alternative, one that shook the Christian worldview profoundly, presented itself in the sixteenth century when the necessity of turning from a long-held geocentric cosmology and adopting a heliocentric one instead became clear to the scientifically informed. This "Copernican turn" did not happen with ease, as the events surrounding the trial of Galileo make clear. In *The Copernican Revolution* (1957), historian of science Thomas S. Kuhn describes the tensions of that era in powerful terms:

> Copernicanism was potentially destructive of an entire fabric of thought. . . . More than a picture of the universe and more than a few lines of Scripture were at stake. The drama of the Christian life and the morality that had been made dependent upon it would not readily adapt to a universe in which the earth was just one of a number of planets. Cosmology, morality, and theology had long been interwoven in the traditional fabric of Christian thought described by Dante at the beginning of the fourteenth century. . . . Copernicanism required a transformation in man's view of his relation to God and of the basis of his morality.[12]

Something of similar proportions is under way in contemporary culture. Much is at stake in how Catholicism will adapt to the changed circumstances of our day, including the intellectual developments associated with "the linguistic turn." Without going into great detail about these matters, it will be useful here to review some of the main features and results of this philosophical movement, which is associated with the names of thinkers that include Ludwig Wittgenstein, Martin Heidegger, Ferdinand de Saussure, and Jacques Derrida, among others. (Because of the technical nature of this subject, some readers may prefer to skip the next section or two and resume the argument with the section entitled "Linguistic Philosophy: Temptation and Resource" or "Plurality, Ambiguity, and Moral Theology." Others may prefer to resume

---

12. Thomas S. Kuhn, *The Copernican Revolution* (Cambridge, Mass.: Harvard University Press, 1957), pp. 192–93.

reading even later, when the fruits of the linguistic turn are applied to concrete issues concerning sexuality in "Beyond the Linguistic Turn: The Radical Conversion of Catholic Consciousness.")

HISTORY OF THE "LINGUISTIC TURN"

In the introduction to his work *The Linguistic Turn* (1967), philosopher Richard Rorty gives credit for coining the phrase "the linguistic turn" to Gustav Bergmann, who had observed in 1953 that there was something radically new about the way philosophers influenced by Wittgenstein were going about their work. From Wittgenstein they had learned to notice how close and special is the relationship between philosophy and language, and this insight thoroughly transformed the way they approached philosophical problems.[13] Rorty sums up thirty years of linguistic philosophy as having caused a "thoroughgoing rethinking of certain epistemological difficulties which have troubled philosophers since Plato and Aristotle." In a footnote he adds that these difficulties are due to a "'spectatorial' account" of knowledge, one presupposing that the mind can have direct access to knowledge "without the mediation of language."[14] Rorty's later work, particularly *Philosophy and the Mirror of Nature*, continues the critique of such an epistemology and moves the discussion into the territory known as "hermeneutics," which broadly speaking, is the science of interpretation.[15]

Writing twenty years after Rorty published *The Linguistic Turn*, and half a century after the advent of "linguistic philosophy," theologian David Tracy, in *Plurality and Ambiguity* (1987), substantially agrees with Rorty that the significance of the linguistic turn is epistemological and that the category of hermeneutics is central to grasping its significance. Tracy claims that the current cultural period is a "critical" one, in the sense that we find ourselves—like Augustine in his day, or Schleiermacher and Hegel in theirs—needing "to find new ways of interpreting ourselves and our traditions."[16] That Tracy

13. See Richard Rorty, ed., "Introduction," *The Linguistic Turn: Recent Essays in Philosophical Method* (Chicago: University of Chicago Press, 1967), p. 9. Bergmann's 1953 essay, "Logical Positivism, Language, and the Reconstruction of Metaphysics," is included in Rorty's anthology (pp. 63–71).

14. Ibid., p. 39.

15. Richard Rorty, *Philosophy and the Mirror of Nature* (Princeton, N.J.: Princeton University Press, 1979).

16. David Tracy, *Plurality and Ambiguity: Hermeneutics, Religion, Hope* (San Francisco: Harper & Row, 1987), p. 8.

himself has made the linguistic turn is clear when he say such things as "all understanding is linguistic through and through," and "[t]here are no ideas free of the web of language."[17] In other words, all that we know is dependent on symbolic codes and texts.

Tracy uses psychological, social, and spatial imagery to discuss the developments in thought that have been subsumed under the metaphor of "the linguistic turn," which all have to do with attempts "to explain the uneasy relationships among language, knowledge, and reality."[18] Such theories, he observes, have the effect of "interrupting" conversations that would otherwise naïvely consider "knowledge" and "reality" without attention to the plurality and ambiguity bound up with *all* understanding because of its linguistic, social, and historical character.

Tracy's discussion can be summarized in three main points. First, the function of the linguistic turn has been "therapeutic" in that the new direction removed illusions that went with its chief predecessors, positivism and romanticism. Second, the linguistic turn marks the difference between "modern" and "postmodern" thought. Whereas the former was still traditional in the way it saw language as a more or less stable *instrument* employed by a relatively unified self, the latter views language much less instrumentally, recognizing a dividedness in the self that threatens all previous assurances. After the linguistic turn there is no going back to a situation of untroubled confidence in what Tracy calls "the power of reflection to eliminate error and render consciousness translucent if not transparent."[19] Tracy's third point is that the change has occurred in three stages, brief consideration of which will further clarify what the linguistic turn involves.

The first stage of the linguistic turn concentrated on the *use* of language. As Tracy observes, Wittgenstein and Heidegger showed that language "is not an instrument that I can pick up and put down at will," but instead "is always already there, surrounding and invading all I experience, understand, judge, decide, and act upon." Wittgenstein's distinct contribution was to stress the *social character* of language and therefore of understanding; his insight into the plurality of "language games" and "life forms," in Tracy's estimation, "freed much Anglo-American philosophy from the seductions of positivism." Heidegger's achievement was to call attention to the *historicity* of all understanding. His views on "language as the house of being," Tracy declares,

17. Ibid., p. 43.
18. Ibid., p. 47.
19. Ibid., p. 77.

"helped to free much Continental philosophy from idealistic and romantic self-interpretations." These contributions "de-centered" the human self and put in question the anthropocentric worldview that had characterized the modern period.[20]

The contributions of Saussure, the structuralists and semioticians, and the deconstructionists all belong to Tracy's second stage of the linguistic turn, which viewed language as *system*. Saussure's basic insight was that language is a system of differential relations. One can see this by noting that the difference of a single phoneme is what gives the word "turn" its meaning, in distinction from similar words such as "burn" or "churn." Structuralists and semioticians applied this theory about language to other systems of signs and structures, such as myths and societies. More recently, the poststructuralists, or deconstructionists, have taken Saussure's insight concerning the differential nature of linguistic relations and drawn the conclusion that *no* system of linguistic, textual, or social structures is either closed or fully analyzable. All meaning depends on the "traces" of signifiers that are "absent" from a given text and yet "present" in their effects. What this implies, Tracy says, is that "[a]ny claims to full presence, especially claims to self-presence in conscious thought, are illusions that cannot survive a study of language as a system of differential relations." Summarizing the contribution of the most famous practitioner of deconstructionism, Tracy declares: "Like a Zen master, [Jacques] Derrida has exposed an illusion, the illusion that we language-sated beings can ever be fully present to ourselves or that any other reality can be fully present to us either."[21]

With Derrida's renewed attention to difference and rhetoric having thus undermined the structuralist hopes for thoroughgoing understanding of linguistic, mythic, and social systems, the second stage of the linguistic turn has been completed, and a third stage begun. Going beyond concern with language as *use* and language as *system* (or differential nonsystem), many philosophers are now preoccupied with language as *discourse*. This stage deals with what goes on when "someone says something to someone." The move to "discourse analysis" is seen in Edward Said's literary criticism, Paul Ricoeur's work on metaphor, Michel Foucault's study of the relations between "power" and "truth," and Jacques Lacan's rewriting of psychoanalysis, to mention

20. Ibid., pp. 49–50. For an important critique of anthropocentrism, see James M. Gustafson, *Ethics from a Theocentric Perspective,* 2 vols. (Chicago: University of Chicago Press, 1981, 1984).

21. Tracy, *Plurality and Ambiguity,* p. 59.

some notable examples. There is a renewed concern with how language is actually employed; we are pursuing social, historical, ethical, and political questions with a new recognition that the rhetorics we experience influence our motivations and actions. Fascination with language itself has been transcended, and attention is now given to the whole relational transaction of human efforts to understand and communicate, which is what the rich concept of "discourse," with its bivalent meanings of "reasoning" and "speaking," entails. We are only beginning to recognize the implications of this last stage of the turn, which include Foucault's insight that "every discourse bears within itself the anonymous and repressed actuality of highly particular arrangements of power and knowledge."[22]

PLURALITY, AMBIGUITY, AND MORAL THEOLOGY

Tracy's narrative is spare, and it leaves out some of the interesting moves in Anglo-American philosophy that are relevant to the concerns of moral theologians, such as the development of speech-act theory. But nevertheless it correctly states the main results of this half century of conceptual change: we postmoderns have a new sense of plurality and ambiguity about our knowledge of anything, including ourselves and our most revered traditions. This development has greatly complicated life for moral theologians:

1. With respect to *epistemology*, aspirations to perfect certainty and absolute stability must be tempered; we can at best strive for relatively adequate knowledge in our given social-historical circumstances.
2. With respect to discussions of *moral agency* and responsibility, our efforts cannot avoid critical analyses of social, historical, political, psychological, and economic factors.
3. With respect to *our professional work*, the plurality and ambiguity of our own situation as moral theologians must be recognized; the element of self-critique is essential.

Clearly a "postmodern" moral theology has been under way for some decades now, but we cannot gloss over how difficult the undertaking currently is, given the context of our labors in a religious institution that has only lately begun to come to terms with *modernity*, let alone *postmodernity!*[23] Small

22. Ibid., p. 79.
23. See Joseph A. Komonchak, "Issues Behind the Curran Case," *Commonweal* 114 (January 30, 1987): 43–47.

wonder, it may seem, that the Catholic forces opposing the Copernican turn, which were officially freed up by the reinstatement of Galileo in 1979, should lately find another outlet by opposing moral theologians who, with varying degrees of self-awareness, are taking their lessons from the linguistic turn.[24]

But to paint the picture thus as simply one of intransigent classicist "power" versus historically conscious, relatively adequate "truth," would be to miss the main point of the linguistic turn, namely, the existence of plurality and ambiguity on *both* sides of such struggles. There is some validity in characterizing the current time as a contest between abusive power and new, relatively adequate understandings of religious and moral truth, but this validity is not without ambiguity. The many who object to Vatican attempts to stifle today's ethical debates need strategies of hope and resistance to keep our enterprise going productively in these discouraging days.[25] We should pray fervently for the "moral equivalent" of *Divino Afflante Spiritu,* the 1943 encyclical that finally affirmed the validity of critical biblical scholarship and implicitly vindicated Henry Poels, the biblical scholar whose firing from the Catholic University of America in 1910 was discussed in the last chapter. In the meanwhile we should also seek to do justice to the concerns that motivate the best of those who are employing, perhaps too desperately, their own strategies of resistance against the results of the linguistic turn, against the terrors felt to be unleashed by this latest in a long series of "revolutionary" philosophical discoveries.

Although some church officials are overly controlling in their mode of governance, in many instances their actions are conscientious ones. This seems to have been the case with Pope Paul VI in deciding to endorse the opinion of the minority of the papal "birth control commission" when he promulgated the encyclical *Humanae Vitae* in 1968.[26] Especially where sexual ethics is concerned, Catholic conservatism can be regarded as a "holding action" designed to prevent the sort of chaos prevalent where the values of the "sexual revolu-

24. Pope John Paul II, "Faith, Science, and the Search for Truth," *Origins* 9 (November 29, 1979): 389–92. From a historical perspective it is interesting to note that the year 1979 also saw the beginning of correspondence between the Congregation of the Doctrine of the Faith and Charles E. Curran, which led eventually to his being removed from the ranks of officially authorized Catholic theologians in 1986.

25. In *Plurality and Ambiguity* Tracy recommends strategies of "resistance, attention, and hope" as preferable to the simplistic options of optimism and pessimism (p. 72).

26. See Robert Blair Kaiser, *The Politics of Sex and Religion* (Kansas City, Mo.: Leaven Press, 1985); and Peter Hebblethwaite, *Paul VI: The First Modern Pope* (Mahwah, N.J.: Paulist, 1993).

tion" are expressed without discipline and cause great harm, until such time as a practical and easily communicated contemporary Christian alternative has been constructed. The problem is that although this reconstructive work is well under way, it has been greatly hindered by the repressive approach to church governance, whether well intentioned or not. In the process many Catholics have come to agree with novelist Mary Gordon, who declared some years ago: "I have always felt it a safe proposition that whatever position the Vatican takes on the sexuality of women, I'm in a good place on the other side."[27] In the final section of this chapter I shall deal more directly with the connections between the debates on sexual teaching and the "linguistic turn," but first I shall describe several ways in which linguistic philosophy and the secular ethics influenced by it have affected moral theology more generally.

LINGUISTIC PHILOSOPHY: TEMPTATION AND RESOURCE

The work of the early stages of linguistic philosophy resulted in a spate of discussions in moral philosophy that we label under such headings as "emotivism," "prescriptivism," and "meta-ethics." The discussions have had valuable results, but they have also led to problems, the most serious of which is described by Oxford philosopher Mary Warnock as follows:

> One of the consequences of treating ethics as the analysis of ethical language is . . . that it leads to the increasing triviality of the subject. . . . One aspect of this trivializing of the subject is the refusal of moral philosophers in England to commit themselves to any moral opinions. . . .[T]he concentration upon the most general kind of evaluative language, combined with the fear of committing the naturalistic fallacy, has led too often to discussions of grading fruit, or choosing fictitious games equipment, and ethics as a serious subject has been left further and further behind.[28]

Such findings are all the more serious in view of the fact that moral philosophy's fascination with linguistic rigor and clarity developed during the period

---

27. Mary Gordon, "Baby M: New Questions About Biology and Destiny," *Ms.* (June 1987): 28.

28. Mary Warnock, *Ethics Since 1900*, 3rd ed. (Oxford: Oxford University Press, 1978) 136–37. Similarly, G. J. Warnock declares in the introduction to *Morality and Language* (Totowa, N.J.: Barnes & Noble, 1983) that he had concluded by 1962 that "certain doctrines about language were actually retarding progress [in moral philosophy] by directing attention the wrong way" (p. 7).

of the Holocaust and the post–World War II arms race. I share Warnock's concern that the inclination to analyze linguistic phenomena without regard to normative considerations and practical implications is a temptation we ought to resist. Whenever the linguistic turn leads to an obsession with language that is detached from the questions and struggles of ordinary life, there is danger of distraction and trivialization. But to recognize this danger is by no means to deny that studies of words and speech acts can be of value to moral theology. My theme, after all, is ambiguity, not villainy, and to balance the account I shall now mention five ways in which insights from secular moral philosophy have enriched moral theology.

Emphasis on Discourse

In the first place, linguistic philosophy has called attention to the category of *discourse* and to the variety entailed in the discourses employed and studied by moral theologians. One of the most valuable insights related to this emphasis involves a social ideal expressed by James M. Gustafson in terms of "a community of moral discourse."[29] Gustafson originally used the phrase when speaking of the potential for a university to be a locus for interdisciplinary ethical reflection, but theologians have also used it to describe the church, seen as ideally a community that searches, in dialogue, for moral wisdom. Much has been written about the complementary roles of hierarchical magisterium, theologians, and faithful alike in this ongoing process of discovery through discourse. Thanks to the linguistic turn, we are coming to appreciate the dialogical nature of knowledge, and thus to prize open discussion as essential for progress toward relative adequacy on practical moral questions. Catholic theologians have expressed this ideal of a community of moral discourse in various ways. John P. Boyle, for example, has observed that "the traditional doctrines of indefectibility and infallibility of the Church . . . stand in tension with others which assert that the eschaton is not yet." This means that

> [t]he Church's perception and thematization of moral values is therefore in need of correction and reformulation, especially at the level of specific moral directives. . . . Given the multiplicity of the gifts of the Spirit in the Church, the community must be one of ongoing moral discernment as it seeks the implications of its Christian commitment for its life.[30]

29. James M. Gustafson, "The University as a Community of Moral Discourse," *Journal of Religion* 53 (1973): 397–409.
30. John Boyle, "The Natural Law and the Magisterium," in *Readings in Moral Theology*

Boyle's words reflect the insight of the linguistic turn that knowledge, which is inherently hermeneutical, social, and historical, is never perfect but always in process.

Likewise, Gerard J. Hughes, in a study of method in moral theology that is greatly influenced by linguistic moral philosophy, makes a convincing case for the need and possibility of "open moral debate" in a church that esteems tradition and authority.[31] The American bishops have begun to model this ideal of the "community of moral discourse" in the consultative processes whereby they drafted their pastoral letters *The Challenge of Peace* and *Economic Justice for All*. On the other side, efforts to inhibit the process of ethical discourse, whether by firing, canceling speaking engagements, or other variations on the theme of silencing, have increasingly been called into question by theologians who recognize that reasoned argument is essential to the doing of moral theology. Currently it is authoritarianism and its reverse, uncritical disdain for authority, that seem most threatening to the ideal of the church as a "community of moral discourse," and these threats are best countered by establishing a climate where the values of open moral debate and respect for authoritative teaching are both promoted.[32]

Acceptance of Plurality

A second result of the linguistic turn is the appreciation of *plurality* in various dimensions of social and intellectual life. Plurality is opposed to authoritarianism and to monisms of all sorts, but is it also destined to degenerate into relativism? This is the question that naturally arises when moralists encounter plurality. Tracy maintains that the recognition of plurality, in combination with attention to the ambiguity of history and society, leads ideally to decisions about which visions of the good life are more relatively adequate than others, and although these judgments are not absolute, they are far from relativistic. Hughes devotes attention to plurality also in his study of method in moral theology and argues that pluralism in ethics is both inevitable and

---

No. 3: The Magisterium and Morality, ed. Charles E. Curran and Richard A. McCormick (New York: Paulist, 1982), pp. 444–45.

31. Gerard J. Hughes, *Authority in Morals: An Essay in Christian Ethics* (Washington, D.C.: Georgetown University Press, 1978), p. 129.

32. Richard A. McCormick states the case for such a balance in *The Critical Calling: Reflections on Moral Dilemmas Since Vatican II* (Washington, D.C.: Georgetown University Press, 1989).

desirable—inevitable because the evidence needed for making ethical judgments is complex and always to some degree incomplete, and desirable because of the "almost inexhaustible variety of human nature and the rich diversity of the many ways in which human beings can find fulfillment."[33] Hughes is careful to distinguish pluralism from relativism, maintaining that "acceptable pluralism" must yield the fruits of "happiness and justice," which assumes that some "culturally neutral" criteria of adequacy are available to judge these fruits, despite the difficulties inherent in cross-cultural comparisons. That Hughes and others are making the effort to clear the ground for pluralism in a religious institution traditionally marked by uniformity even in smaller matters is an indication that moral theology has entered the postmodern age.[34] Hughes's concluding words define rather well the agenda for theoretical progress in Catholic moral theology:

> It is my final conclusion that taking the concept of human nature seriously . . . leads inevitably to an ethical theory which is neither relativist nor monolithic. It seems to me that only such a theory can be integrated with any appeal to an authoritative tradition in a religion which has to be preached to all men.[35]

Ethical Critique of Language

Hughes's infelicitous use of the so-called generic masculine in the above passage is what led me to say the agenda was put only "rather" well, and this point leads directly to a third contribution the linguistic turn has offered moral theology, namely, attention to the way *language itself* either serves or inhibits human well-being. We have come to realize that in a certain sense the limits of our language define the limits of our thought, and that it matters a great deal if common discourse renders women invisible when generalizations are made about "the nature of man," the ethical ideal of "brotherhood,"

33. Hughes, *Authority in Morals,* p. 111. Among magisterial documents expressing an openness to pluralism is Pope Paul VI's 1971 encyclical *Octogesima Adveniens* (*A Call To Action*), which states: "It is up to the Christian communities to analyze with objectivity the situation which is proper to their own country, to shed on it the light of the Gospel's unalterable words and to draw principles of reflection, norms of judgment and directives for action from the social teaching of the Church" (#4).

34. Of interest in this regard is the issue of *Concilium* edited by Jacques Pohier and Dietmar Mieth, *Christian Ethics: Uniformity, Universality, Pluralism* (New York: Seabury, 1981), which assembles various essays in support of the claim that moral pluralism has obtained throughout the history of Christianity.

35. Hughes, *Authority in Morals,* p. 121.

and "the salvation of mankind."[36] This is well-covered ground by now, and more and more people are convinced that not only our nouns and pronouns for persons but also our words for God have ethical significance in a world where gender has figured so prominently in unjust patterns of distributing the rewards and burdens of life.[37]

Attention to Language and Power

Close on the heels of attention to the morality of language itself has been a fourth result of the linguistic turn, namely, recognition of the *politics of language use.* We are asking the question of discourse: Who has been saying what to whom? And we are coming to appreciate what it has meant that powers of definition, powers of absolution, powers of declaring this or that morally significant, powers of indicating by omission that this or that is *not* morally significant, have resided with an elite corps within the church, which has presumed that silence and compliance are the main duties of the rest of the faithful. Tracy's summary of Foucault's findings is indeed relevant to the discourse called moral theology or Christian ethics:

> What these analyses show is that every discourse bears within itself the anonymous and repressed actuality of highly particular arrangements of power and knowledge. Every discourse, by operating under certain assumptions, necessarily excludes other assumptions. Above all, our discourses exclude those others who might disrupt the established hierarchies or challenge the prevailing hegemony of power.[38]

To recognize that systems involving power have had detrimental effects is not to deny that they have also had good, even very good, effects. I am not saying that the Catholic sacramental system, moral theological tradition, or hierarchical church organization should be scrapped in favor of some struc-

---

36. See Benjamin Lee Whorf, *Language, Thought, and Reality,* ed. John B. Carroll (Cambridge, Mass.: Massachusetts Institute of Technology Press, 1956).

37. See, for example, Casey Miller and Kate Swift, *Words and Women* (Garden City, N.Y.: Anchor Press, 1977); Beverly W. Harrison, "Sexism and the Language of Christian Ethics," in *Making the Connections: Essays in Feminist Social Ethics,* ed. Carol S. Robb (Boston: Beacon, 1985), pp. 22–41; and Anne E. Patrick, "Toward Renewing 'The Life and Culture of Fallen Man': 'Gaudium et Spes' as Catalyst for Catholic Feminist Theology," in Judith A. Dwyer, *"Questions of Special Urgency"* (Washington, D.C.: Georgetown University Press, 1986), pp. 55–78.

38. Tracy, *Plurality and Ambiguity,* p. 79.

tureless religious encounter group. But I am saying that we cannot, in a post-modern age, assume uncritically that all is well in the religious institution that has been our spiritual home. This point is hardly novel; the Second Vatican Council's *Dogmatic Constitution on the Church* reminds us that the church is both holy and "always in need of being purified" (*Lumen Gentium* #8), though how this need should be interpreted and addressed is a matter of some dispute.

For the sake of truth and justice, we should listen to those who have been marginalized from the dominant systems of moral reflection in our tradition. Despite the staggering methodological challenges entailed, moral theologians are beginning to do this, for the profoundly theological reason voiced by Tracy: that "the poor, the oppressed, and the marginalized—all those considered 'nonpersons' by the powerful" have been seen "by the great prophets to be God's own privileged ones."[39] Moral reflection has in fact been going on among officially silenced groups. Women have had a discourse that is increasingly receiving systematic and public expression. So also have various non-European Christian peoples; so indeed have sexual minorities.[40] Moral theology is cautiously listening to these "discourses of otherness" and is beginning to learn from them. In a related development, moral theology is also coming to recognize the contribution to ethical reflection made by great poets, novelists, and dramatists, particularly since the eighteenth century, when both secular and religious ethics began to grow more distant from the concerns of ordinary people.[41]

Recognition of Ambiguity

Finally, a fifth result of the linguistic turn is the recognition of the *radical ambiguity* inherent in all efforts, past and present, to articulate moral truth.

---

39. Ibid., p. 81.

40. See, for example, Barbara Hilkert Andolsen, Christine Gudorf, and Mary Pellauer, eds., *Women's Consciousness, Women's Conscience: A Reader in Feminist Ethics* (Minneapolis: Seabury, 1985); Ursula King, ed., *Feminist Theology from the Third World: A Reader* (Maryknoll, N.Y.: Orbis, 1994); John Coleman, "The Homosexual Revolution and Hermeneutics," in *The Sexual Revolution,* ed. Gregory Baum and John Coleman (Edinburgh: T & T Clark, 1984), pp. 55–64; and Mary Hunt, *Fierce Tenderness: A Feminist Theology of Friendship* (New York: Crossroad), 1991.

41. See James T. Laney, "Characterization and Moral Judgments," *Journal of Religion* 55 (1975): 405–14, for elaboration of the claim that post-Kantian ethics led to a "moral-emotional vacuum [that] came to be filled by the novel" (p. 413).

This seems the most theologically significant result of all, for this insight removes any justification for trusting blindly in human language and authorities and should leave us more vividly aware that God alone is the proper object of ultimate trust and loyalty.[42] To illustrate the importance of these several ways that the linguistic turn is influencing moral theology, I shall discuss below some contributions by a thinker who is not only well read in both Catholic moral theology and contemporary philosophy but is also attentive to "discourses of otherness," particularly those of women, sexual minorities, divorced and remarried persons, hospital patients, women religious, and seminary students.

I have in mind the theologian who was mentioned earlier in this chapter in connection with her views on the decision of the leaders of the Sisters of Mercy to comply with the Vatican ultimatum to halt discussion of changes in hospital policy regarding sterilization. Margaret Farley's recognition of the ambiguities of that case and the issues of power and powerlessness it involved provides a clear example of the practical fruits of the linguistic turn for moral theology and for the church. Philosophical abstractions about the politics of discourse come to life in Farley's account, quoted earlier, of why the leaders of her religious community submitted to the Vatican directive:

> The decision of the Sisters of Mercy must still be reviewed and critiqued by those within the Community and without. The answer to the question, "Why did this group of women agree to be silenced?" seems to me to be this: "In order that theirs and other voices may ultimately prevail." The danger, of course, is that the silence will grow, and that power in the Church will be more and more isolated, especially from the experience of women. But this story is unfinished.[43]

Once again we see how moral theology is building on the insight that knowledge, which is inherently hermeneutical, social, and historical, is never perfect but always in process. The case also shows that this fact need not paralyze our powers of judgment, but rather can allow for finite decisions to be made in trust and hope, with a conscience consoled by the assurance that God's mercy will compensate for the ambiguity entailed.[44]

42. The qualities of trust and loyalty are associated with the theory of faith developed by H. Richard Niebuhr in *Radical Monotheism and Western Culture* (New York: Harper & Row, 1960).

43. Farley, "Power and Powerlessness," p. 119.

44. My use of the term "consoled" is influenced by H. Richard Niebuhr, who writes at the conclusion of an illuminating essay entitled "The Ego-Alter Dialectic and the Conscience," in

Farley's work provides other examples of the influence of the linguistic turn on moral theology. Her 1986 book *Personal Commitments* analyzes a concept of great religious and moral importance in light of insights gained from a variety of theologians and philosophers, including speech act theorists.[45] Significantly, the book is informed by the discourse of ordinary struggling individuals as well and even aspires to be useful to a nonspecialist audience. Farley agrees with the speech act theorists that a commitment to love is a "performative utterance," and she maintains also that such a commitment "assumes a fundamental ground of moral obligation in the reality of persons."[46] She does not, however, assume that the "reality of persons" is a static item that can be the basis for absolute pronouncements about conduct. The fruits of the linguistic turn are evident in her observation that

> [i]f . . . the norm of a just love is the concrete reality of the beloved, everything will depend on how we interpret this reality. Our knowledge of human persons generally, as well as of individual persons, obviously differs and changes, for our interpretation of human experience is importantly historical and social.[47]

This recognition of historicity and ambiguity leads Farley to seek a middle course between absolutizing "the obligation to keep our commitments" and relativizing it "out of existence in favor of a general obligation to avoid harmful consequences or produce good ones."[48] Her solution is to argue that a commitment to love does entail an enduring obligation, but the framework in which that love is expressed may in certain circumstances need to be changed:

> Within our promise, then, lies the basis for our being released from it and the basis for our continuing to be bound. A just love, committed unconditionally,

---

Journal of Philosophy 42 (1945): 352–59: "The choice does not lie between the good conscience of a self which has kept all its laws and the bad conscience of the transgressor, but between the dull conscience which does not discern the greatness of the other and the loftiness of his demands, the agonized conscience of the awakened, and the consoled conscience of one who in the company of the spirit seeks to fulfill the infinite demands of the infinite other" (p. 359).

45. Margaret A. Farley, *Personal Commitments: Beginning, Keeping, Changing* (San Francisco: Harper & Row, 1986). It is interesting to note the degree to which this work makes use of the insights of imaginative artists as well as of philosophers and theologians. There are references to John A. Searle and Thomas Aquinas, but also to Alan Paton, Alice Walker, and Henrik Ibsen.

46. Ibid., pp. 136–37 (n. 1).

47. Ibid., p. 82.

48. Ibid., p. 69.

may require that its framework be lived to the end; but it may also require that its framework be changed.[49]

Farley's characterizing of the norm as one of "just love" recalls an earlier work of hers, also influenced by the linguistic turn. This is her 1975 essay "New Patterns of Relationship: Beginnings of a Moral Revolution," which demonstrates how changed views about gender require a reexamination of moral language, especially concepts of love and justice. Her analysis shows not only how productive the work of philosophical ethics can be but also how profound and far-reaching are the changes involved as our culture moves from the "old order" of male dominance and female subordination to a "new order" of mutuality between the sexes. Farley compares this twentieth-century development to other monumental "turns" of thought in Western history:

> Indeed, so profound are these changes and so far-reaching their consequences that one is tempted to say that they are to the moral life of persons what the Copernican revolution was to science or what the shift to the subject was to philosophy.[50]

What Farley did not articulate, but what I trust has become clear by now, is that it is the linguistic turn that made possible the contemporary critique of the inadequate notions of human nature sustaining the old order. I think she is especially correct to associate new understandings of gender and sexuality with the "Copernican revolution." Indeed, as the final section of this chapter endeavors to show, this sixteenth-century upheaval is even more closely linked with the current "moral revolution" than she indicated, and it also has striking affinities with the linguistic turn.

BEYOND THE LINGUISTIC TURN:
THE RADICAL CONVERSION OF CATHOLIC CONSCIOUSNESS

To summarize the historical material above: I have followed Tracy in describing the linguistic turn as the name given the various intellectual developments resulting from fifty years of attention to language (as use, as system or differential nonsystem, and as discourse), agreeing with him that the movement has so complicated our understanding of knowledge and ourselves

49. Ibid., p. 99.
50. Margaret A. Farley, "New Patterns of Relationship: Beginnings of a Moral Revolution," *Theological Studies* 36 (1975): 628.

that we have crossed over from modernity into a territory called postmodernity. I have indicated that this change has affected moral theology especially in regard to our understandings of moral epistemology, moral agency, and the limits of our own enterprise. I have argued that certain risks associated with these new developments are worth taking, since the linguistic turn has enriched our discipline by its attention to discourse, its recognition of plurality and ambiguity, and its acknowledgment of the moral significance of language forms and the politics of discourse. Finally, I have intimated that the last item, attention to the politics of discourse, already opens into a stage *beyond* the linguistic turn because discourse analysis attends to other realities besides language. What then is this new stage we have reached? What are we finding beyond the linguistic turn?

Many things, surely, but paramount among them is a renewed call to the radical sort of "turning" our tradition has always commended, which we term *metanoia,* or conversion. What this means for moral theology I shall now indicate, showing how some of the intellectual moves on the far side of the linguistic turn may help us to speak more adequately to certain moral questions of our time. My clues for this analysis come not only from moral theologians but also from hermeneutical theorists. These reflections, in fact, are an exercise of what Tracy terms the "analogical imagination," one that has benefited from the theory of knowledge-in-process delineated in Mary Gerhart and Allan Russell's 1984 volume *Metaphoric Process.*[51]

I shall explore two related analogies, one of which concerns striking similarities-in-difference between the linguistic turn and other great "turns" of Western history, while the other concerns the similarities-in-difference between sexuality and language. To begin with the latter, some recent moral theology discusses sexual ethics in terms of an analogy between sex and language.[52] The basis for the analogy is that sex has the potential for highly meaningful communication, and that sexual conduct should respect this teleology. The analogy has provided room for a natural law ethic to maneuver beyond physicalism and procreationism, without being cast adrift on a sea of relativism. Although the analogy needs more critical scrutiny, it does have

51. See David Tracy, *The Analogical Imagination: Christian Theology and the Culture of Pluralism* (New York: Crossroad, 1981); and Mary Gerhart and Allan Russell, *Metaphoric Process: The Creation of Scientific and Religious Understanding* (Fort Worth: Texas Christian University Press, 1984).

52. See, for example, André Guindon, *The Sexual Language: An Essay in Moral Theology* (Ottawa: University of Ottawa Press, 1976).

possibilities, one of which deserves particular attention. Obviously sex figures in human communication and relationships, but perhaps less obviously and yet very importantly it also figures in the Catholic believer's *relationship with God,* especially in the form of sexual abstinence and self-discipline.

Over the centuries, sexual discipline has been central to the *language of Catholic spirituality,* much as dietary discipline has been central to the language of Jewish piety. In neither case has the discipline in question been the only dialect of the language of religious devotion, but its prominence can be seen in the way membership in the community, understood broadly to include also an individual's sense of whether or not one is a "good" member, is defined, as it were, by conformity to the standard grammar and syntax. E. P. Sanders has shown how useful attention to the practical patterns that define membership in a community of faith can be for understanding the first-century situation, and when I reflect on our Catholic tradition in this light it seems clear that conformity on sexual matters has long been a prominent factor in the functioning of Catholicism.[53] We all know persons who have found it necessary "to leave the church" over decisions to marry non-Catholics or divorced persons, for example, but never over decisions to go into the liquor business or nuclear weapons industry, though in certain other communions such moves would lead to exclusion. We sense that the response of a gay man who protested Vatican statements on homosexuality by mailing his baptismal certificate back to his bishop is not the sort of thing that would be done by a Catholic who was upset over teachings on racial or economic questions. When we consider how deeply Catholics have internalized the traditional sexual ethos and how strongly this has been enforced compared to other moral teachings, it is hardly surprising that many just and charitable persons who are sexual nonconformists have chosen to say they "are no longer Catholic," or "are not good Catholics," whereas dyed-in-the-wool racists have less often been plagued with doubts about their Catholic identity.[54]

Furthermore, when we pursue the analogy between sex and language, we find that a core dimension of the language of Catholic spirituality has been a discourse of silence, or of very restricted speech, when it comes to the matter

53. E. P. Sanders, *Paul and Palestinian Judaism: A Comparison of Patterns of Religion* (Philadelphia: Fortress Press, 1977). For a recent discussion of the connection between piety and Christian ethics, see James M. Gustafson, *Ethics from a Theocentric Perspective,*1:201–4, 2:9–11.

54. J. F. Powers depicts this problem, using the case of racism, in "The Trouble," in *The Prince of Darkness and Other Stories* (Garden City, N.Y.: Doubleday, 1958), pp. 19–31.

of sexual expression. Indeed, the tradition has tended to hold that the safest course is to associate sexual pleasure with sin, allowing an important exception in the case of licit marital love that is open to procreation or, in recent decades, that is not artificially closed to procreation. This traditional presumption that sexual pleasure is sinful in so many circumstances, however, is increasingly being questioned today, much as the Ptolemaic view of a geocentric universe was found in the sixteenth and seventeenth centuries to be less and less adequate to what astronomers were discovering about the planets.

We know that the long-standing identification of a great deal of ordinary human sexual experience with moral evil has been challenged by the findings of biologists, psychologists, feminists, and other critical social theorists, and I want here simply to note that the changes in attitudes about sex that seem so reasonable to postmodern thought are of great *religious* as well as moral significance. Having reached the point where the analogy of language and sex intersects with the line of thought that sees connections between the linguistic turn and other revolutionary changes in Western thought, we can say of these postmodern views on sex much the same thing that we noted Thomas Kuhn said regarding the findings of Copernicus:

> Copernicanism was potentially destructive of an entire fabric of thought. . . .
> More than a picture of the universe and more than a few lines of Scripture were
> at stake. The drama of the Christian life and the morality that had been made
> dependent upon it would not readily adapt to a universe in which the earth was
> just one of a number of planets. Cosmology, morality, and theology had long
> been interwoven in the traditional fabric of Christian thought described by
> Dante at the beginning of the fourteenth century. . . . Copernicanism required
> a transformation in man's view of his relation to God and of the basis of his
> morality.[55]

Indeed, a revolutionary change in understandings of God and humanity, as well as of sin and virtue, is now in progress in our religious culture, and we seem to be in that very uncomfortable phase when a less adequate model is being patched up and defended by some because a more adequate model has not yet been recognized as compatible with central religious beliefs.[56] Copernicus's notion of a "moving earth" resulted in a "de-centered universe," required a massive reinterpretation of the biblical tradition, and led to many

---

55. Kuhn, *Copernican Revolution*, pp. 192–93.
56. Aspects of this tension are evident in various essays from the *Concilium* volume (191) *Changing Values and Virtues*, ed. Dietmar Mieth and Jacques Pohier (Edinburgh: T & T Clark, 1987).

changes in Christian religious practice. Similarly, the notions of "moving language" and "moving human nature," both fruits of the linguistic turn, have exposed the plurality and ambiguity in all knowledge and have "de-centered" the human subject. Again we need a massive reinterpretation of tradition and numerous changes in religious practice. Feminist scholars have been about this work for more than two decades, and the recognition accorded an especially fine 1992 study by Elizabeth A. Johnson, *She Who Is: The Mystery of God in Feminist Theological Discourse,* testifies to the importance of these labors not simply for the church but for the wider human community as well.[57]

As we muster the courage and energy to continue the work of reinterpretation and renewal, it may help to look back in our tradition and notice an important similarity between the revolutionary developments in the sixteenth and twentieth centuries and the radical development early in Christian history involving another great turn, the "turn to the Gentiles." One thing common to all three cases is the phenomenon of intense resistance to new ideas, which happened because the ideas shook not just a world of thought but also a world of practice, specifically religious practice. We have always known that the welcoming of non-Jews into first-century Christian communities raised enormous issues of religious practice, and we have also come to realize that the reason why Copernicus's ideas were judged so harshly, first by the Protestant reformers and then by the Catholics, is that these notions put in question the whole biblical worldview upon which the ethos of medieval Christianity had reposed.[58] So, likewise, the contemporary Catholic resistance to new ideas of moral theologians who have been influenced by the linguistic turn—whether these ideas have to do with tubal ligation, or artificial contraception, or same-sex love, to mention a few controversial subjects—

---

57. New York: Crossroad, 1992; according to the *National Catholic Reporter* (May 21, 1993), p. 5, *She Who Is* received the $150,000 Grawemeyer award from the University of Louisville, Kentucky, and the Louisville Presbyterian Theological Seminary. As the *NCR* notes, this award "recognizes ideas that can be applied practically to improve society." Johnson, a Sister of St. Joseph, has indicated that the Grawemeyer prize money will be used by her religious community "to support members working in shelters for battered women and children or to finance scholarships in inner-city schools where members teach." The Fordham University professor has also contributed *Women, Earth, and Creator Spirit* (New York: Paulist, 1993), which explicitly addresses the doctrine of creation in relation to the contemporary ecological crisis and marginalization of women, and an earlier study based on conferences she gave in the Republic of South Africa, *Consider Jesus: Waves of Renewal in Christology* (New York: Crossroad, 1990).

58. Kuhn, *Copernican Revolution,* p. 192.

goes deeper than simply a case of intransigent patriarchy holding on to what vestiges of power it can. Also at play are theological and pastoral factors that can profitably be distinguished from the "patriarchal conspiracy hypothesis," though they are related to it in certain ways.

The theological factors concern especially the doctrines of God and creation. For example, more work needs to be done to lift up the connections between classical sexual teachings that stress procreation and the Neoplatonic God-concept that helped to usher in the Copernican worldview in the first place. Here is Kuhn's description of this God-concept:

> The Neoplatonist's God was a self-duplicating procreative principle whose immense potency was demonstrated by the very multiplicity of the forms that emanated from Him. In the material universe this fecund Deity was suitably represented by the sun whose visible and invisible emanations gave light, warmth, and fertility to the universe.[59]

Feminist theology, informed by the discourse of women who can testify vividly to the human costs of boundless fecundity, must be a prime resource for articulating a more adequate concept of Divine Reality for our times.

Likewise, a reinterpretation of the doctrine of creation is needed before a more adequate ethics of sex and reproduction can be fully embraced by the church, because currently for many believers passivity in relation to the origins of human life seems necessary for God to be its author, which in turn is necessary for life to have meaning at all. In Jewish and Christian understanding, the doctrine of creation has supported the conviction that life is good and meaningful. The Genesis story has had a powerful influence in shaping Western religious sensibility, serving as a basis for a way of life that respects persons as created in God's image.

So too the myth of the origin of individual life as the result of special divine creation has been very powerful, particularly among Catholics whose piety was shaped from an early age by the first item in the Baltimore Catechism: "Who made you?" "God made me." This is important in view of the way a religious perspective functions to sustain a world of meaning and an ethical way of life for the believers of any tradition. As anthropologist Clifford Geertz has argued, the "religious perspective" involves symbols that establish

---

59. Ibid., p. 129. For a discussion of a "renewed notion of sexual fecundity" that seeks to overcome the one-sided emphasis on biological fertility, see André Guindon, *The Sexual Creators: An Ethical Proposal for Concerned Christians* (Lanham, Md.: University Press of America, 1986).

and reinforce a conviction that there is an "unbreakable inner connection" between the way things are and the way one ought to live.[60] Applying this insight to the contemporary situation, it seems clear that the meaning systems of some Catholics and Protestants depend on a literal interpretation of symbols of creation. For such Christians, life would have no meaning if it were not the result of God's *direct* intervention. This bedrock feature of religious sensibility cashes out in absolutist defense of embryonic human life and in passionate espousal of creationist theories of the origin of species. When the options are framed as either the security of literal acceptance of religious myth and authority, on the one hand, or else the loss of meaning that results from corrosive critical reason, on the other, it is not hard to see why some people prefer the former. Theologians know that these are by no means the only options available, but we face an enormous task of translating "second naïveté" understandings of creation from the discourse of systematic theology into terms that make sense to believers schooled in precritical understandings of these mysteries.[61]

There are also a number of pastoral factors that require attention. If the classical association of sexual pleasure with sin is no longer adequate, what will take its place? How shall we redefine sexual ethics in a realistic and effective way? How shall we speak to God? How shall we present our bodies as "a living sacrifice" (Rom. 12:1)? Of course, it will still be necessary to discipline our sexual energies, though now for reasons of justice rather than traditional taboos; a significant degree of sexual restraint will always be *part* of the language of religious devotion.[62] But more central to the spirituality needed at this juncture of history will be an asceticism that disciplines our *attention* and

60. Clifford Geertz, *Islam Observed: Religious Development in Morocco and Indonesia* (Chicago: University of Chicago Press, 1971), p. 98.

61. Paul Ricoeur's term "second naïveté" is discussed in his study *Symbolism of Evil* (Boston: Beacon, 1967), pp. 347–57. John Shea applies this idea to key Christian doctrines in *Stories of God: An Unauthorized Biography* (Chicago: Thomas More Press, 1978). Insights from both thinkers are related to the abortion issue in Anne E. Patrick, "Virtue, Providence, and the Endangered Self: Some Religious Dimensions of the Abortion Debate," in *Abortion and Catholicism: The American Debate*, ed. Patricia Beattie Jung and Thomas A. Shannon (New York: Crossroad, 1988), pp. 172–80.

62. For examples of approaches that stress *justice* as a norm for sexual ethics, see Margaret A. Farley, "Sexual Ethics," in *Encyclopedia of Bioethics*, ed. Warren T. Reich (New York: Free Press, 1978), 4:1575–89; eadem, *Just Love* (forthcoming); Beverly W. Harrison, *Making the Connections*, ed. Carol S. Robb (Boston: Beacon, 1985); Carter Heyward, *Our Passion for Justice* (New York: Pilgrim Press, 1984); and Joan Timmerman, *The Mardi Gras Syndrome: Rethinking Christian Sexuality* (New York: Crossroad, 1984).

controls our *greed*. Is it not the case that unreasonable levels of accumulation and unjust patterns of consumption are responsible for much of the evil we experience on this planet today? Is not our basic problem due to a failure to see what life is really like for neighbors who are *other* than ourselves? The revolution that moral theology must continue to be about involves not only the liberation of otherwise comfortable Catholics from various sorts of sexual oppression, which is important enough, but also the liberation of *all* who are oppressed for whatever reasons, especially by racism, militarism, and economic injustice.

It needs to be noted, however, that the secular culture's uncritical celebration of eros is not an acceptable alternative to classical Christianity's tendency to identify so much "ordinary human sexual experience" with sin. Indeed, especially under the conditions of patriarchy, the celebration of eros is problematic insofar as it contributes to violent, abusive, and irresponsible sexual conduct.[63] For this reason I have some sympathy for the traditionalist inclination to hold the line on classical moral norms about sex. Despite serious limitations, these norms do prevent much harm. However, these norms are not widely observed, their intellectual underpinnings are inadequate, and the absoluteness and rigidity with which they have been communicated are themselves factors that contribute to addictive and oppressive patterns of sexual conduct. Therefore it seems much wiser to face the "Copernican" fact that classical teaching on sex is not adequate in light of modern knowledge and set about the task of describing a reasonable contemporary sexual ethic. In the process, a criterion for judging the adequacy of such an ethic must be the impact it is likely to have on those who suffer most from hunger, poverty, violence, and political marginalization.

From a moral and religious perspective, it seems to me that the great turn beyond "the linguistic turn" must be the "turn to the oppressed." This process of conversion is under way in many quarters, and we are experiencing its difficulty, much as the early church suffered the conflicts involved in the "turn to the Gentiles." Because we in this century of the Holocaust are aware of the tragic consequences of the polemics that went on in the first century, we have

63. Authors who have stressed this problem include Lisa Sowle Cahill, *Women and Sexuality* (New York: Paulist, 1992); Karen Lebacqz, "Love Your Enemy: Sex, Power, and Christian Ethics," in *The Annual of the Society of Christian Ethics* (Washington, D.C.: Georgetown University Press, 1990), pp. 3–23; and Kathleen M. Sands, "Uses of the Thea(o)logian: Sex and Theodicy in Religious Feminism," *Journal of Feminist Studies in Religion* 8 (Spring 1992): 7–33.

reason to give thanks especially to those pastoral leaders and moral theologians who are struggling to articulate new visions of sexual, economic, and political ethics that do not break finally with our traditional heritage even as they challenge us to a *metanoia* more fundamental than our catechisms ever suggested would be required.[64]

Negotiating the linguistic turn, in sum, should result in our proceeding with a new consciousness of pluralism, ambiguity, tradition, and hope. For me this consciousness includes the conviction that when attentiveness to the "otherness" in all who are oppressed has been creatively combined with our best understanding of the mysterious "Otherness" that sustains us in life and in hope, it will happen that Peter will once again give expression to a new vision of what God finds acceptable. Thanks to the narrative in Luke-Acts, we do have a precedent in our tradition for monumental change in the language of piety. In Acts 10 we read of Peter's dialogue with the Spirit just prior to meeting Cornelius: "But Peter said, 'By no means, Lord; for I have never eaten anything that is profane or unclean.' The voice said to him again, a second time, 'What God has made clean, you must not call profane'" (Acts 10:14–15 NRSV). Moral theologians, currently in a relation of tension with Peter over various questions of sexual and reproductive ethics, should understand that we are nonetheless contributing to some future Petrine "discourse" on the subject, which will not be the last word, though we have reason to hope it will be a more relatively adequate word than has lately been spoken.

In the meanwhile, charity, patience, and humility are called for on all sides of the controversy, and no small amount of prudence, courage, and wisdom as well. Chastened by linguistic philosophy, troubled by awareness of its past complicity in injustice, Catholicism today seems poised at a moment of choice between competing visions of religious devotion, moral goodness, and right action. Since the invitation to radical conversion is as much about our being as our doing, I turn next to the matter of virtue, which is at the heart of the Christian life.

---

64. For a systematic analysis of Christian conversion, see Stephen Happel and James J. Walter, *Conversion and Discipleship: A Christian Foundation for Ethics and Doctrine* (Philadelphia: Fortress, 1986); for a challenging invitation to conversion, see Christine E. Gudorf, *Victimization: Examining Christian Complicity* (Philadelphia: Trinity Press International), 1992.

CHAPTER THREE

Changing Paradigms of Virtue:
The Good Life Reconsidered

> From them I learned all that a child should learn of honour and charity and
> generosity. But of South Africa I learned nothing at all.

These are the thoughts of Arthur Jarvis, the young white protagonist of
Alan Paton's novel *Cry, the Beloved Country,* voiced as he reflects on his
upbringing by well-meaning parents in a land of systemic injustice.[1] His
words suggest the paradox at the heart of this chapter on virtue, namely, that
our very ideals of moral goodness can contribute to evil in the world, if they
are pursued without attention to the ways our lives are complicit in the unjust
sufferings of others.

What I am suggesting is that the radical conversion to which contemporary Christians are called involves not simply a resolution to pursue classical
virtues more earnestly, but rather a willingness to reconsider the matter of
virtue altogether and to acknowledge that valued habits of character are, like
other finite realities, ambiguous and in need of critical scrutiny. Indeed, as a
result of such scrutiny, we are experiencing today a tension between differing
sets of ideals for Christian character, which reflects the broader tension
between the contrasting styles of faith and ethics discussed in chapter 1.

Since Christian understandings of value and virtue developed over time,
their continuing development is to be expected.[2] What matters in a period of
change such as ours is that the normative questions be pursued with courage

---

1. Alan Paton, *Cry, The Beloved Country* (New York: Charles Scribner's Sons, 1948), p. 174.
2. See Dietmar Mieth and Jacques Pohier, eds., *Changing Values and Virtues* (Edinburgh:
T & T Clark, 1987).

and honesty: What changes in our ideas of goodness *should* be promoted by Christians? What configuration of values and virtues is needed for today's world? How should we contribute to the process of transforming inadequate notions of moral goodness for the sake of God's realm?[3] Before normative questions can be resolved, however, it is necessary to gain some understanding of how virtue is related to the individuals who comprise society and to the society that shapes individuals.

VIRTUE: HISTORICAL, SOCIAL, AND NARRATIVE-DEPENDENT

In the past, questions of personal virtue were discussed in isolation from topics of social ethics. Virtue, however, is a thoroughly social phenomenon, for groups are distinguished by the traits and dispositions they foster in their members. Besides recognizing the *historicity* of virtue, or the fact that ideals for character are shaped and modified over time, an adequate theory will appreciate its *sociality* as well. This involves acknowledging that an agent's social context determines to some degree the ideals for character he or she will develop. Societies promote ideals through such means as laws, rewards and punishments, rituals and prayers, and, above all, narratives. Myths, legends, histories, biographies, fables, dramas, and other works of fiction convey clear messages about what sorts of characters are valued or despised. Whether or not individuals personally embody the traits prized by the group, they generally internalize the values contained in important cultural myths and judge themselves in light of these common norms.

Narrative serves two functions in a culture. It communicates and reinforces the values and virtues esteemed by the culture and it criticizes notions of virtue once their favored status is seen as problematic. Consider, for example,

---

3. In using this term "realm" I am deliberately avoiding the English word "kingdom," which has traditionally been used to translate the Greek *basileia*, a biblical metaphor that carries for most Christians positive associations with an ideal state where God's values govern life. The metaphor is associated with truth, love, justice, and peace, but the term also carries negative associations with male dominance (a king is by definition a man) and with the violence and militarism linked with establishing and maintaining sovereignty in the past. Thus, many today prefer to speak of the "commonwealth" or "realm" of God and to avoid "kingdom" imagery. In *Hispanic Women: Prophetic Voice in the Church* (San Francisco: Harper & Row, 1988), Ada María Isasi-Díaz and Yolanda Tarango suggest another alternative—namely, "kin-dom"—to indicate "that when the fulness of God becomes a day-to-day reality in the world at large, we will all be sisters and brothers—kin to each other" (p. 116).

the value of obedience to authority. When it became known that this was the defense employed by Nazi war criminals at Nuremberg after World War II—"I was only following orders"—society had to rethink whether obedience deserved quite the place it had enjoyed in the then prevalent paradigm of virtue. Thus, it is not surprising that narratives satirizing military discipline, such as Joseph Heller's 1961 novel *Catch-22*, came to prominence in the postwar period. Meanwhile Christian thinkers were working in a more systematic way on the problem of overemphasis on duty and obedience, with the result that emphasis shifted away from obedience in favor of the category of responsibility.[4]

In stressing the social dimensions of virtue I do not mean to suggest that every agent in a society will adopt a uniform set of ideals, for especially in modern pluralistic cultures, value options are constantly competing for adoption by individuals, with agents choosing among this plurality and *to some extent* designing their own value paradigms.[5] Certainly, ideals for character vary among members of any society. But the element of choice is not completely autonomous, because social realities strongly influence an individual's sense of value and virtue, establishing the limits within which personal freedom operates. As I indicated in the discussion of conscience in chapter 1, it is now generally recognized that the human person is constitutively social. We simply would not develop as human beings in the absence of social relationships; our very selves are structured by the values bound up in the linguistic and mythic patterns of the cultures in which we are raised. Narratives are especially efficient at shaping us because they express the worldview and ethical system of a group in a way that at once engages our emotions, intellect, and imagination, effectively conveying the message of what is valuable and what values should be given priority.

Among contemporary Christian ethicists, Stanley Hauerwas is particularly known for emphasizing the historical and social dimensions of virtue and for attending to the role that stories play in shaping communities and individuals. His position is summarized in the following claim: "Our capacity to be

4. See Albert R. Jonsen, *Responsibility in Modern Religious Ethics* (Washington, D.C.: Corpus Books, 1968), for a general treatment of this development and an analysis of four representative thinkers: Dietrich Bonhoeffer, Bernard Häring, Robert Johann, and H. Richard Niebuhr. Also illustrative of this development is Dorothee Soelle, *Beyond Mere Obedience*, trans. Laurence W. Denef (New York: Pilgrim Press, 1982).

5. The modern trend toward "consumerism" in religious identity formation is discussed by Thomas Luckmann in *The Invisible Religion: The Problem of Religion in Modern Society* (New York: Macmillan, 1967), pp. 98–99.

virtuous depends on the existence of communities which have been formed by narratives faithful to the character of reality."[6] Hauerwas stresses the primary function of narrative in relation to virtue, namely, its role in forming communities and selves. But the norm of adequacy to reality in his statement suggests the importance of the secondary function of narrative, that of correcting the limitations of operative myths by critiquing inadequate ideals for character. John Barbour demonstrates this second function in his 1984 study *Tragedy as a Critique of Virtue,* where he combines insights from Hauerwas, classics scholar James Redfield, and his own literary investigations to explain the role played by tragic novels in critiquing dominant ideals of virtue. Such works as Joseph Conrad's *Nostromo* and Robert Penn Warren's *All the King's Men,* Barbour indicates, portray the human cost of attempting to live out certain ideals for character to their fullest, thus inviting reconsideration of societal norms.[7]

In the present chapter I shall build on what Hauerwas and Barbour have said by describing a conflict between two competing paradigms, or exemplary sets of ideals for virtue, which are now in tension within Catholicism. One of these sets of ideals is captured in the term "patriarchal," and the other can be called "egalitarian-feminist." My assumption is that the latter is gaining ascendancy in Catholic consciousness and that this accounts for the increasingly defensive articulations of the patriarchal paradigm by those in power who espouse it. After laying out this typology, I shall illustrate the two functions of narrative with respect to paradigms of virtue—namely, shaping selves and critiquing ideals when they have gone too far—by discussing two stories. The first is a newspaper account of a beatification ceremony that took place in 1985, and the second is a substantial work of fiction, *The Good Conscience* by Carlos Fuentes.[8] In this novel Fuentes uses a genre linked with issues of character formation, the *Bildungsroman,* to critique the constellation of attitudes concerning Christian virtue that I term the patriarchal paradigm. In the final sections of this chapter, I treat the relationship of the egalitarian-feminist paradigm to the conciliar emphasis on "the universal call to holiness" and discuss the emergence of a narrative tradition that reflects this developing understanding of what goodness entails.

---

6. Stanley Hauerwas, *A Community of Character* (Notre Dame: University of Notre Dame Press), p. 116.

7. John D. Barbour, *Tragedy as a Critique of Virtue* (Chico, Calif.: Scholars Press, 1984).

8. Carlos Fuentes, *The Good Conscience,* trans. Sam Hileman (New York: Noonday, 1961).

THE CURRENT CONFLICT OF CATHOLIC PARADIGMS FOR VIRTUE

The ongoing debate concerning "authority and dissent" in the Catholic Church, evident in the United States in Vatican disciplinary action against such figures as Professor Charles Curran, Archbishop Raymond Hunthausen of Seattle, and twenty-four nuns who signed a 1984 *New York Times* advertisement calling for discussion of abortion policy, has not often been analyzed in relation to Catholic ideals for character. But these cases from 1986, and others like them in North America and abroad, are symptoms of the tension between competing understandings of virtue, for what is at issue is precisely what it means to be a "good Catholic." Each side in these controversies has a different normative constellation of values and virtues, one that tends to line up with either the patriarchal paradigm or the egalitarian-feminist one. The "fit" is never exact, of course; typologies are abstract heuristic models that are by definition artificial, and concrete reality is always much more complex than theory.

Before I sketch this typology, it is appropriate to comment on my use of the terms "patriarchal" and "egalitarian-feminist." As I mentioned in the introduction, I am using the term "patriarchy" in a specialized ethical sense to designate social patterns and structures of domination and subordination, especially (but not exclusively) those involving unjust attitudes toward females. I employ the term feminism in a broad sense to indicate a position that involves (1) a solid conviction of the equality of women and men, and (2) a commitment to reform society so that the full equality of women is respected, which requires also reforming the thought systems that legitimate the present unjust social order. Given this understanding of feminism, it is, strictly speaking, redundant to use the term "egalitarian-feminist," but I do so in order to distinguish the type of feminism I have in mind from other sorts with which it might be confused, such as "liberal," "romantic," or "separatist."[9] As I have stated, my hope is that increasing numbers of both sexes

---

9. In earlier versions of this material I designated the newer paradigm simply as "egalitarian," in order to stress the basic theological affirmation that males and females are both created in the divine image and possess equal dignity. More recently I have also considered calling it "liberationist" or "feminist-liberationist." No phrase is fully adequate or without problems. The use of "egalitarian" may carry overtones of classical liberalism, which I fault for its inadequate critique of the social and economic systems within which equal rights are to be respected. The use of "liberationist" alone misses the crucial dimension of women's experience that "feminist" carries (and indeed much early work by liberation theologians betrayed an unquestioned androcentrism), and the use of "feminist" alone seems at once too narrow and too open to mistaken associations with sorts of feminism I find problematic for various rea-

will claim the ethical stance of feminism in this broad sense, for not to do so is to be complicit with sexism.

A patriarchal paradigm for virtue has long dominated Catholic thinking. Its shape has been affected by the otherworldly spirituality, the theological and social patterns of domination and subordination, the misogyny, and the body-rejecting dualism characteristic of Western culture.[10] This paradigm understands virtue to involve the control of passion by reason and the subordination of earthly values to heavenly ones. It articulates many ideals for character but tends to assume that these are appropriately assigned greater emphasis according to one's gender and social status. All Christians should be kind, chaste, just, and humble, but women are expected to excel in charity and chastity, men are trained to think in terms of justice and rights, and subordinates of both sexes are exhorted to docility and meekness. For various reasons this paradigm came to function in a way that saw chastity as the pinnacle of perfection, absolutizing this virtue as defined by physicalist interpretations of "natural law" and stressing its necessity for salvation. In this model charity and justice may be said to be more important, but in reality chastity is most important. This claim might be denied by defenders of the patriarchal paradigm, but such denial is unconvincing in view of their continued insistence that there is no "smallness of matter" where sexual sin is concerned, whereas violations of charity and justice admit of varying degrees of gravity.[11]

---

sons, including inattention to matters of race and class. The sort of feminism I espouse is, like that of Rosemary Radford Ruether, Elisabeth Schüssler Fiorenza, and Elizabeth Johnson, one that seeks to be a "critical theology of liberation." It builds on a theological conviction that equal human dignity is the Creator's design for our lives and draws especially on the prophetic biblical tradition and the preaching of Jesus about God's reign, which calls for considerably more radical approaches to injustice than does classical liberalism. I have lately noted a somewhat parallel use of terminology in Mary Jo Weaver, *Springs of Water in a Dry Land* (Boston: Beacon, 1993), where she describes pre– and post–Vatican II paradigms as "hierarchical and egalitarian, or to borrow terminology from the women's movement, patriarchal and feminist" (p. 64). For related discussions of definitions and method, see Anne E. Carr, "The New Vision of Feminist Theology: Method," in *Freeing Theology: The Essentials of Theology in Feminist Perspective*, ed. Catherine Mowry LaCugna (San Francisco: HarperSanFrancisco, 1993), pp. 5–29; Rosemary Radford Ruether, *Sexism and God-Talk* (Boston: Beacon, 1983); and Elisabeth Schüssler Fiorenza, "Feminist Theology as a Critical Theology of Liberation," *Theological Studies* 36 (1975): 605–26.

10. For analysis of the connection between this paradigm and the violence of conquest and colonialism, see Pablo Richard, "1492: The Violence of God and the Future of Christianity," in *1492–1992: The Voice of the Victims*, ed. Leonardo Boff and Virgil Elizondo (Philadelphia: Trinity Press International, 1990), pp. 59–67.

11. The Vatican "Declaration on Certain Questions Concerning Sexual Ethics" (1975)

Biblical grounding for the patriarchal paradigm comes in part from interpreting the beatitude "Blessed are the clean of heart, for they will see God" (Matt. 5:8) in a way that internalizes sexual taboos and establishes sexual purity as a focal sign of religious devotion. For this paradigm, "purity of heart" is interpreted in a narrow, sexual sense, rather than in the broader (and more biblically accurate) sense of singleness of purpose.[12] The paradigm is based on a metaphor of domination, which emphasizes control of the lower by the higher; the unruly body must be dominated and tamed by "dispassionate" reason. Further scriptural warrant is found in the Pauline declaration, "I punish my body and enslave it" (1 Cor. 9:27 NRSV). The rigid emphasis on control from above extends beyond sexual matters to include social ones as well; hence the high value placed on obedience in this model. In fact, the idea of hierarchical *control* of the "mystical body" closely parallels the premium placed on domination of the flesh by the will in traditional understandings of chastity. It would seem also that the tendency to apply military "solutions" to political problems may be a secular manifestation of the same paradigm.

In contrast to the anthropological dualism of the patriarchal paradigm, the egalitarian-feminist paradigm understands reason itself to be embodied, and women and men to be fully equal partners in the human community. Instead of *control,* the notion of *respect* for all created reality is fundamental to this paradigm, which values the body in general and the humanity of women in particular, and promotes gender-integrated ideals for character. Rather than

---

reiterates this rigorous teaching of manualist moral theology: "the moral order of sexuality involves such high values of human life that every direct violation of this order, is objectively serious" (#10); cited here from Anthony Kosnik et al., *Human Sexuality: New Directions in American Catholic Thought* (New York: Paulist, 1977), p. 308. The full English translation of the text from *L'Osservatore Romano* (January 22, 1976) is included as an appendix to the Kosnik volume, which was a study commissioned by the Catholic Theological Society of America in 1972. This study investigates a number of questions in light of magisterial teaching and new evidence from biblical and theological scholarship as well as the empirical sciences. Its conclusions are cautiously revisionist, and it calls for ongoing research. Other studies that depart from the classicist absolutism expressed in the 1975 Vatican Declaration and published shortly thereafter include Philip S. Keane, *Sexual Morality: A Catholic Perspective* (New York: Paulist, 1977), and Charles E. Curran, *Issues in Sexual and Medical Ethics* (Notre Dame: University of Notre Dame Press, 1978).

12. For a biblically informed, egalitarian-feminist discussion of this beatitude, see Michael H. Crosby, *Spirituality of the Beatitudes: Matthew's Challenge for First World Christians* (Maryknoll, N.Y.: Orbis, 1987), pp. 159–77. Observes Crosby: "In the sermon on the mount, the lesson is reinforced that if the eye is pure or simple, so is the heart. If one is absorbed in the experience of God's reign and will, the whole personality will be endowed with light's perfection . . ." (p. 160).

understanding power as control over others, this paradigm operates with a sense of power as the energy of proper relatedness.[13] Discipline is still valued, but it is less rigidly understood. Ideals of love and justice are not segregated into separate spheres of personal and social ethics, with responsibility for realizing them assigned according to gender; instead love and justice are seen to be mutually reinforcing norms that should govern both sexes equally.

Perhaps because of the exaggerated attention given by advocates of the patriarchal paradigm to sexual purity, advocates of the egalitarian-feminist model tend not to emphasize the virtue of chastity per se, although a reinterpretation of this virtue may be inferred from what they have written on love and justice, and also on particular sexual questions. The newer paradigm sees sexuality as a concern of social justice as well as of personal virtue, and it attends particularly to the beatitude "Blessed are they who hunger and thirst for righteousness, for they will be satisfied" (Matt. 5:6). It recognizes that the focal sign of religious devotion should not be the directing of one's energy to controlling bodily impulses and other people, but rather must involve a stance of ongoing commitment to the well-being of oneself and others, which has material as well as spiritual components and entails building social relations of respect, equality, and mutuality.

Both paradigms recognize that suffering is part of the Christian life, but they understand the last beatitude quite differently. The patriarchal paradigm tends to foster an apocalyptic mentality, in which the "righteous" see themselves enduring persecution from godless enemies in this world, but ultimately vindicated in the next. The egalitarian paradigm acknowledges that forces of evil long structured into unjust power relationships will seek to destroy those who dedicate themselves to the campaign for just social and economic relationships. But, with Jesus' own paschal experience in mind, advocates of this model recognize that the struggle has in principle been won, even here and now on earth, thanks to the graciousness of the Ground and Source of life and the continued involvement of God in human history.

Presently the egalitarian-feminist paradigm is capturing the imaginations of many Christians, through a process involving new narratives and critiques of old narratives. To illustrate this aspect of the dynamics of change, I turn

13. For Christian feminist discussions of power, see Beverly Wildung Harrison, *Making the Connections,* ed. Carol S. Robb (Boston: Beacon, 1985); Carter Heyward, *Our Passion for Justice: Images of Power, Sexuality, and Liberation* (New York: Pilgrim Press, 1984); and Anne E. Patrick, "The Ambiguity of Power," in *Walking in Two Worlds,* ed. Kay Vander Vort, Joan H. Timmerman, and Eleanor Lincoln (St. Cloud, Minn.: North Star Press, 1992), pp. 159–66.

now to an example of a narrative designed to foster the patriarchal paradigm, and show why such stories are losing their power for contemporary believers.

A NARRATIVE WITH FADING POWER

Throughout its history the Catholic Church has communicated ideals of character by designating certain persons as saints or "blessed ones." To appreciate how stories of the saints have supported the patriarchal paradigm of virtue, consider this brief item from the *New York Times* for August 16, 1985.

> KINSHASO, Zaire, Aug. 15—Pope John Paul II today beatified a Roman Catholic nun who chose to be killed rather than surrender her virginity. The nun, Marie Clementine Anwarite, demonstrated the "primordial value accorded to virginity" and an "audacity worthy of martyrs," the Pope said. He said he forgave the man, a Col. Piere Colombe, who killed the nun during an incident in Zaire's civil war in 1964. (page A-4)

This report is reminiscent of the story of St. Maria Goretti, who was canonized in 1950 for having repulsed the sexual advances of the youth who stabbed her to death in 1902. Catholic students at the time of her canonization were encouraged to see in this teenage victim an exemplar for girls, a model of virtue whose concern was not for her physical well-being but rather for the spiritual values at stake. A biographer quotes the saint as declaring during the encounter with her assailant, "'No, God does not wish it. It is a sin. You would go to hell for it,'" words that reveal much about the values Maria espoused and the religious world she inhabited.[14] This was a world where sexual pleasure outside of sacramental marriage, if deliberately indulged, was always grounds for damnation, a world where death was preferable to yielding to rape. The Vatican's selection of this young woman for canonization in 1950 was clearly an effort to articulate the value of premarital abstinence in a society that was questioning the absoluteness of this norm. Moreover, the saint's preeminent concern for the spiritual welfare of her assailant ("It is a sin. You would go to hell for it") reinforced the emphasis on a young woman's responsibility for the sexual behavior of a dating couple typical for Catholic education of the day. Maria Goretti was one of several vir-

---

14. M. Buehrle, s.v. "Goretti, Maria, St." in *New Catholic Encyclopedia* (New York: McGraw Hill, 1967), 6:632. See also Eileen J. Stenzel, "Maria Goretti: Rape and the Politics of Sainthood," in *Violence Against Women*, ed. Elisabeth Schüssler Fiorenza and Mary Shawn Copeland (Maryknoll, N.Y.: Orbis, 1994), pp. 91–98.

ginal youths whose example was commended to Catholics in mid-century, including the Italian schoolboy Dominic Savio and the Jesuits John Berchmans, Aloysius Gonzaga, and Stanislas Kostka. If their hagiographers are to be believed, none of these saints ever indulged a sexual thought, but only the female paid for her virginity with her life. One can gauge the progress of the shift from the patriarchal paradigm of virtue to the egalitarian-feminist one by comparing the general acceptance of the Maria Goretti model in the post-war Catholic culture with the objections that surface so easily among believers when the Anwarite beatification story is considered today.

Several aspects of this news report from 1985 are disturbing. Paramount among them is the flagrant injustice of the basic situation of attempted rape and actual murder. This situation is faced daily by women around the globe, with all too many suffering one or both aspects of the threatened evil: forced sexual contact and death. Moreover, we know that unjust patterns of relationships between the sexes contribute to the frequency with which women experience such predicaments, and that schooling in so-called feminine virtues of docility and submissiveness to male authority increases the likelihood that a woman will suffer this violence.

Also disturbing is the explicit value statement, "'the primordial value accorded to virginity,'" with its clear implication that a woman's life is of lesser value than a physical condition that is not typical for most women. Marie Clementine's virginity was, to be sure, "consecrated virginity," and the religious significance of this should not be ignored. Nonetheless, the aspect of formal religious dedication should not obscure the basic fact that a woman was lifted up as a model for the emulation of the faithful because "'she chose to be killed rather than surrender her virginity.'"

Now any person's right to physical integrity, privacy, and sexual autonomy is a high value. But is this value greater than that of the person's life? The threat of death is not necessarily removed by a woman's submission to rape, but if we assume that some virginal victims are presented with two real alternatives, the Anwarite beatification explicitly raises the question of whether rape is a greater evil than death.

But is this to put the question wrongly? One might object that the chief value at stake in these instances was not virginity per se but rather God's will. There is point to this objection insofar as the question of subjective culpability or merit is concerned, for the formal value of God's will is preeminent for believers. The obligation to follow a certain conscience is exceptionless. But to recognize this formal value does not answer the substantive question concerning what God "wills" a woman to do when threatened with death if she does not submit to rape. Answers to this question can hardly be universal or absolutely certain, for as with other ethical dilemmas, the right choice must be discerned in view of the relevant circumstances, values, and principles involved in each case. This leads to further questions: Is such overriding emphasis on sexual "purity" a good thing? Is it right to emphasize one response to the threat of violent attack by a rapist ("Take my life, but not my virginity") by idealizing it to the extent that virginity assumes a "primordial value" for females, one greater than their own lives, with the result that other responses, which might be equally moral, are ruled out of consideration by devout women?[15] These questions bring one to the point where concerns about virtue and action intersect most conflictedly in contemporary Catholicism because they hinge on the issue of discerning God's will, and on the question of what constitutes the basis for claims of the hierarchy to have certain knowledge on all matters of sexual ethics.

Furthermore, these stories invite questions about what they imply concerning the nature of rape. Do they recognize that rape is primarily an act of hostility and aggression, or do they contribute to the prevalent and inaccurate myth that somehow a victim derives pleasure from being seized and "taken," thereby reinforcing the tendency to blame the victim of this crime?[16] Furthermore, what does the lack of attention to the social causes of male sexual aggression imply? One might have hoped that by 1985, if not 1950, church leaders would recognize that past teachings about the "unnaturalness" of masturbation and homosexuality and the "naturalness" of rape—these very classic teachings based on inadequate Aristotelian understandings of human reproductive biology—feed into the insecurities of young males and con-

15. One wonders what Augustine would have thought of the language used to praise Marie Clementine, for his insight in *City of God* (1.18) is entirely absent from the report of the ceremony: "[B]odily chastity is not lost, even when the body has been ravished, while the mind's chastity endures" (trans. H. Bettenson; Harmondsworth: Penguin, 1972), p. 28. Despite the body-rejecting dualism implied in his analysis, Augustine rightly recognizes that chastity involves a disposition of the subject that perdures despite bodily violation. His analysis betrays his male bias, however, especially in the assertion that an act of rape "perhaps could not have taken place without some physical pleasure on the part of the victim" (1.16, p. 26). It can only be lamented that in the late twentieth century Catholic women were being exhorted to an even more regressive understanding of chastity than that of the fifth-century Augustine.

16. For an informed contemporary ethical and pastoral analysis of these matters, see Marie Fortune, *Sexual Violence: The Unmentionable Sin* (New York: Pilgrim Press, 1983). Also valuable is Emilie Buchwald et al., eds., *Transforming a Rape Culture* (Minneapolis: Milkweed Editions, 1993).

tribute directly to patterns of seduction and rape.[17] Finally, why would any woman prefer death to the violation of her virginity? Such a choice on a woman's part is largely a function of her socialization; it makes sense in light of the ideals for character dominant in her culture, values she has appropriated to govern her decisions.

The Anwarite case clearly shows the influence of culture and narrative on character. Early in the history of Christianity, the biblical emphasis on sexual purity among the Hebrews, the doctrine of Mary's perpetual virginity, beliefs that Jesus avoided sexual activity, and emphasis on eschatological virginity, combined with a body-rejecting dualism already present in Greco-Roman culture to yield an ethos that encouraged the development of persons who saw their own bodies as the locus of a contest between the powers of good and evil, with goodness demanding a vigilant campaign against one's sexual inclinations. Over the centuries new stories entered the culture—stories of virgin martyrs, ascetic monks and nuns, repentant profligates, and the like—all of which joined with legal practice and an otherworldly eschatology to create a world where a decision to die rather than lose one's virginity made quite good sense.

A person growing up in such a world understands that an ideal character chooses no sexual pleasure before marriage and limits it very strictly within marriage. Such a person tends to judge the self according to this norm, whether or not he or she achieves it. Now this view of chastity may have done more good than harm in the past. What is clear today, however, is that an ideal of character with this notion of chastity as its lynchpin is no longer accepted uncritically by Christians, although a clearly delineated alternative understanding of this still-important virtue has yet to be fully articulated. Catholic society today is reassessing its ideals of character with respect to sexuality, even though the transformation has not been the focus of much attention in discussions of virtue among theorists of the moral life. Instead,

---

17. In *Women and Sexuality* (New York: Paulist, 1992), Lisa Sowle Cahill criticizes the excessive physicalism of moral theology that ranks sexual sins according to whether or not they conform to the "procreative structure" of the act, observing that in this regard Aquinas neglected "his own principle that the human faculties of reason and freedom are higher and more distinctive than physical characteristics and processes, for if the distinctively personal aspects of sex were recognized (over and above what humans have in common with animals), then certainly rape and incest would be recognized as greater sins against human dignity than contraception, masturbation, and consensual homosexuality. Moreover, this narrow adherence to a physicalist norm of 'the natural' in sexual matters would hardly have been possible in a culture which respected the dignity of women as well as men, and which recognized that incest and rape are usually crimes perpetrated against females by males" (pp. 9–10).

Catholic moral theologians have concentrated on gingerly trying to question absolute prohibitions of certain sexual acts without unleashing a plague of ecclesiastical penalties on their lives. We are at a moment in history when one understanding of chastity is increasingly recognized as inadequate and when a more adequate one has not come fully into focus.

At this juncture, however, we can recognize that the task of moral theology in bringing a new interpretation of chastity into an egalitarian-feminist paradigm of virtue has been made easier because of ethical reflection already done by two groups working mainly outside the circle of traditional moral theology. These are feminist scholars of religion and literary artists, particularly novelists, who have been testing various ideals for character ever since the novel was invented.[18]

A now classic feminist critique of ideals for virtue is Valerie Saiving [Goldstein]'s article "The Human Situation: A Feminine View."[19] Saiving argues that traditional Christian understandings of sin and virtue reflect experiences typical for those males who enjoy some status and power in society. For such men, pride has been recognized as the most harmful inclination, with temptation to sensual indulgence at others' expense also a recurrent danger. Thus, exhortations to cultivate humility and self-sacrifice are appropriate. But to universalize this analysis, and especially to apply it to women, is to exacerbate the moral problems most of them face. For, given the disparate experiences of the two sexes, the temptations of women tend to be somewhat different from those of men. Instead of pride being the greatest danger, for women the chief temptation is to fail to have a centered self, to yield up responsibility for one's identity and actions to other persons and environmental factors. Whereas generally speaking men are tempted to abuse their power, women tend to abdicate their possibilities for using power well by surrendering it for the sake of approval and security. What women in patriarchal society need is not exhortations to humility and self-sacrifice, much less stories of saints who preferred death to rape. Women need instead, as do men and children, new models of virtue and new stories that communicate them. These models and

18. For an account of this relationship between fiction and moral philosophy, see James T. Laney, "Characterization and Moral Judgments," *Journal of Religion* 55 (1975): 405–14. Laney argues that the rise of the novel coincided with a turn taken by moral philosophy toward concentration on action and away from emotional and characterological matters. Novelists, he suggests, provided a way for reflection on these matters to continue in the culture.

19. Originally published in *Journal of Religion* (1960), the article also appears in Carol Christ and Judith Plaskow, eds., *Womanspirit Rising* (New York: Harper & Row, 1979), pp. 25–42.

stories are beginning to emerge, but it will be some time before they have supplanted the patriarchal narratives on a wide scale.

In the meanwhile, a second resource for the constructive work still to be done by storytellers and theologians is the large body of serious fiction that critiques the inadequacies of the patriarchal paradigm of virtue. A particularly interesting example is *The Good Conscience,* an early work by the Mexican novelist Carlos Fuentes.

CHASTITY AND THE PSYCHOLOGY OF SOCIAL INJUSTICE

Originally published in 1959, *The Good Conscience* provides an incisive analysis of the ambiguity of Catholic teaching and practice with respect to values and virtues. A prominent theme in this narrative is the co-optation of Christian moral energy in the service of an unjust social structure. Because in the culture depicted in this novel Christian morality has been reduced to preoccupation with sexual purity, the wealthy Mexican class into which the story's hero, Jaime Ceballos, is born succeeds in distracting itself from the poverty and injustice surrounding it, and to which its own defensive greed and narrow understanding of family contribute. The novel depicts Jaime's transformation from a sensitive, idealistic child, who befriends a fugitive labor organizer and a Marxist Indian youth, into a hardening egoist who will follow in the footsteps of the hypocritical uncle whose values he has always despised. At the book's end we find Jaime dealing with the guilt he feels over having failed to show love and respect for his parents, by visiting a brothel after his father's funeral. There he commits a sin that can be more easily named and absolved in the confessional than the pride and insensitivity to others that have become part of his character. Thus, by reducing the moral life to a routine of sexual sin and confession Jaime comes to have a "good conscience," as the work's ironic title puts it. Earlier scenes establish the connection between affirming one's own embodiment and rejoicing in the mysteries of creation and God's love. They also show how such feelings are linked with a disposition to care for others, whereas alienation from the body is associated with alienation from other people. Indeed, through the lives of Jaime and his family, Fuentes shows how moral theology and pastoral practice that overemphasize sexual sins contribute to neurotic patterns of individual behavior as well as to social injustice. With the rest of life removed from the arena of sin and grace, the injustice of social systems and cultural values never comes to attention.

The Good Conscience demonstrates how the patriarchal paradigm of virtue is implicated in some of the most besetting problems of Catholicism today: injustice to women and the blindness of the middle and upper classes to matters of social and economic justice. From there, to draw out explicitly the connection between this paradigm and systemic injustice and violence, it is a short step to defending one's sense of family and property with whatever means it takes. We see in this novel what rigid patriarchal authority has done to one family system, and we can infer what it has done and is doing to the church. Jaime's was a home in which the truth could not be spoken and where sexuality was a taboo subject. What Fuentes's narrator says of this home brings to mind how pastors and moral theologians alike have been silenced on matters of sexuality: "The first rule in this family was that life's real and important dramas should be concealed."[20]

THE NEW PARADIGM AND THE UNIVERSAL CALL TO HOLINESS

Up to this point I have focused on the social context of virtue and the dynamics of transformation of ideals for character, emphasizing how the interplay of cultural factors, especially models and stories, affects the ranking of values and virtues. My argument implies that the virtue of chastity needs to be reinterpreted in light of a new overall paradigm of Christian virtue in which justice assumes central importance.[21] The shift from a patriarchal paradigm to an egalitarian-feminist one can be compared to an adjustment of a kaleidoscope in which the elements of the configuration remain but are arranged in a new pattern. Everything remains, and everything is changed. This shift is occurring as part of the post–Vatican II renewal and is linked quite directly with the conciliar emphasis on the universal call to holiness, which is developed in the fifth chapter of *The Dogmatic Constitution on the Church (Lumen Gentium)*.[22] We see in this document from 1964 indications of a move away from a class system in which clergy and vowed members of

20. Fuentes, *Good Conscience,* p. 26.

21. For a discussion of "A Social-Justice Context for Rethinking Sexuality," see Joan Timmerman, ed., *The Mardi Gras Syndrome* (New York: Crossroad, 1984), pp. 50–68. Margaret A. Farley shows the usefulness of such an emphasis in her revisionist natural law approach to "An Ethic for Same Sex Relations," in Robert Nugent, ed., *A Challenge to Love* (New York: Crossroad, 1983), pp. 93–106.

22. Cited here from Walter M. Abbott, ed., *The Documents of Vatican II* (New York: The America Press, 1966), pp. 14–96.

religious communities were considered called to holiness of a sort unattainable by other Christians. As with all the conciliar documents, the insights of *Lumen Gentium* are not fully developed in the text itself, which contains compromises reflecting differences among council participants on various questions. Much of the conciliar reform agenda was left to subsequent living to be worked out, and this is certainly the case with ambiguities found in *Lumen Gentium*.

The tension of paramount interest here concerns that between a two-tiered approach to holiness, on the one hand, and a unified approach, on the other. The direction of change seems to be away from a long-entrenched elitism and toward the democratization of holiness, judging from the chapter titles and their arrangement. After an opening chapter on the mystery of the church, *Lumen Gentium* next discusses the people of God and then the hierarchical structure of the church, with special reference to the episcopate. There follow chapters on the laity, the call of the whole church to holiness, and religious.[23] One of the most striking things to note is how the chapter on the universal call to holiness employs language that will be echoed in a subsequent document on the renewal of canonical religious communities, *Perfectae Caritatis* (1965). Thus, in chapter 5 of *Lumen Gentium* we read:

> The Lord Jesus . . . preached holiness of life to each and every one of His disciples, regardless of their situation. . . Thus it is evident to everyone that all the faithful of Christ of whatever rank or status are called to the *fulness* of the Christian life and to the *perfection of charity*. . . . In the various types and duties of life, one and the same holiness is cultivated by all who are moved by the Spirit of God. . . . (##40–41, emphasis added)

These points are then developed by specific references to bishops, priests and other "ministers of lesser rank," "married couples and parents," "widows and single people," "laborers," and all who are suffering and oppressed.

That this document does not represent the complete eclipse of elitism by a

---

23. The reason for particular stress on the episcopate was to complete the work of the First Vatican Council, which had been halted in 1870 before the enhanced authority of the papacy could be placed in its proper collegial context. I omit discussion of the final two chapters of *Lumen Gentium*, for, despite the import of their subjects (eschatology and Mary), they are not so directly related to the topic at hand as the first six chapters. For a discussion of the need to rethink the history of religious life in light of new insights, see Susan Marie Maloney, "Historical Perspectives on Women Religious: Implications for Creating a Feminist Theology of Religious Life," in *Women and Theology*, ed. Mary Ann Hinsdale and Phyllis H. Kaminski (Maryknoll, N.Y.: Orbis, 1995), pp. 136–57.

democratizing tendency is clear, however, from what is said about the "evangelical counsels" of poverty, chastity, and obedience, the practice of which is said to provide a "shining witness and model of holiness" (#39). Persons with the gift of celibacy "can more easily devote their entire selves to God alone with undivided heart," and "Mother Church rejoices at finding within her bosom men and women who more closely follow and more clearly demonstrate the Savior's self-giving by embracing poverty with the free choice of God's sons, and by renouncing their own wills. . . . Thus they liken themselves more thoroughly to Christ in His obedience" (#42). This concluding paragraph of the chapter "The Call of the Whole Church to Holiness" shades into the final chapter "Religious," in which the older elitism is implied in such passages as, "Religious should carefully consider that through them . . . the Church truly wishes to give an increasingly clearer revelation of Christ."

Although it is not quite stated that vowed religious are in an objectively superior state to other Christians, the cumulative effect of such comparative phrases as "more clearly," "more closely," "more easily," and "more thoroughly," is to convey this impression. The problem here is that the basic insight of the universal call to "one and the same holiness," understood as the "perfection of charity," is embedded in a text still governed by dualistic hierarchical thinking, which finds it impossible to distinguish difference without asserting superiority and inferiority. It is as if in one paragraph the council fathers dismantle the religious class system only to rebuild it in the next.

Without wanting to get bogged down in the nuances and ambiguities of these conciliar statements, I would assert that part of the unfinished agenda of the Second Vatican Council involves freeing the notion of "evangelical counsels" from the rigidly controlled definitions of canonical religious life and seeing them once more as invitations to all disciples to live the ideals of charity in the circumstances of their lives. A more thorough democratization of the Catholic understanding of holiness need not dispense with celebrating the unique gifts of the different religious orders and congregations, but it should not celebrate them by suggesting that superior qualities, whether of clarity of revelation, ease of following Christ, or whatever, are found in these situations. I hope there will always be communities of Christians who focus their energies on prayer and apostolic activities, some of which find it helpful to practice celibacy, communal ownership of property, unfailing hospitality, explicit dedication to nonviolence, and so forth, but I believe our times call for an end to romantic praise of elitist notions of poverty, chastity, and obedience, which lend themselves so readily to fundamentalism and authoritarianism. It would be good if the currently needed character traits associated with the traditional three vows could be restored as ideals for the whole church in language intelligible to everyone: solidarity with the poor and oppressed, sexual integrity and justice, and dedication and coresponsibility in the use of one's talents and energies for the common good of the earth and its inhabitants. Terminology is not the issue here so much as the need to renew and reform the canonically recognized religious orders and congregations without ranking these sorts of Christian living as superior to the life forms of other Christians. It is all one holiness; everyone is called to the "perfection of charity."

Under the patriarchal paradigm of virtue, however, charity has to some extent been subordinated to a preoccupation with chastity, which is rigorously interpreted as abstinence from all nonmarital sexual thoughts and actions. This disciplining of sexual energy has served for many Christians as a focal sign of the love of God and has supported neighbor-love in important ways, particularly by promoting marital fidelity and by discouraging forms of sexual activity that can cause great harm. But the limits of this patriarchal understanding of chastity are considerable, including the disrespect for embodiment and for female humanity that have accompanied it, the narrowing of the moral life to matters of sexuality in the popular imagination (as Fuentes's novel shows so well), and the elitism resulting from the rhetoric associated with clerical and religious celibacy. Moreover, there is some evidence that rigidly antisexual religious training can have the paradoxical result of promoting sexual addictions and sexual violence, and that excessive preoccupation with sustaining the "nuclear family" can lead to neglect of the wider human community.[24] Clearly there is need to reinterpret the demands of chastity in a way that minimizes these problems, and fortunately the shift from a patriarchal to an egalitarian-feminist paradigm of virtue is contributing to this task. I shall not attempt here a full delineation of the new paradigm, but simply mention several points about the shift:

1. *Classical theological and moral virtues remain in the new paradigm.* The egalitarian-feminist position is quite compatible with affirming that "faith, hope, and love remain . . . but the greatest of these is love" (1 Cor. 13:13); likewise it has no reason to dispense with the classical wisdom that recognizes prudence, justice, fortitude, and temperance to be required for excellence of character. What is suggested by the shift is that chastity should be recognized to be at least as closely related to justice as it is to temperance, if not more so. Instead of seeing chastity as simply a subcategory of temperance, which rein-

---

24. See Patrick J. Carnes, *Don't Call It Love: Recovery from Sexual Addiction* (New York: Bantam, 1991).

forces an exaggerated emphasis on control, we need to regard chastity as an expression of right relationships. To assert this is not to deny that managing sexuality is required, but rather to affirm that the reasons for exercising such discipline are what matter most. Perfectionistic concern for controlling thoughts and impulses contributes to obsession and even addiction, while asking about the effects of sexual choices on the well-being of oneself and others can provide incentive for a balance of restraint and enjoyment, governed by values that include honesty, respect, pleasure, care, mutuality, and fidelity.

2. *The egalitarian-feminist reconfiguration of virtue places more emphasis altogether on justice, and less on control than the patriarchal paradigm.* This eclipse of the rigid ideal of "control" applies whether it is focused on other persons (obedience as interpreted by patriarchy) or bodily impulses (chastity as interpreted by patriarchy). Undoubtedly there are many sexually addicted persons today who still identify with the prayer of the early Augustine, "Make me chaste, but not yet." On the contemporary scene, however, I suspect there is even greater resonance among spiritually sensitive persons for a prayer on the order of, "Make me deeply committed to the cause of the world's hungry and oppressed, but not yet."[25] In both cases, the disclaimer "but not yet" amounts to an admission of the need for grace to overcome the fears that accompany the desire to live more chastely or justly. In any event, the new paradigm's emphasis on justice as central to the perfection of the Christian moral life should be seen as today's understanding of the way charity, the greatest of all virtues, needs to be expressed. The new vision of goodness requires relinquishing the patriarchal "ethic of control" in favor of an egalitarian-feminist "ethic of respect, trust, and risk."[26]

3. *The dislodging of chastity from being seen as the epitome of "virtue," indeed synonymous with the notion itself in popular discourse, requires reconsidering its demands in light of the ideal of justice, or right relationships.* Presently this virtue suffers from trivialization in the religious and wider cultures, which is a symptom of the need both for its reinterpretation and for its integration into a

25. This version of Augustine's prayer is one I remember from school days; the original is from *Confessions* 8.7: "Da mihi castitatem et continentiam, sed noli modo."

26. This designation is influenced especially by Marie Augusta Neal's concept of a "socio-theology of relinquishment," discussed in her volume *The Just Demands of the Poor* (New York: Paulist, 1987) and Sharon Welch's *A Feminist Ethic of Risk* (Minneapolis: Fortress, 1990).

more comprehensive ethical picture. With respect to virtue theory, the need is to delineate the qualities of character that epitomize sexual holiness among embodied spirits of differing ages, sexual orientations, and relational situations. The "taboo mentality" of physicalist moral theology is clearly inadequate; but the uncritical indulgence of secular hedonism is no better—indeed it is arguably worse in terms of the human costs of the unjust and addictive behaviors it encourages. The task now is to develop a rational and coherent set of ideals for character with respect to sexuality that will encourage integration of these energies into a life project that is honest, centered, responsible, and just.[27]

Reconstructive work on the virtue of chastity needs above all to restore the ideal to the whole community rather than restrict it to an elite corps of "religious professionals." To accomplish this it will first be necessary to repent the harm caused by inadequate notions of chastity, which have rendered the church complicit in perpetuating injustices of various types, particularly mistreatment of homosexuals, abuse of children, unnecessary strain on marriages, and violence toward women.

JUSTICE AND NEW NARRATIVES OF VIRTUOUS LIVES

There remains the matter of providing new models that demonstrate—with a power scholarly prose can never attain—the goodness and beauty of lives governed by the egalitarian-feminist paradigm of virtue. What does holiness look like when lives bear witness to the heroic practice of justice? In recent decades there have been many stories of such models. These contemporary examples of holiness are of three principal types, two of which involve classical categories of sanctity, namely, martyrs and confessors of the faith. The third type corresponds to the "holy founders" of religious communities,

---

27. Works contributing to this task include Joan Timmerman, *The Mardi Gras Syndrome* (1984) and *Sexuality and Spiritual Growth* (New York: Crossroad, 1992); Lisa Sowle Cahill, *Women and Sexuality* (New York: Paulist, 1992); Margaret A. Farley, *Just Love* (forthcoming); Christine E. Gudorf, *Body, Sex, and Pleasure* (Cleveland, Oh.: Pilgrim Press, 1994); and Patricia Beattie Jung and Ralph F. Smith, *Heterosexism: An Ethical Challenge* (Albany: State University of New York Press, 1993). Jean Porter's study *The Recovery of Virtue: The Relevance of Aquinas for Christian Ethics* (Louisville: Westminster/John Knox, 1990), lifts up the importance of justice in Aquinas's theory of human good and notes that, for Aquinas, sins involving "standard sexual intercourse between a man and a woman, are violations of justice as well as temperance" (p. 118).

the saints whose legacy included social organizations that carried their religious vision into the future.

Martyrs of Justice

The contemporary martyrs of justice are many. Ordinary believers find the holy women who endured rape *and* martyrdom in El Salvador in 1980 because of their solidarity with victims of injustice certainly as worthy of canonization as Marie Clementine Anwarite. Indeed, the distinctions of virginity or sexual relatedness (or violation), and vowed or nonvowed canonical status seem far less important to people generally than the exemplary solidarity with the oppressed so evident in the lives and deaths of Maryknoll missionaries Maura Clarke and Ita Ford, lay volunteer Jean Donovan, and Ursuline sister Dorothy Kazel.[28] Their deaths, as do those of many others in this century, bear out the findings of French thinker Bruno Chenu and his colleagues who observe in a 1990 study that Christian martyrdom has varied considerably under different historical circumstances.[29]

According to these authors of *The Book of Christian Martyrs,* the first period of martyrdom began with the dawn of Christianity and continued until Constantine's imperial Edict of Milan made Christians safe from persecution in 313. Saints such as Polycarp, Perpetua and Felicitas, and other early martyrs are distinguished for explicitly confessing Christ and then suffering the consequences meted out to them by powerful opponents of the new religious movement. The second era extended from the late Middle Ages through the nineteenth century. Its martyrs are known for witnessing to conscience in various European and missionary contexts, for making "the sacrifice of their lives in faithfulness to their convictions."[30] Examples from this period include Joan of Arc, Jan Hus, Thomas More, and nineteenth-century martyrs in Madagascar and Uganda. Finally, what distinguishes the martyrs of the present era from those of the two earlier periods is the fact that in the twentieth century Christians have been martyred not primarily because of their religious or moral convictions but because of their commitment to the well-being of other persons. These martyrs "are no longer just defenders of

28. See Ana Carrigan, *Salvador Witness: The Life and Calling of Jean Donovan* (New York: Simon & Schuster, 1984); and Judith Noone, *The Same Fate as the Poor* (Maryknoll, N.Y.: Maryknoll Sisters, 1984).

29. Bruno Chenu, Claude Prud'homme, France Quéré, and Jean-Claude Thomas, *The Book of Christian Martyrs* (New York: Crossroad, 1990).

30. Ibid., p. 97.

the authentic faith but defenders of life. Those who fall, like Martin Luther King and Oscar Romero, are often the pioneers in a fight for the dignity of the poorest, for the essential rights of the oppressed."[31] Among several other contemporary martyrs of justice whose stories are recounted in this volume are Maximilian Kolbe, the Polish Franciscan who gave his life in place of the father of a family who had been selected for extermination at Auschwitz in 1941; Dietrich Bonhoeffer, the Lutheran theologian who was killed in 1945 for his involvement in a failed plot against Hitler; and Alice Domon and Léonie Duquet, two French nuns who "disappeared" in Argentina in December 1977 because of their solidarity with women of the Plaza de Mayo.

Truth Tellers

Confessors of the faith could perhaps today be termed "truth tellers." They are heirs to an ancient prophetic tradition, that of the ones who are recognized, sooner or later, to have spoken the values of God to a culture set on other things. These women and men suffer for announcing the reality they see and experience, but in ways short of the physical death that martyrs endure. One thinks of the courageous homosexuals who "come out" as gay or lesbian in a culture that largely receives their gift of truth with scorn or indifference. Of course, it is premature to "canonize" individuals while they are still alive, but many persons are already taking inspiration from the way Catholics such as Mary Hunt, Brian McNaught, John McNeill, and Barbara Zanotti are making the graces of their lives available to a community that has officially declared same-sex love outside the realm of holiness.[32] Other candidates for prophecy abound. There are the "whistleblowers" who risk livelihoods and social acceptance to report health hazards and ecological irresponsibility in the workplace. There are the bishops who take stands against capital punishment or in favor of reexamining positions the Vatican would prefer to consider closed, such as contraception and women's ordination. There are the church professionals who publish critiques of injustice

31. Ibid., p. 163.
32. See Mary E. Hunt, *Fierce Tenderness: A Feminist Theology of Friendship* (New York: Crossroad, 1991); Brian McNaught, *On Being Gay: Thoughts on Family, Faith, and Love* (New York: St. Martin's Press, 1988); John McNeill, *The Church and the Homosexual* (Kansas City: Sheed, Andrews & McMeel, 1976); idem, *Taking a Chance on God: Liberating Theology for Gays, Lesbians, and Their Lovers, Families, and Friends* (Boston: Beacon, 1988); and Barbara Zanotti, ed., *A Faith of One's Own: Explorations by Catholic Lesbians* (Trumansburg, N.Y.: The Crossing Press, 1986).

within the religious institution, getting specific about needs for reform in a way that imperils their own careers. There are the victims of sexual abuse and domestic violence who have been willing to tell their stories and confront their oppressors for the sake not only of personal healing but also the well-being of others in systems based on denial and fear. When the stories of victims who have "gone public" out of compassion for themselves and others (and not for reasons of greed) become more widely known, there will be less incentive to maintain a conspiracy of silence that has too long protected unhealthy aspects of the religious system.

The test of time is, of course, needed to sift through the ambiguities of the activities of these and other sorts of truth tellers; not everyone who speaks with honesty has enough charity and compassion to warrant being considered an exemplar of the new paradigm of virtue. But many struggling individuals are inspiring us with new examples of what goodness can look like. The life stories of these individuals deserve to be much more widely known.

Such persons as Teresa Kane, for instance, are providing a new image of goodness that reflects the egalitarian-feminist paradigm. Her words of welcome to Pope John Paul II in Washington, D.C. in October 1979 were controversial precisely because as an elected leader of U.S. nuns Kane was expected to reflect the traditional virtues of the "good sister," which are captured rather well in the Victorian image of woman as "the angel in the house."[33] But Kane's attention to a deeply felt sense of responsibility and of God's presence in her life had taught her to transcend this patriarchal socialization to uncritical passivity and docility. As President of the Sisters of Mercy of the Union and also the Leadership Conference of Women Religious (a national organization of officers of women's religious congregations), Kane had asked to speak with John Paul II about the insights and needs of the women she represented. After repeatedly being refused this private conversation by those who choreographed the papal visit, Kane decided to use the one opportunity she had for conveying a message she deemed it urgent for him to hear, a formal welcome during a prayer service for nuns at the National Shrine of the Immaculate Conception. After extending a greeting, she went on to ask the pope to examine church practice regarding women's roles:

33. The phrase originated with the poet Coventry Patmore; for a discussion of the problematic tendency to view women as either angels or monsters, see Sandra M. Gilbert and Susan Gubar, *The Madwoman in the Attic: The Woman Writer and the Nineteenth-Century Literary Imagination* (1979; New Haven: Yale University Press, 1984), pp. 20–36.

Your Holiness, the women of this country have been inspired by your spirit of courage. We thank you for exemplifying such courage in speaking to us so directly about our responsibilities to the poor and the oppressed throughout the world. . . .

As women, we have heard the powerful messages of our church addressing the dignity and reverence for all persons. . . . Our contemplation leads us to state that the church in its struggle to be faithful to its call for reverence and dignity for all persons must respond by providing the possibility of women as persons being included in all ministries of our church.[34]

Kane's action was unexpected and controversial, but it epitomized the sort of response someone operating under the new paradigm of virtue might make under the circumstances, particularly in the way it balanced conflicting values within limited circumstances. There was the duty to express welcome and respect; there was the obligation to represent the injustices experienced by those who had chosen her as leader. Both concerns found their way into the course she took, and she succeeded in the Christian ideal of "speaking the truth in love" (Eph. 4:15 NRSV). Although her words were offensive to those who confuse papal opinion with the divine will, to those of an egalitarian-feminist cast of mind they were reminiscent of the prophetic tradition described in 2 Peter 1:21 (and translated into inclusive language and contemporary theological terms) thus: "no prophecy ever came by human will [alone], but rather human beings moved by the Holy Spirit spoke under the influence of God."[35]

Of course, biblical prophets tended to grate on the nerves of religious leaders, and so also do contemporary truth tellers such as Kane, Andrew Greeley, Leonardo Boff, and Claire Murphy. Greeley's style is much more confrontational than Kane's, but his willingness to present social scientific data and theological opinion in whatever way he thinks will be helpful to the people of God reflects his deeply felt sense of pastoral responsibility.[36] Leonardo Boff, a Brazilian theologian, named the injustices in ecclesiastical operations too

34. Kane's words are cited here from *The Washington Post* (October 8, 1979), p. A-27. See also Annie Lally Milhaven, ed., *The Inside Stories: 13 Valiant Women Challenging the Church* (Mystic, Conn.: Twenty-Third Publications, 1987), pp. 1–23.

35. Translation by Joseph J. Arackal, *Praying in Inclusive Language: Morning and Evening Prayer* (Belle Plaine, Minn.: Patmos Publications, 1991), p. 226.

36. Greeley's publications include scholarly and popular nonfiction as well as a number of mass market novels; a recent instance of significant "truth telling" is "How Serious Is the Problem of Sexual Abuse by Clergy?" *America* 168 (March 20/27, 1993): 6–10.

clearly in the volume *Church: Charism or Power,* and was subsequently harassed by Vatican officials until he resigned from the priesthood and Franciscan order in 1992, expressing his desire to devote his energies to the poor and oppressed rather than to fighting the church bureaucracy.[37] Claire Murphy is less well known than these other truth tellers, but her willingness to share her story is extremely important because her experience provides evidence for ecclesiastically recognized ambiguity on a moral question declared clear and settled by Catholic authorities. During the 1960s, when this Irish nun was a missionary in Nigeria, she received oral contraceptives from the Vatican in order to prevent pregnancy in case she were raped by soldiers involved in the Biafran war. She chose not to use the pills and initially kept silent about the experience. She has more recently shared it with the wider public for the sake of other Catholic women whose life circumstances require not becoming pregnant, but who have been declared guilty of material wrongdoing for taking such prudent measures.[38]

Organizers of Movements for Social Justice

Finally to be considered are the organizers of movements for social justice. These women and men are analogous to the "holy founders" of active religious communities, who inspired others to join in their vision and labors,

37. Boff's phrase from this book, "a Church striving for a new type of holiness," reflects the shift in paradigms of virtue quite directly; quoted here from John W. Diercksmeier's translation (New York: Crossroad, 1985), p. 123. Like McNeill, Boff accepted Vatican demands to keep silent until the frustration became intolerable.

38. In an article for the *Los Angeles Times,* which appeared in the Minneapolis *Star Tribune* (August 30, 1992), p. 20A, Tamara Jones reported from Dublin: "'The Vatican had sent me a whole cupboard full' of birth control pills, Sister Claire recalled with a thin-lipped smile. 'It was OK to protect the nuns against rape by the soldiers, but not the girls in our school.' She threw out the pills and kept quiet." Of related interest is a report in the *National Catholic Reporter* for July 16, 1993, which described an article in the July 3 issue of *La Civilta Cattolica,* a journal whose contents are reviewed by the Vatican. There the Jesuit thinker Giacomo Perico went on record as approving the use of contraceptives as "a legitimate form of self-defense that does not violate church teaching" when women are at great risk of being raped, as was the case in Bosnia-Herzegovina at the time the article was published. The *NCR* quotes Perico as declaring: "For the woman who is raped, sexual relations has nothing to do with an act of love between husband and wife." The implication is that official teaching against birth control is concerned with consensual conjugal sex; Perico's position is important because it moves away from the rigid physicalism of classical teaching and opens the possibility of considering the range of differences between the extremes of ideal married love and terrorist wartime rape.

with the eventual result being an enduring apostolic society. Groups of this sort were not always immediately recognized as "religious" in the canonical sense, and indeed they sometimes made a point of emphasizing their distinction from those congregations that were subject to ecclesiastical regulation, at least initially. The Daughters of Charity are an outstanding example of such a group. In contemporary society these points are not made explicitly, and the similarities between such groups as the Catholic Workers, Pax Christi, NET-WORK, or New Ways Ministry, and traditional religious congregations escapes notice, largely because a common sex-segregated life of publicly professed celibacy has been seen as the chief characteristic of religious communities, and these groups are based on other things. They all, however, draw their inspiration from the gospel, and their members make important commitments of time, talent, material resources, and emotional energy to the ideals of the *basileia,* the reign of God proclaimed by Jesus. Catholic Workers live a common life and provide food for the hungry and homeless in various cities. Pax Christi members support each other in promoting nonviolence through educational efforts and other activities. NETWORK, a social justice lobby founded by nuns in 1971, helps to focus the political energies of men and women within and beyond canonical communities in their efforts to influence public policy in Washington. New Ways Ministry, especially through publications and educational programs, seeks to provide "a bridge ministry of justice and reconciliation for gay and lesbian Catholics and the larger church community."[39]

Moreover, the steadfast agents of social change who attract others to the work they are about succeed in multiplying their own impact for good in much the same way that the holy founders (and reformers) of traditional orders and congregations did in the past. Again, as is the case with the "truth

---

39. Quoted from Robert Nugent and Jeannine Gramick, *Building Bridges: Gay and Lesbian Reality and the Catholic Church* (Mystic Conn.: Twenty-Third Publications, 1992), p. ix. Another organization, NAWR/NARW, is particularly interesting because its brief history illustrates the development of a more inclusive organization on the foundations of one originally intended for nuns. Founded as the National Assembly of Women Religious in 1970, this organization initially was limited to diocesan sisters' councils and "grass-roots" individual members of religious congregations. It soon adopted an explicit commitment to a gospel vision of justice and in 1982 changed its name to National Assembly of Religious Women, intending thereby to dismantle past barriers to the collaboration of "lay" and "community" women and to acknowledge that the adjective "religious" should not be limited to describing the latter. All Catholic women, in fact, are lay in the important sense of not belonging to the clerical state, and are religious in the basic sense of belonging to the People of God. (The Greek term *laos* simply means "people.") Funding difficulties led to the disbanding of NARW in 1995.

tellers," there is more ambiguity here than with the recognized martyrs of justice, simply because the gift of one's life over decades is less completely evident at any one time than when a holy person suffers a violent end. But the characteristics that enabled such Christians as Dorothy Day and César Chávez to involve others (often at considerable personal cost) in their work for social justice are already proving inspirational to persons of various backgrounds, and their stories are strengthening the new paradigm of virtue.[40]

This new paradigm, with its focus on justice, is actually quite traditional in the biblical sense, for in the Hebrew Scriptures the terms "justice" and "holiness" are synonymous. In our postcritical age, however, there is increasing recognition of the fact that notions of justice (and other virtues) need to be critiqued and refined as moral insight deepens. New historical circumstances and new knowledge have altered our views on what sorts of dispositions and behaviors are harmful and beneficial to the human community. With respect to the ideals of love and justice, for example, Margaret Farley has argued persuasively that both must be reinterpreted in light of radically new patterns of relationship between women and men. Under the "old order," which presumed the inferiority of females and understood God's will to require the subordination of women to men, understandings of love and justice did not include the possibility of criticizing sexism. Modern recognition of women's full human dignity, however, is bringing into being a "new order" that requires new interpretations of these traditional principles. Thus, with respect to Christian love, Farley proposes that its component of "equal regard" is empty if it does not include real equality of opportunity, its dimension of "self sacrifice" is false if tied in with misconceptions about alleged female passivity, and its aspect of "mutuality" is inadequate if based on analogues found "in the mutuality of relationships between parent and child, ruler and subject, master and servant" rather than on a recognition of the equality of women and men.[41] With respect to justice she argues that adequate understandings of both individual and common good require a shift from strict hierarchical models of social organization to more egalitarian

40. See, for example, Mel Piehl, *Breaking Bread: The Catholic Worker and the Origin of Catholic Radicalism in America* (Philadelphia: Temple University Press, 1982); June E. O'Connor, *The Moral Vision of Dorothy Day: A Feminist Perspective* (New York: Crossroad, 1991); and Joan London and Henry Anderson, *So Shall You Reap: The Story of César Chávez and the Farm Workers' Movement* (New York: Thomas Y. Crowell, 1970).

41. Margaret A. Farley, "New Patterns of Relationship: Beginnings of a Moral Revolution," *Theological Studies* 36 (December 1975): 632–33.

ones. She notes that "the good of the family, church, etc. is better served by a model of leadership which includes collaboration between [male and female] equals" than one which places a single male leader at the head of the community."[42] In the end, new understandings of justice and love are found to be mutually reinforcing norms for this Christian feminist ethic:

> [I]nterpersonal communion characterized by equality, mutuality, and reciprocity may serve not only as a norm against which every pattern of relationship may be measured but as a goal to which every pattern of relationship is ordered. Minimal justice, then, may have equality as its norm and full mutuality as its goal. Justice will be maximal as it approaches the ultimate goal of communion of each person with all persons and God.[43]

Certainly more work needs to be done translating such insights about the principles of love and justice into new understandings of the related virtues. Notre Dame theologian Richard P. McBrien has contributed to this task by stressing the virtue of "social justice," which he defines as "that virtue which is dedicated to the reordering of society, to the changing of institutions, systems, and patterns of behavior which deny people their basic human rights and which thereby destabilize society."[44] Some persons who exemplify this virtue will be explicitly committed to feminism, while others may state their commitment to justice in more general terms, such as the "option for the poor" or "solidarity with victims of oppression." In any case, the commitment to a gender-inclusive vision of justice and the willingness to press for social change distinguish this sort of justice from patriarchal notions of virtue that promote "rendering others their due" within social systems that are not themselves adequately scrutinized. This virtue of social justice is evident in those who have taken to heart the invitation of Jesus to "hunger and thirst" for justice, which the 1971 Synod of Bishops interpreted as requiring that we "reflect on the society in which we live and on its values" and "renounce these values when they cease to promote justice for all men [*sic*]."[45]

42. Ibid., p. 645.
43. Ibid., p. 646.
44. McBrien, "Social Justice: It's in Our Bones," unpublished address for Archdiocese of Saint Paul and Minneapolis Presbyteral Assembly, Collegeville, Minn. (June 25, 1991).
45. Synod of Bishops, "The Ministerial Priesthood" and "Justice in the World," (Washington, D.C.: National Conference of Catholic Bishops, 1971), p. 46. The sexist language of this official translation is typical of church documents (and other publications as well) from the period, a problem I discuss in "'Toward Renewing the Life and Culture of Fallen Man': *Gaudium et Spes* as Catalyst for Catholic Feminist Theology," in Judith A. Dwyer, *"Questions of Special Urgency": The Church in the Modern World Two Decades after Vatican II* (Washington, D.C.: Georgetown University Press, 1986), pp. 55–78.

Such reflection and the grace of God's Spirit have led the saints of the twentieth century down the paths to martyrdom, prophecy, and the creation of new religiously based societies for the promotion of justice. There is ambiguity in all of this, and only time will finally sort out authentic virtue from its counterfeit. In the meanwhile, what is involved in the transition from the patriarchal paradigm to the egalitarian-feminist one is well captured in the image with which Flannery O'Connor concluded her short story "Revelation." After narrating the events that invite a bigoted woman named Eva Turpin to change from self-righteousness to a more authentic religious stance, O'Connor describes a vision Eva has when a purple streak of light remains in the sky at the close of an eventful day:

> She saw the streak as a vast swinging bridge extending upward from the earth through a field of living fire. Upon it a vast horde of souls were rumbling toward heaven. There were whole companies of white-trash, clean for the first time in their lives, and bands of black niggers in white robes, and battalions of freaks and lunatics shouting and clapping and leaping like frogs. And bringing up the end of the procession was a tribe of people whom she recognized at once as those who, like herself and [her husband] Claud, had always had a little of everything and the God-given wit to use it right. She leaned forward to observe them closer. They were marching behind the others with great dignity, accountable as they had always been for good order and common sense and respectable behavior. They alone were on key. Yet she could see by their shocked and altered faces that even their virtues were being burned away.[46]

Eva's conversion needs also to be ours. All human moral striving is relative in the light of divine goodness and mercy, and changing times require changing emphases and interpretations of what human goodness entails. The honor and charity and generosity Arthur Jarvis learned from his parents can contribute to unspeakable evil if not connected to knowledge of the material and political circumstances of *all* his South African neighbors and to a commitment to the well-being of those who are most oppressed among them. The classical virtues are of abiding importance, but what they require and which ones are especially needed will vary with different historical circumstances. Martyrdom affords the clearest case of the shifting paradigm of virtue, and it is particularly instructive to note why certain priests and ministers of the gospel slain in this century are so important to devout Christians. Clerical and professedly religious figures have a particular visibility and are

---

46. In Flannery O'Connor, *Everything That Rises Must Converge* (New York: Farrar, Straus & Giroux, 1965), pp. 217–18.

held to high standards of morality within and beyond the Christian community. But if Martin Luther King, Jr., and Oscar Romero (and the other ministers, male and female, who lost their lives in El Salvador) had simply
epitomized the patriarchal paradigm of virtue, they could have preached,
taught, and led services until they retired or died of natural causes. Their violent ends can be seen to testify to the extremely high stakes in today's conflict
about what it means to be a good religious leader, which is only to up the ante
a bit on what it means to be a good Christian. Their deaths proclaim that
social justice must take precedence over unjust "law and order," and basic
human rights are more important than "property rights." The "good life," we
are instructed by their holy deaths, is a life poured out in compassion and
labor for the sake of making it possible for those who are the poorest and
most oppressed to enjoy the material and political conditions that allow
human beings to flourish as the Creator intends.

CHAPTER FOUR

Contested Authority:
The Cases of Charles Curran
and the Vatican 24

An honest reading of the Gospels shows Jesus critically evaluating each claim or exercise of authority in relation to the demands of God's rule and order in human society, and accepting or rejecting it accordingly. It might be argued that this is because of his divinity and his messianic role, yet it is noteworthy that it is precisely in these actions that the Gospels present him as a model for Christian conduct throughout the ages.

—Monika K. Hellwig[1]

If the good life is one devoted to making it possible for human beings to flourish as the Creator intends, the questions that surface next are clear: How can we *know* the Creator's intentions? Who has access to God's design for human beings?

Christianity has traditionally responded in a complex manner. On the one hand, there is the admission that we can never know God's will with absolute and full certainty. As St. Paul recognized: "Oh, the depth of the riches and wisdom and knowledge of God! How inscrutable are his judgments and how unsearchable his ways! 'For who has known the mind of the Lord or who has been his counselor?'" (Rom. 11:33–35). The link between theology and ethics is inescapable, and the first thing to say about human knowledge of the divine will is that it will always be limited and imperfect.

---

1. Monika K. Hellwig, "Catholic Faith and Contemporary Questions" (Tulsa: University of Tulsa Warren Center for Catholic Studies, 1988), p. 6.

THE RELEVANCE OF REVELATION

Christians, however, have balanced this insight about the inscrutability of "God's mind" (itself an anthropomorphic metaphor for a transcendent reality) with strong claims to know God's will quite well, as is evident from their respect for the principles of the decalogue and the teachings of Jesus. How have they justified this paradoxical position? The answer to this question involves the doctrine of divine revelation, which affirms that God has communicated to humankind the knowledge necessary for salvation. Thus, the *Dogmatic Constitution on Divine Revelation* of the Second Vatican Council declares: "Through divine revelation, God chose to show forth and communicate Himself and the eternal decisions of His will regarding the salvation of men" (*Dei Verbum* #6). While acknowledging that God can be known through created realities, the conciliar fathers affirm the classic position that revelation enhances the knowledge of religious truths available through reason, providing a degree of certitude otherwise unattainable. In the second chapter of this document, they address the process of revelation and emphasize the importance of Christ, the apostles, and their successors the bishops, in this process:

> In His gracious goodness, God has seen to it that what He had revealed for the salvation of all nations would abide perpetually in its full integrity and be handed on to all generations. Therefore Christ the Lord, in whom the full revelation of the supreme God is brought to completion (cf. 2 Cor. 1:20; 3:16; 4:6), commissioned the apostles to preach to all men that gospel which is the source of all saving truth and moral teaching . . . . But in order to keep the gospel forever whole and alive within the Church, the apostles left bishops as their successors, "handing over their own teaching role" to them. (*Dei Verbum* #7)

Thus, the official Catholic doctrine on revelation establishes a connection between the inscrutable, transcendent divine will and the contemporary church authorities. Drawing out the literal meaning of *traditio,* which is "handing over," the authors of *Dei Verbum* go on to affirm that "sacred tradition, therefore, and sacred Scripture of both the Old and the New Testament are like a mirror in which the pilgrim Church on earth looks at God, from whom she has received everything, until she is brought finally to see Him as He is, face to face (cf. 1 Jn. 3:2)" (#7).

It is significant that *Dei Verbum* does not attend to the first pole of the paradox here, namely, the imperfect quality of all knowledge of God and God's will, even though its use of the mirror image recalls St. Paul's recognition that his apostolic knowledge and vision were limited: "At present we see indistinctly, as in a mirror, but then face to face. At present we know partially; then I shall know fully, as I am fully known" (1 Cor. 13:12). Indeed, it has been characteristic of Catholicism to celebrate the gifts of truth it enjoys without emphasizing the theological fact of its limitations in relation to divine transcendence. This understandable if problematic tendency has been seen historically in the anathemas of church councils prior to Vatican II, as well as in the persecution of heretics. More recently it has been expressed in such official documents as Pope John Paul II's 1993 encyclical *Veritatis Splendor* and the *Catechism of the Catholic Church,* which became available in the United States in 1994.[2] Summary statements from the catechism forge a connection between God and the hierarchical magisterium in such a way that the balancing Pauline insight is obscured, if not forgotten:

> God has revealed himself fully by sending his own Son, in whom he has established his covenant forever. The Son is his Father's definitive Word; so there will be no further Revelation after him. (#73)

> The task of interpreting the Word of God authentically has been entrusted solely to the Magisterium of the Church, that is, to the Pope and to the bishops in communion with him. (#100)

This emphasis on the revelatory process continuing in history beyond the apostolic age is distinctive of Catholicism, as indeed is the emphasis on the pope and bishops, whose teaching authority is captured in the Latin term *magisterium.*[3]

It is safe to say that Catholics generally, including those who differ with the

---

2. Pope John Paul II, *Veritatis Splendor* (October 5, 1993); *Catechism of the Catholic Church* (Collegeville, Minn.: Liturgical Press, 1994). The catechism itself recognizes the limited nature of human abilities to speak about God, especially in paragraphs 39–43, but its theological affirmation of mystery and transcendence does not carry over into subsequent discussions of God's will as known by church authorities.

3. The word *magisterium* simply means teaching authority, and, as Richard P. McBrien notes in *Catholicism* (Minneapolis: Winston Press, 1980), it can apply in a wide sense to a gift pertaining to the entire People of God, commissioned at baptism to participate in Christ's work as prophet, priest, and king. He observes further that Thomas Aquinas had distinguished two principal sorts of magisterial authority, that of the bishop and that of the theologian (p. 68). Recent usage, however, tends to favor a stricter definition, employing *magisterium* in the sense of "hierarchical magisterium," that is, the teaching authority of the pope and bishops. For a full analysis of the development of Catholic doctrine on this matter, with emphasis on the nineteenth and twentieth centuries, see John P. Boyle, *Church Teaching Authority: Historical and Theological Studies* (Notre Dame: University of Notre Dame Press, 1995).

hierarchical magisterium on certain aspects of moral teaching, affirm the above assertions from the recent catechism, when they are properly interpreted. As the discussion of contrasting styles of faith and ethics in chapter 1 and the delineation of recent philosophical developments in chapter 2 both indicate, however, this matter of interpretation is controversial. Does one hold to a virtual identification of God's word and God's will with papal judgments? This is the position of Catholic Fundamentalism, promoted by many in our time. But another position is arguably more orthodox, for it attends to the pole of divine transcendence at the same time as it affirms the immanence of God's word in the historical religious institution and its authoritative teachings. This is the position of Catholic Revisionism, which affirms papal and episcopal authority but also insists that because official judgments can never fully express God's will, and indeed may suffer from imperfections, there devolves on all Christians the obligation to discern moral truth under the guidance of God's Spirit, always with careful attention to authoritative teaching but never to the point of abdicating their own responsibility for moral discernment.

What this means in practical terms is that official teaching is authoritative insofar as it is convincing. As the conciliar *Declaration on Religious Freedom* puts it, "The truth cannot impose itself except by virtue of its own truth, as it makes its entrance into the mind at once quietly and with power" (*Dignitatis Humanae* #1). Reasonable teaching is persuasive on its own merits, without needing to be reinforced by coercive measures. But this is precisely the point that current Vatican officials deny by their actions. In the face of widespread nonreception of the teaching of *Humanae Vitae* and other related moral doctrines, Roman officials have used the power of their office to shore up unconvincing arguments in support of teachings on sexual and reproductive ethics and the status of women.

Notable examples of this coercion include censorship of moral theologians and pressures against church personnel whose differences with official positions are judged to be out of line. In the face of this Vatican administrative policy, revisionist moral theology has a difficult task, namely, to uphold the traditional values of faith and reason in the face of a fundamentalist tendency to conflate human and divine authority, virtually to the point of idolatry. Obedience is the contested virtue, and its interpretation makes all the difference.

What does obedience require and when should it override other considerations? Fundamentalism, which reflects the domination-subordination model of human relationships characteristic of patriarchy, understands obedience primarily as a matter of *submission*. It maintains that the obedience of good

Catholics must be total, since conformity with official teaching is symbolic of docility to God. Abdication of human reasoning is idealized in this paradigm, because the point is to submit to what is understood as Divine Wisdom. Thus, the interpretation of moral obligation is left to the religious authority figures.

Revisionism, on the other hand, which advocates the mutuality model of human relationships characteristic of egalitarian-feminism, implicitly views obedience under a different metaphor, that of *hearing* rather than submission. This emphasis expresses the etymology of the term, which derives from the Latin *ob* and *audire,* words that in combination suggest the idea of "hearing toward." In this paradigm the image of the obedient Christian is one of attentiveness, of listening with care for clues to the divine will. In a great many cases revisionist moral judgments will be identical with those of the magisterium, but revisionism does not understand the moral life as primarily a matter of submitting to the voice of authority. Instead, this stance is one of listening more broadly, of attending not only to magisterial teaching but also to what is going on in the situation at hand and what is likely to result from the choices under consideration.[4]

Clearly these two models depend on disparate understandings of revelation itself. As with biblical fundamentalism, ecclesiastical fundamentalism tends to focus on the "products" of revelation, even going so far as to locate the divine in verbal formulas. By contrast, revisionism sees the verbal formulas (whether biblical, conciliar, or papal) more as records of a revelatory "process" than as divine utterances per se. Richard McBrien's treatment of this theological topic is illustrative of such an approach. In *Catholicism,* McBrien asserts that revelation is essentially "the self-communication of God," which is experienced in a mediated way, that is, historically and sacramentally.[5] This fact of mediation entails that any experience of God must be interpreted before it is expressed; thus, the records of revelatory experiences such as one finds in the Bible are somewhat removed from the divine self-communication itself and are limited by the cultural forms available for their interpretation

4. My attention to these differences has been influenced by H. Richard Niebuhr, who contributed a very helpful discussion of the importance of metaphor in the experience of moral agency in *The Responsible Self* (New York: Harper & Row, 1963). It should also be noted that support for the revisionist interpretation of obedience is found in such classic texts as Aquinas's treatment of practical reason and prudence in the *Summa Theologiae* (I–II. Q 94. a 4 and II–II. Q 47. a 2) as well as in the Second Vatican Council's *Declaration on Religious Freedom* (*Dignitatis Humanae* #14, quoted at the conclusion of chapter 1).

5. McBrien, *Catholicism,* pp. 234–35. The second chapter of this work, "Faith, Theology, and Belief" (pp. 23–77), analyzes distinctions that are basic to McBrien's theology of revelation.

and expression. This insight has been a source of hope for feminists from biblical traditions, who have succeeded to some degree in retrieving the liberating truth of sacred texts from the patriarchal language of biblical authors.[6]

Official Catholic teaching on revelation does not emphasize the hermeneutical difficulties involved in dealing with divine revelation, whether in the form of scripture or tradition, but as the insights from linguistic philosophy discussed in chapter 2 make clear, conflicts of interpretation are entailed whenever human beings consider the meaning of texts. Indeed, *Dei Verbum*'s acknowledgment of the fact that tradition develops in a complex process implies as much:

> This tradition which comes from the apostles develops in the Church with the help of the Holy Spirit. For there is a growth in the understanding of the realities and the words which have been handed down. This happens through the contemplation and study made by believers, who treasure these things in their hearts (cf. Lk. 2:19, 51), through the intimate understanding of spiritual things they experience, and through the preaching of those who have received through episcopal succession the sure gift of truth. For, as the centuries succeed one another, the Church constantly moves forward toward the fulness of divine truth until the words of God reach their complete fulfillment in her. (#8)

Significantly, this passage also implies a distinction between the truth the church is able to articulate at any given point in its history and the "fullness of divine truth," which is a goal rather than a possession. Given the finitude and the complexity of the traditioning process, and given the historical record of the controversies that have enabled church teachings to reach their present stage, the fact that disputes about doctrines and their interpretation are raging today should not be surprising.

Today's conflicts, as I discussed in the preceding chapter, reflect the tensions involved in shifting from a patriarchal understanding of virtue to an egalitarian-feminist one. Although in general I applaud the transition and would hasten its successful completion, I also recognize the finitude of the new paradigm, the fact that it too falls short of the fullness of divine truth. Thus, in arguing that the patriarchal paradigm of virtue and the patriarchal relational model are obsolete and harmful, I acknowledge that they have served as vehicles of social order and historical evolution. The relational order

6. Ground-breaking and highly influential examples of such scholarship include Phyllis Trible, *God and the Rhetoric of Sexuality* (Philadelphia: Fortress Press, 1978) and Elisabeth Schüssler Fiorenza, *In Memory of Her: A Feminist Theological Reconstruction of Christian Origins* (New York: Crossroad, 1983).

of mutuality promoted by feminism represents a decided improvement over patriarchy, but no social advance is without ambiguities. For this reason it is important to understand the current conflict in Catholic moral theology as a complex matter, with no party possessing the fullness of truth. The controversy is also a momentous one for the earth and its peoples. This became evident once again at the United Nations conference on population in Cairo in 1994, when Vatican representatives joined forces with conservative Muslim countries to impede international efforts to lower the rates of growth in human population.[7]

It is difficult to analyze a storm of controversy while it is in progress, but something can be gained from tracking its force and direction. Below, then, I shall discuss two instances where Catholics influenced by the new paradigm of virtue have challenged Vatican authority on matters of moral doctrine and encountered strong pressures to desist. These are both cases that came to a head in the mid-1980s: that of Charles Curran, the moral theologian whose dismissal from the Catholic University of America has already been mentioned in chapter 1; and that of a group of women religious known as the Vatican 24, whose signatures on a *New York Times* advertisement published by the organization Catholics for a Free Choice during the 1984 U.S. presidential election nearly caused their expulsion from their communities. The chapter concludes with a brief look at some ancient and contemporary sources of wisdom on the issues entailed in these cases.

CHARLES CURRAN AND A CHURCH COMING OF AGE

Charles Curran has been a controversial figure since 1968, when he organized a statement of U.S. theologians objecting to the teaching on contraception of the encyclical *Humanae Vitae* and published it as an advertisement in

---

7. Publicity at the time of the conference stressed Vatican objections to any aspects of the U.N. Plan of Action that impinged on official teachings concerning contraception and abortion. In the end, however, the Vatican endorsed the conference document except for two offending passages, which reflects a significant degree of cooperation, especially in view of its total refusal to affirm conclusions of previous conferences in 1974 and 1984. Shortly after the recent meeting, David S. Toolan, an editor of the Jesuit weekly *America*, observed in "Hijacked at Cairo" that the Vatican, "rallying conservative Islamic patriarchalists to its side, . . . committed the mistake of positioning itself, at least in the eyes of the Western press, as hostile to the cause of women. In a strange way, a penchant for the perfect became the enemy of the good, and any chance of strengthening the Program of Action in the area of development vanished into the smoggy Cairo air" ([October 1, 1994]: 3).

the *Washington Post*. From that time on, conservatives pressed for his removal from the School of Theology of the Catholic University of America, despite the wide support he enjoyed from scholarly colleagues and the university's stated commitment to academic freedom. While many continue to laud his writings and actions as instances of prophetic commitment to truth, others object to his confronting magisterial authority in the secular media and maintain that the withdrawal of his "canonical mandate" (that is, the official permission) to teach theology in 1986 was not only just and pastorally required but long overdue. Since then he has held visiting professorships at Cornell University, the University of Southern California, and Auburn University, before finally receiving a tenured appointment at Southern Methodist University in 1991.[8]

Scholars and journalists have analyzed this case from many angles—ecclesiological, canonical, and historical, to name a few. Moral theology has of course been prominent in these discussions, particularly with respect to points of difference on sexual questions and the issue of public dissent from official hierarchical teaching.[9] Something one notices about the ethical treatment of this case is that it tends to focus on the morality of *actions*. The questions are ones such as: Is artificial contraception or sterilization ever permissible or is it always wrong? Was Curran right to organize the theological protest challenging *Humanae Vitae* in 1968? Was Cardinal Josef Ratzinger right to have Curran removed from his teaching post in 1986? Such questions all concern the dimension of the moral life that has predominated in modern ethics, namely, judgments about the rightness or wrongness of particular acts. As I indicated in the last chapter, however, ethics must also attend to matters of character and virtue.

The connection between virtue, vision, and action has been succinctly put

8. The appointment at Auburn University was accepted with expectation of tenure, but the president of that university yielded to pressure from conservative influences and denied Curran the permanent post, thereby drawing censure from his faculty. Curran has published his record of the case leading to his departure from Catholic University, including correspondence between himself and church officials in *Faithful Dissent* (Kansas City, Mo.: Sheed & Ward, 1986). For the AAUP report, "Academic Freedom and Tenure: The Catholic University of America," see *Academe* 75/5 (September-October 1989): 27–40. Curran has probed these matters further in *Catholic Higher Education, Theology, and Academic Freedom* (Notre Dame: University of Notre Dame Press, 1990).

9. See, for example, Kenneth A. Briggs, *Holy Siege: The Year That Shook Catholic America* (San Francisco: HarperSanFrancisco, 1992); and William W. May, ed., *Vatican Authority and American Catholic Dissent* (New York: Crossroad, 1987).

by Stanley Hauerwas: "[W]e can only act in the world we see, a seeing partially determined by the kind of beings we have become. . . ."[10] This line of thinking helps explain what is involved in the Curran case. Fundamentally this controversy is symptomatic of a developmental crisis in the church, one that involves a significant change in value priorities and ideals for character. What is ultimately at stake is our church's vision of what it means to be a good Catholic.

Although there are ambiguities on both sides of the debate, the value paradigm associated with Curran's position not only retains essential elements of Catholicism but also represents a more adequate way of *being* moral and religious than does the one associated with the official Vatican position. Given the context of modernity, in which believers must respond to the mystery of existence in a "world come of age," as Dietrich Bonhoeffer phrased it, Curran's stance represents a more mature and responsible way of being Catholic than does the way Vatican officials would enjoin theologians and faithful alike to be and behave.[11] In support of this claim, I shall first indicate how the disciplinary action taken against Curran in 1986 reflects an effort on the part of Vatican authorities to impede the paradigm shift from a patriarchal to an egalitarian-feminist understanding of virtue, and then show how Curran's position is consistent with contemporary standards of professional ethics for the theologian.

As I have stressed in earlier chapters, it is the nature of typologies to be abstract and artificial. They are not depictions of reality or "boxes" for locating individuals, but rather heuristic categories to aid our interpretation of complex situations. In the instance at hand, the typology helps account both for the force and the persevering nature of opposition to Curran, whose theology accommodates significant revision of moral teaching and incorporates egalitarian-feminist values, and whose practice of "loyal dissent" lacks the kind of submissive docility that patriarchal authorities deem essential in subordinates. Nor is it mere coincidence that the moral questions Curran was asked to change his mind about concern sexuality; in various ways he has exposed the inadequacies of past ideals of chastity, objecting to the absolutism and physicalism of older norms and promoting instead a view of chastity that incorporates personalist values and takes into account the find-

10. Stanley Hauerwas, *Vision and Virtue: Essays in Christian Ethical Reflection* (Notre Dame: Fides/Claretian, 1974), p. 69.
11. Dietrich Bonhoeffer discusses this concept in *Letters and Papers from Prison,* ed. Eberhard Bethge, trans. Reginald H. Fuller (1953; London: SCM Press, 1956), pp. 162–64.

ings of modern science and the experience of the faithful.[12] This is to challenge the long-dominant patriarchal paradigm head-on. Furthermore, to continue articulating his opposition when asked by legitimate superiors to desist was directly counter to the role that clerics have long been expected to play in the Roman communion.

Moreover, Curran's evident piety and reasonableness are an added threat, for the patriarchal paradigm has retained its power in part by convincing believers that goodness lies only within the bounds prescribed by those wielding religious authority. When virtue is evident beyond those bounds, the plausibility structure of the patriarchal paradigm is undermined. For this reason it is significant that Curran's bishop, Matthew Clark of Rochester, New York, stressed the theologian's virtues in the press release issued when the threat of Curran's dismissal from Catholic University became public in March 1986:

> Father Curran is a priest whose personal life could well be called exemplary. He lives simply and has a remarkable ability to combine a life of serious scholarship with a generous availability to a great variety of persons. My personal observations, supported by the testimony of many, is that Father Curran is a man deeply committed to the spiritual life. I am personally aware of his commitment and know by testimony of others that he is a respected spiritual guide for people who seek counsel in their journeys of faith.
>
> As a theologian, Father Curran enjoys considerable respect not only in our diocese but across this country. He is unfailingly thorough and respectful in his exposition of the teaching of the church. Indeed, I have heard it said that few theologians have a better grasp of or express more clearly the fullness of the Catholic moral tradition. In instances when Father Curran offers theological views which appear to be at a variance with the current official statements of the church, he always does so in a responsible manner. He is respectful of authority in the church in a most Christian manner.[13]

It is perhaps even more significant that Clark in no way retracted this praise in the tersely worded statement of August 18, 1986, in which he bowed to Roman authority in the matter:

12. Curran's positions on sexual ethics are developed in several of his works, including *Faithful Dissent* (1986); *Issues in Sexual and Medical Ethics* (Notre Dame: University of Notre Dame Press, 1978); and *Tensions in Moral Theology* (Notre Dame: University of Notre Dame Press, 1988).

13. Quoted in Curran, *Faithful Dissent,* p. 279.

In recognition of the ultimate authority of the Holy Father, who has confirmed this decision, and in a spirit of collegiality with him, I accept the decision as the final word on this matter and urge all members of our community to accept it in a similar spirit.

So that there will be no confusion, I state as well that the decision does not affect Father Curran's good standing as a priest of the Diocese of Rochester where he will always be welcome to exercise his priestly ministry.[14]

This support of Curran as priest is important, for it testifies to the very paradigm shift I have been describing. In order to be a good priest it is no longer necessary, as was generally thought in the past, to agree with rigid traditional norms for sexual behavior and to submit unquestioningly to patriarchal authority. Clark himself chose to submit, but in the process he implicitly acknowledged the possibilities for Christian virtue associated with the new paradigm.

Important as this gradual change from a patriarchal to an egalitarian-feminist paradigm of virtue is for Catholic life, it is by no means the only ethical factor involved in the controversy. Also relevant are the professional obligations of the Catholic theologian, and on this matter Curran and the Vatican differ profoundly, as is evident when one compares his writings with those of Cardinal Ratzinger, Prefect of the Congregation for the Doctrine of the Faith, the curial official who oversaw the process of withdrawing Curran's canonical mandate. Whereas from a "managerial" standpoint Ratzinger maintained that the theologian's lines of accountability are strictly vertical, the primary duty being to align one's teaching with that of the hierarchical magisterium, for Curran the lines of accountability also include a horizontal dimension, involving responsibility to exercise independent judgment about the intellectual adequacy of a given teaching and its probable effects on the lives of the faithful and to make public one's dissent if there is serious reason to do so.

This difference in perception of role and accountability reflects the above-treated difference between understandings of virtue, with unquestioning submissiveness fitting the patriarchal paradigm and willingness to dissent fitting the egalitarian-feminist paradigm. It reflects as well the heightened sense of professional identity on the part of theologians and the general trend in Christian ethics since World War II to emphasize the category of responsibility in preference to previously stressed categories of duty and obedience, which, with their associations with complicity in state-sponsored evil, were recognized as highly ambiguous by postwar analysts of the crimes of that period.

14. Ibid., p. 286.

Catholic thinkers who popularized this postwar emphasis on responsibility include Curran's teacher at the Academia Alfonsiana in Rome, Bernard Häring, whose approach to moral theology is centered in the concept of responsibility,[15] and the influential Belgian, Cardinal Léon-Joseph Suenens, whose emphasis on "coresponsibility" in the church invited the conciliar fathers and Catholics generally to leave behind an ecclesiology that to some extent encouraged believers to be passive consumers of religious services in favor of one that expanded their sense of Christian duty to include active concern for the quality of church life.[16] That theologians such as Curran would feel responsible also for the quality of church *teaching* is a natural outcome of this emphasis, as well as of the increasing professionalization of the discipline of theology.

It is curious that although the term "professional" first derived from descriptions of those who professed religious vows, in our day it is more commonly associated with secular careers than religious callings. As Dennis M. Campbell points out, however, originally the vocations of law, medicine, and divinity were all associated with the vowed clergy working in medieval universities, in contrast to the technically skilled lay workers associated with the guilds:

> Although the traditional learned professions did not remain exclusively clerical, their roots in the religious orders decidedly shaped the way they were conceived and practiced. The use of the term "laity" to refer to those untrained in any one of the professions is indicative of their clerical foundations. Originally the term "laity" was used to distinguish ordinary people from the clergy; it came to refer to those not belonging to a profession.[17]

Among the characteristics he associates with a traditional understanding of a profession, Campbell includes engagement with an essential and unique social service, specialized knowledge and skill in its application, autonomy and self-regulation, and an ethical code.[18] There are many indications that in the latter half of the twentieth century theologians have gained a new sense of

---

15. See Albert R. Jonsen, *Responsibility in Modern Religious Ethics* (Washington, D.C.: Corpus Books, 1968) for a discussion of Häring in the context of general postwar emphasis in Catholic and Protestant ethics on "responsibility."

16. Suenens's book *Coresponsibility in the Church* (New York: Herder & Herder, 1968) proved very influential among American Catholics, particularly women religious, who at the time were involved in the renewal mandated by Vatican II.

17. Dennis M. Campbell, *Doctors, Lawyers, Ministers: Christian Ethics in Professional Practice* (Nashville: Abingdon, 1982), p. 20.

18. Ibid., pp. 21–24.

professional identity. This is evident in the growth of organizations such as the Catholic Theological Society of America, the College Theology Society, the Canon Law Society of America, and the Catholic Biblical Association, as well as in various publishing projects such as the international journal *Concilium*.[19] Although theologians have by no means developed as extensive a body of literature on issues concerning the practice of their profession as have, for example, health care professionals, it is clear that many are invoking norms of truth and justice as they ask about the purposes and results of their work. The 1982 volume published jointly by the professional organizations of canon lawyers and theologians, *Cooperation Between Theologians and the Ecclesiastical Magisterium*, is but one outstanding example of the way an enhanced professional identity and sense of coresponsibility in the church have led theologians to probe their role and its obligations.[20]

In view of all this, it is not surprising that what Campbell says in general about the professional's sense of personal responsibility applies so well to the case of Curran:

> The true professional cannot be a functionary; accountability for both the procedures and results of his or her work is recognized and accepted. . . . The professional's primary concern and commitment is to *communal interest* rather

19. The Catholic Theological Society of America was founded in 1946, immediately after World War II. Among its stated purposes were: "to promote an exchange of views among Catholic theologians . . . to further studies and research in sacred theology," and "to relate theological science to current problems." These phrases are quoted by C. L. Salm in his article on the CTSA in the *New Catholic Encyclopedia*, 3:330. The canon lawyers had organized earlier, in 1939, but the Canon Law Society of America constitution was amended in 1969 to reflect the conciliar emphasis on coresponsibility. Note the "horizontalization" of accountability implied in the society's revised statement of purpose: "to promote the use of every method of serving God's people that comes under the concept of law. Mindful that Church laws ought to be pastoral in character and made only to serve the people of God, we accept our responsibility as Christians trained in Canon Law to continue research and study and to assist any members of Christ's Body singularly or collectively, laity or clergy, who will welcome the deliberations, research, and common opinion of this society." I quote here from J. E. Lynch's article on the CLSA, *New Catholic Encyclopedia*, 16:48.

20. Leo J. O'Donovan, ed., *Cooperation Between Theologians and the Ecclesiastical Magisterium* (Washington, D.C.: CLSA/CTSA, 1982). In June 1989 the National Conference of Catholic Bishops approved the document that had been based on the work of O'Donovan's committee, "Doctrinal Responsibilities: Approaches to Promoting Cooperation and Resolving Misunderstandings Between Bishops and Theologians," modified after much consultation among the U.S. bishops as well as influence by the Vatican Congregation for the Doctrine of the Faith. The document and background information are found in "Bishops and Theologians' Promoting Cooperation, Resolving Misunderstandings," *Origins* 19/7 (June 29, 1989): 97–110.

than merely to the self. . . . The professional is expected to think about the consequences of a given case in the context of a society's needs and interests.[21]

It is just such a sense of professional responsibility that Curran cites as having led him and eighty-six other Roman Catholic theologians to voice public dissent to aspects of the encyclical *Humanae Vitae* in 1968:

> We were concerned that some Catholics would be upset by our statement, but we thought that the good of many others and the good of the church called for us to do what we did, so that Catholics would know that they did not have to choose between practicing artificial contraception and being loyal Roman Catholics.[22]

The fact that over six hundred other Catholic theologians, of the approximately twelve hundred polled at the time, endorsed the statement testifies to the broad extent of such an enhanced sense of professional responsibility as early as 1968. Subsequent instances of respectful dissent on the part of various theologians in this country and abroad should thus be understood to reflect both the professionalization of specialists trained in theological disciplines and the more general trend in Christian ethics since World War II to emphasize categories of responsibility rather than duty or obedience. Daniel Maguire, who is associated with the 1968 statement on *Humanae Vitae* and also with more recent dissent on the subject of abortion and public policy, has expressed the latter point eloquently:

> Theological ethics has moved from micro- to macro-ethics. We are now less like those German chaplains who accompanied the *Wehrmacht* in the invasion of the Netherlands warning the soldiers against the Dutch prostitutes while overlooking the Second World War and the Holocaust. We are less inclined to ignore the institution of slavery while quibbling about the number of slaves that can be humanely carried on a slave ship.[23]

Although the Vatican now appears to favor a return to the paternalism, passivity, and conformism that Cardinal Suenens argued so strongly against at the time of Vatican II, it seems unlikely that many theologians will abandon their sense of coresponsibility in and for the church. Indeed, the paradigm shift from patriarchal ideals for virtue to egalitarian-feminist ones has progressed too far for ecclesiastical penalties to subvert this process of change.

21. Campbell, *Doctors, Lawyers,* pp. 24–25.
22. Curran, *Faithful Dissent,* p. 18.
23. Daniel C. Maguire, "Service on the Common," *Religious Studies Review* 10 (1984): 14.

Theologians are unwilling to internalize the identity of minor or functionary that coercive measures seem designed to promote. On the contrary, they are willing to suffer for what they take to be the values of truth and the good of the church.

The fact that the Curran controversy reflects the deep-seated conflict between patriarchal and egalitarian-feminist paradigms is evident in both the rhetoric and substance of the correspondence between both sides. Influenced by the new model, Curran assumes that mutuality and dialogue are necessary for the good of the church. He regards himself as coresponsible, with his superiors, for the quality of Catholic teaching and life, and he repeatedly articulates the need for mutually respectful dialogue. His correspondence reveals a self-understanding that presupposes a basic equality with the Vatican officials, whose authority he nonetheless respects, and a sense of shared concern for the welfare of the faithful and the Catholic tradition.

Thus he states in an important letter to Cardinal Ratzinger, dated August 10, 1983: "In the course of our correspondence I have constantly reiterated that the quality of the dialogue is poor." Later in the same letter he declares: "There can be no true dialogue on this matter unless the Congregation itself is willing to say what are the norms that should govern dissent in the Church. I do not think that my request for clarification of this central issue can be looked upon as unreasonable."[24] The "reasonableness" of Curran's request presupposes, however, that mutuality of concern for the faithful and a fundamental equality of relationship are shared by him and the Vatican officials. Rome, however, does not hold these presuppositions; rather, the Vatican sees Curran as a recalcitrant subordinate, a "minor" who must submit to the wisdom of his elders, as it were, just as a youth should submit to paternal authority, or a wife to the authority of her husband in patriarchal marriage. This difference in perception of the relationship between Curran and the Vatican is evident in the letters from Cardinal Ratzinger. His phrases do not speak of mutuality and dialogue but instead employ the words of an officer to a subordinate:

> [W]e still await your complete reply [Dec. 2, 1983]. . . . [W]e again asked for your cooperation [Apr. 13, 1984]. . . . [T]he Congregation now invites you to reconsider and retract those positions which violate the conditions necessary for a professor to be called a Catholic theologian [Sept. 17, 1985]. . . . [O]ne who dissents from the Magisterium as you do is not suitable nor eligible to teach Catholic Theology.[25]

24. Curran, *Faithful Dissent*, pp. 211, 222.
25. Ibid., pp. 224, 227, 250, 268.

In view of the Cardinal's refusal to describe norms for dissent or to argue against those norms offered by the U.S. bishops in 1968, from the perspective of the egalitarian-feminist paradigm one can understand why Curran would feel he had been treated unfairly. Thus, after the unfavorable judgment came from Rome in March of 1986, Curran reiterated the emphasis on dialogue and justice he had voiced earlier:

> I still remain quite disappointed with the dialogue that has ensued between the Congregation and myself on this matter. Both good theology and justice demand that the Congregation explicitly state what are the norms governing the legitimacy or the possibility of dissent from such noninfallible teaching and then indicate how I have violated these norms. In 1979, I proposed five questions and my answers to these questions in an attempt to find out what might be the norms that the Congregation is proposing, but there has never been a response to these questions. Later I expressed my willingness to accept the criteria for dissent proposed by the United States bishops in 1968, but again the Congregation was unwilling to accept these norms."[26]

Although I am not persuaded of the accuracy of Ratzinger's accusation that Curran "effectively treats the position of the Magisterium as he would the opinion of an ordinary theologian,"[27] the accusation is telling in that it objects to a kind of mutual accountability to truth the Cardinal clearly does not want. From his vantage, it will not do for all theological formulations, whether originating in papal, conciliar, or individual theologians' minds, to be tested according to the best norms for truth and adequacy available at a given point in history.

Bishops, of course, both as individuals and in regional conferences, function in relationship to centralized Vatican authority in ways parallel to theologians and have themselves felt Roman discipline. Their pastoral practice is closely scrutinized by agents bent on preserving the patriarchal church order and classical religious mentality, and penalties have resulted for those who seem too lax. The collegiality advocated by Vatican II to balance the emphasis on papal authority articulated by the "unfinished" Vatican I thus finds itself threatened by powerful Roman officials who perceive the role of bishops and theologians alike as necessarily conformist rather than collegial in any meaningful sense. In the patriarchal model of government according to which they operate, submission, not consensus, is the goal, and coercion and fear are used to obtain submission when policies are not inherently reasonable. Vati-

26. Ibid., p. 266.
27. Ibid., p. 203.

can actions against Curran, Archbishop Raymond Hunthausen of Seattle, and others seem intended to restore things to the way they were in a time when believers were viewed as children, not adults. The restorationist agenda comes close to seeking the situation nostalgically recalled by Mrs. Farebrother in George Eliot's nineteenth-century masterpiece *Middlemarch:* "Every respectable church person had the same opinions."[28]

One of the most besetting sins of modern Catholicism has been precisely the effort to preserve such a mentality. As Richard A. McCormick observes, the Vatican is in danger of betraying the rich intellectual heritage of Catholicism by settling for "ideology," that is, "the idea that conformity with past papal formulation is the sole or ultimate test of truth."[29] The fact that sexual issues are involved in the dispute is relevant, for coming of age, growing to responsible maturity, requires integrating sexuality into the rest of life. The unwillingness of Rome to tolerate any rethinking of traditional teachings on sexuality seems directly related to the political objective of preserving an authoritarian church order, one quite foreign to the conciliar insight that "[t]ruth can impose itself on the human mind only in virtue of its own truth, which wins over the mind with both gentleness and power" (*Dignitatis Humanae* #1).

U.S. POLITICS, CATHOLICS FOR A FREE CHOICE, AND THE VATICAN 24

The long period of tension between Professor Curran and the Vatican coincided with an era when social change in the United States contributed to pressures for and against the liberalization of public policy concerning abortion. In 1973 the Supreme Court decision in *Roe v. Wade* established national parameters for abortion laws that were considerably more permissive than

28. George Eliot, *Middlemarch* (Harmondsworth: Penguin, 1976), pp. 199–200. Kenneth A. Briggs traces the actions taken to limit Hunthausen's authority in Seattle in *Holy Siege,* noting that "the archbishop was to his fellow bishops what Father Curran was to his fellow theologians. Both were representative rather than radical exceptions; both were held in high esteem; both exemplified the 'new' church in conflict with the 'old'" (pp. 14–15). Theologians from Seattle University responded to the Hunthausen case by inviting scholars to reflect on the issues in a series of symposia during 1987–89. Papers from these conferences are published in Patrick J. Howell and Gary Chamberlain, eds., *Empowering Authority: The Charisms of Episcopacy and Primacy in the Church Today* (Kansas City, Mo.: Sheed & Ward, 1990).

29. Richard A. McCormick, "The Vatican Document on Bioethics: Some Unsolicited Suggestions," *America* (January 17, 1987): 39.

had previously been the case in many states, and catalyzed a significant reaction among opponents of abortion. The policy debate had since the 1960s been couched in the language of "pro-life" versus "pro-choice," and the official position of the U.S. Catholic hierarchy was strongly identified with the pro-life movement.[30] Since many Catholics had more nuanced positions on abortion and abortion policy than the hierarachy articulated, and since an even greater number of Catholics differed from the magisterium on the issue of articifial contraception, it is not surprising that the lay organization Catholics for a Free Choice (CFFC) gained support, whether cautious or wholehearted, from those who identified with the goals of the women's movement. Thus, when the first female candidate to run for vice-presidential office in U.S. history, Geraldine Ferraro, a Catholic congresswoman from New York, was attacked during the 1984 election campaign by prominent members of the hierarchy for her tolerant policy position on abortion, the stage was set for a confrontation between church officials and Catholics who dissented from the absolutist pro-life policy stance of the bishops.

This confrontation involved the same strategy for expressing dissent that had led to so much pressure against Curran, namely, the publication of a display advertisement in a secular newspaper. In this case, a full-page advertisement paid for by CFFC appeared in the *New York Times* for Sunday, October 7, 1984. It proclaimed in bold type that "[a] diversity of opinions regarding abortion exists among committed Catholics" and went on to present "A Catholic Statement on Pluralism and Abortion" that declared:

> Statements of recent Popes and of the Catholic hierarchy have condemned the direct termination of pre-natal life as morally wrong in all instances. There is the mistaken belief in American society that this is the only legitimate Catholic position. In fact, a diversity of opinions regarding abortion exists among committed Catholics: a large number of Catholic theologians hold that even direct abortion, though tragic, can sometimes be a moral choice; [and], according to data compiled by the National Opinion Research Center, only 11% of Catholics surveyed disapprove of abortion in all circumstances.

After citing disputed areas such as ensoulment, probabilism, religious liberty, and conscience, the statement maintained that "Catholics—especially priests, religious, theologians, and legislators—who publicly dissent from hierarchical statements and explore areas of moral and legal freedom on the

---

30. For a balanced analysis of the U.S. public discussion of abortion, see Celeste Michelle Condit, *Decoding Abortion Rhetoric: Communicating Social Change* (Urbana: University of Illinois Press, 1990).

abortion question should not be penalized by their religious superiors, church employers, or bishops." It concluded:

> Finally, while recognizing and supporting the legitimate role of the hierarchy in providing Catholics with moral guidance on political and social issues and in seeking legislative remedies to social injustices, we believe that Catholics should not seek the kind of legislation that curtails the legitimate exercise of the freedom of religion and conscience or discriminates against poor women.[31]

Names of ninety-six individuals were published with the statement, including fifteen members of the "Catholic Committee on Pluralism and Abortion" who originated it. Among these were several theologians, of whom Mary Hunt, Daniel C. Maguire, Marjorie Riley Maguire, J. Giles Milhaven, and Thomas A. Shannon specialized in ethics.

In this instance, however, it was not primarily these lay theologians who felt the direct force of Vatican objections to the statement, but rather the clergy and members of religious communities who were among the signatories. Of these, three men quickly yielded to their superiors' requests to withdraw their endorsement in December 1984 and a fourth had settled by May

---

31. The text is reprinted in *Origins* 14 (December 6, 1984), immediately following a November 15, 1984, statement of Archbishop John R. Quinn, then chair of the U.S. Bishops' Committee on Doctrine, "Abortion: A Clear and Constant Teaching" (pp. 413–14), which declares the advertisement to be incorrect, "a personal opinion which directly contradicts the clear and constant teaching of the church on abortion." Two things about Quinn's statement are important. First, it strongly condemns the position taken by the signers and was picked up by the secular and Catholic press in this country, reaching a wider audience than the original *New York Times* readership. Many would judge this a sufficient response on the part of the hierarchy of a nation that treasures free speech and open political debate and would ask whether the action of CRIS violated the principles of collegiality and subsidiarity in relation to the U.S. bishops. Second, evidently the bishops especially objected to the use of the word "legitimate" in the advertisement, which had declared that the official teaching on abortion is "not the only legitimate Catholic position," since Quinn employs the term "legitimate" four times in his brief statement. He insists, for example, that "deliberately chosen abortion . . . is not a legitimate moral choice" and that if discussions about such matters as personhood have "provided a basis for legitimate diversity of opinion," such discussions "have always presumed the church's constant teaching about the immorality of abortion." Two of the signers have defended the use of "legitimate" in different but complementary ways. Rosemary Radford Ruether holds that a "legitimate opinion" is one that is "theologically and ethically defensible" ("Catholics and Abortion: Authority vs. Dissent," in *Abortion and Catholicism: The American Debate,* ed. Patricia Beattie Jung and Thomas A. Shannon [New York: Crossroad, 1988], p. 320). Ann Patrick Ware maintains in "A Case Study in Oppression: A Theological and Personal Analysis" (Chicago: National Coalition of American Nuns, 1993) that the hierarchy confused "legitimate" with "official," which was not the sense intended by the statement (p. 10).

of 1985, but twenty-four women religious held to their basic position.[32] They felt entitled to express the fact that Catholic opinion on abortion was diverse and the belief that discussion about it should not be stifled, nor should Catholics who were politically pro-choice suffer the sort of discrimination that Ferraro had received.

The unwillingness of these women to capitulate to Vatican pressure must have seemed striking to those who expected the threat of expulsion to result in immediate retractions or resignations. In the spring of 1983, Agnes Mary Mansour, a Sister of Mercy, had requested a dispensation from her vows when faced with a Vatican ultimatum to do so or else resign the post she had accepted as director of the Michigan Department of Social Services, which involved administering programs that funded abortions for poor women.[33] The seriousness and suddenness of Mansour's dilemma had alerted other women religious to issues of Vatican power and due process of canon law. Thus, the officers and members of the women's communities involved in the advertisement sought to find a way to avoid the stark options presented in a letter sent November 30, 1984, from Cardinal Jean Jerome Hamer, Prefect of the Vatican Congregation for Religious and Secular Institutes (CRIS). In this letter Hamer enjoined the officers of the communities to direct the signers "to make a public retraction" of the statement or be faced with "an explicit threat of dismissal from the institute."[34] Gradually, over the next two years, twenty-two of the signers found ways to settle the matter with the Vatican that they

32. Frances Kissling provides a chronology of events in "Women Religious and the Catholic Statement, 1984–1986" in the CFFC periodical *Conscience* 7/3 (May/June 1986): 10–11, 14–16. The chronology indicates that terms of settlement varied widely for the women and were handled on a congregation-by-congregation basis, with the first case being reported closed "without retraction" in August 1985. Fifteen cases were still unresolved when a second advertisement appeared in the March 2, 1985, issue of the *New York Times*, a "Declaration of Solidarity" signed by 962 persons from seventeen countries, including "at least 5 priests and 40 women religious," according to Kissling (p. 15). The text included these words: "We, as Roman Catholics, affirm our solidarity with those who signed the statement and agree to stand with all those who face reprisals" (quoted here from *Origins* 15 [1986]: 652).

33. For analysis and documentation concerning the Mansour case, see Madonna Kolbenschlag, ed., *Authority, Community and Conflict* (Kansas City, Mo.: Sheed & Ward, 1986). An interview with Mansour is included in Annie Lally Milhaven, ed., *The Inside Stories: 13 Valiant Women Challenging the Church* (Mystic, Conn.: Twenty-Third Publications, 1987), which also contains interviews with other Catholic women involved in disputes over abortion policy.

34. *Origins* 14 (January 15, 1985): 516. The letter was also signed by Hamer's assistant, Archbishop Vincenzo Fagiolo, whose tendency to conflate papal and divine authority was mentioned in another context in chapter 1.

judged conscientious. For example, six Sisters of Loretto signed the following statement:

> We had no intention of making a pro-abortion statement. We regret that the statement was misconstrued by some who read it in that way. We hold, as we have in the past, that human life is sacred and inviolable. We acknowledge this as teaching of the Church.[35]

Two women, however, refused any conciliatory gestures and went beyond the original statement to articulate a staunch pro-choice position in the media. These were Sisters of Notre Dame de Namur Barbara Ferraro and Patricia Hussey. Eventually they received formal warnings from their congregation's leaders, sent in accord with the canonical procedures for dismissal. Many supporters of the signers hoped for a resolution short of this extremity and were relieved to learn that on June 1, 1988, the Notre Dame officers decided to withdraw the immediate threat of dismissal. Shortly thereafter, Ferraro and Hussey volunteered their resignations anyway, stating that the process had alienated them from their community and canonical religious life.[36]

Thus, the cases of all twenty-four nuns were resolved within four years of the statement's publication. Most of the women had managed to retain community membership without backing down from their claim that signing the statement had been appropriate in the context of the political and social situation in the United States at the time. The episode has received far less scholarly analysis than the Curran controversy, and its complexities warrant much fuller investigation than can be attempted here.[37] There are, however, several

---

35. Quoted here from Ware, "Case Study," p. 34.

36. For a full discussion of their evolving positions, see Barbara Ferraro and Patricia Hussey (with Jane O'Reilly), *No Turning Back: Two Nuns' Battle with the Vatican over Women's Right to Choose* (New York: Poseidon Press, 1990). Analyses published by others include Susan Maloney, "Religious Orders and Sisters in Dissent," *The Christian Century* (March 9, 1988): 238–40; and Jeannine Gramick, "Catholic Nuns and the Need for Responsible Dissent," *The Christian Century* (December 7, 1988): 1122–25.

37. In an early analysis, John R. Gilbert basically defends the advertisement as an instance of Catholic political responsibility and objects to the coercive threats against the nuns who signed. See "Obedience, Authority, and Public Policy," *Sisters Today* 57/7 (March 1986). Discussions by those who signed the advertisement include Mary E. Hunt and Frances Kissling, "The *New York Times* Ad: A Case Study in Religious Feminism," *Journal of Feminist Studies in Religion* 3/1 (Spring 1987): 115–27; Maureen L. Fiedler, "Dissent Within the U.S. Church: The Case of the 'Vatican 24,'" in Mary C. Segers, ed., *Church Polity and American Politics: Issues in Contemporary American Catholicism* (New York: Garland, 1990), pp. 303–12; and the above-cited works by Ferraro and Hussey, Ruether, and Ware. Analyses from the perspective of leaders of women's religious congregations include a chapter by Marian McAvoy, president of

observations relevant to the interests of this chapter that can be made on the basis of available information. These concern the fact of diversity, the recognition of power differences, the increased self-assurance of women as moral and political agents, and the challenges of implementing egalitarian-feminist values within ecclesial structures of governance. All of these factors affect the development of a new understanding of what obedience entails.

The Fact of Diversity

The opening claim of the advertisement is beyond dispute: a diversity of positions on abortion and abortion policy does exist among Catholics.[38] It is also the case that a diversity of opinions on proper levels of involvement in ethically charged political debates exists among Catholics, especially where clergy and members of religious communities are concerned. Diversity was also evident in the judgments the twenty-four threatened signers made in response to the dilemma posed by Cardinal Hamer's ultimatum and in the ways the heads of the various communities responded to Vatican pressures. For the signers Ferraro and Hussey, the experience of working with poor women in West Virginia led to a perceived obligation to allow no compromise with Vatican officials who seemed to them to disregard women's status as moral agents facing complex decisions in tragic circumstances. For Judith Vaughan, social ethicist and director of a shelter for women and children in Los Angeles, the decision was to resolve matters with Rome and remain a Sister of St. Joseph. Likewise, theologians Margaret Farley and Anne Carr and

---

the Sisters of Loretto at the time of the controversy, "The Only Way Available," in Ann Patrick Ware, ed., *Naming Our Truth* (Inverness, Calif.: Chardon Press, 1995), pp. 207–28; and a chapter on "A Rightful Coming of Age," in a volume by two former executive directors of the Leadership Conference of Women Religious, Lora Ann Quiñonez and Mary Daniel Turner, *The Transformation of American Catholic Sisters* (Philadelphia: Temple University Press, 1992), pp. 113–40. Finally, without focusing on specific cases, Margaret A. Farley has published an analysis of "Moral Discourse in the Public Arena," in *Vatican Authority and American Catholic Dissent*, ed. May, pp. 168–86. Her conclusion is that "[w]e have had long centuries in which to learn the counterproductiveness of coercive measures when the issue becomes not truth but power; and long centuries to learn the glory of human freedom, as well as its limits and dangers.... Wisdom may teach us that not every voice can speak for the community; but the truer voices will be better discerned not by excluding dissent but by protecting the most fragile voices in our midst" (p. 184).

38. Many opinion surveys have confirmed this fact. For an example from the year of the statement, see Tom W. Smith's analysis of data from the National Opinion Research Center, "Catholic Attitudes Toward Abortion," *Conscience* 5/4 (July/August 1984): 6–7, 10.

interfaith leader Ann Patrick Ware all continued in their communities and their feminist activities after their cases were closed. One can infer that the other nuns who signed also felt the ambiguities of "settling" with the Vatican were tolerable given the values at stake and the fact that their individual ministries and struggles for justice were continuing on various fronts, while the force of the original statement remained on the record despite the defeat of the Mondale-Ferraro ticket by the Reagan-Bush campaign.

In the pre–Vatican II church it was commonly expected that "good Catholics" all had the same moral opinions. Reintroducing an appreciation for the mystery at the heart of life that John Mahoney has eloquently argued to be a principal task of contemporary moral theology entails that there will be diversity in practical judgments on a range of ethical questions.[39] It is a continuing challenge for Catholics to grow comfortable with this situation, learning to find unity at a deeper level than in uniform judgments on difficult moral dilemmas.

The Recognition of Power Differences

The power differences involved in the case of the *New York Times* advertisement are interesting. Lay theologians suffered reprisals in terms of canceled speaking engagements and pressures in employment contexts, but the main disciplinary action was focused on the clergy and religious.[40] The men, relatively closer in access to ecclesiastical power structures, cooperated rather promptly with the system, whereas the women religious sought an alternative to the action that was demanded by church officials and eventually succeeded insofar as "clarifications" were accepted by Rome rather than the "retractions" originally insisted upon.[41]

39. John Mahoney, *The Making of Moral Theology: A Study of the Roman Catholic Tradition* (Oxford: Clarendon Press, 1987), p. 337.

40. Ann Patrick Ware has described the focus on disciplining clergy and members of religious communities as a significant departure from the ecclesiology of Vatican II. She objects to the fact that lay signers "have been generally ignored and selectively punished," adding that "perhaps the most telling estimate of what the official Church thinks of the laity is contained in this, that the ultimate penalty to members of religious congregations was to have them reduced to the 'lay state' through dismissal (even though in canon law all those who are not ordained are already lay people)" ("Case Study," p. 15). For elaboration of the difficulties experienced by lay signers, especially theologians, see Ruether, "Catholics and Abortion: Authority vs. Dissent."

41. Although Kissling's chronology describes the settlement of Marist brother Ron Pasquariello (reported in May 1985) as a "retraction," the content of his statement and the fact

Also at play were the differences between the officers of the women's communities, who had been chosen as leaders by women of wide-ranging theological and political views, and the community members threatened by Vatican authorities. The officers held canonical authority over their communities but were themselves subject to churchmen. Many of these women were seeking to function in a collegial fashion and at the same time serve a divided membership in a manner that respected individual consciences and sought the common good. The pressures of divergent role expectations were great for these officers, and their situation was further complicated because their national organization, the Leadership Conference of Women Religious (LCWR), had for years been threatened by antirenewal forces within and beyond its membership. Thus, it was a serious moment when LCWR proceeded with its convention program plans in September 1985, despite the fact that two archbishops boycotted the event when they learned that Margaret Farley, one of the signers, had been invited to address the assembly on the topic of moral discernment. According to National Catholic News Service, Archbishop Pio Laghi, Papal Pro-nuncio to the United States, and Archbishop John R. Quinn, head of a pontifical commission studying religious life in the U.S., canceled plans to speak and celebrate the liturgy at the New Orleans assembly of nuns' leaders. This decision did not stifle discussion of ethical and political issues at the convention, which in fact continued in deep and imaginative ways, but it did testify to the complex power dynamics that surrounded the controversy.[42]

The Increased Self-assurance of Women as Moral and Political Agents

The willingness of a range of Catholic women to face opposition from church officials because of their moral and political convictions had not been

---

that it was published in a community newsletter rather than a more public forum suggest that the designation "clarification" applies in his case as well as those of the women religious. The other men, two priests and a religious brother, are understood to have issued public retractions in December 1984. See Kissling, "Women Religious and the Catholic Statement, 1984–1986," pp. 10–11.

42. The news story by Florence Herman and Jerry Filteau ran in the Washington, D.C. *Catholic Standard* for September 12, 1985, under the headline, "Archbishops boycott meeting because of abortion ad signer." Quiñonez and Turner describe the careful thought involved in the LCWR decision and assembly discussions in *The Transformation of American Catholic Sisters*, pp. 133–40.

seen before on such a scale in the U.S. church. In the first place, lay women had organized Catholics for a Free Choice in 1973 in opposition to the hierarchy's heavy involvement with pro-life political forces. For another, a variety of Catholics had felt strongly enough about the one-sidedness of episcopal pronouncements during the 1984 election to endorse the statement that became the *New York Times* advertisement. Many of these signers were far from committed pro-choice activists themselves—even Ferraro and Hussey originally declined to describe themselves in those terms—but their sense of justice had been disturbed by the apparent unwillingness of the hierarchy to tolerate any ambiguity on matters related to female lives and female political candidates. This absolutism was all the more striking in view of the careful distinctions between principles and policy opinions the U.S. bishops had drawn in their pastoral letter *The Challenge of Peace* in 1983, where they acknowledged that their own judgment against any "first use" of nuclear weapons might not be shared by all conscientious persons.[43]

The hierarchy's position in favor of a Human Life Amendment to the U.S. constitution was problematic to many Catholics, and the fact that the bishops scrupulously withheld the first draft of their pastoral letter on the U.S. economy from the public until after the 1984 election angered the Democrats among them, since this meant silence on the very points of church teaching that were favorable to Mondale and Ferraro during a time when some churchmen were virtually shouting their endorsement of the Reagan-Bush forces. It may be the case that the opinions of the hierarchy did not influence the Catholic vote in a decisive way, but many members of the church felt at the time that someone needed to articulate a more complex vision of what the tradition stood for than had been evident in the press during the campaign.[44] Opposition to Ferraro seemed discriminatory to Catho-

---

43. In a note following the statement in paragraph 153, "we judge resort to nuclear weapons to counter a conventional attack to be morally unjustifiable," the U.S. bishops explain: "Our conclusions and judgments in this area although based on careful study and reflection of the application of moral principles do not have, of course, the same force as the principles themselves and therefore allow for different opinions, as the Summary makes clear."

44. Cardinal Joseph Bernardin of Chicago was described in the *St. Paul Pioneer Press* for October 26, 1984, as offering a "mild rebuke" to the anti-Ferraro Catholics led by Archbishop John O'Connor of New York when Bernardin insisted in a Georgetown University speech that a "consistent ethic of life" should not reduce political concern to the single issue of abortion. However, Bernardin's position, which also stressed that Catholics "must 'recognize the different roles played by moral law and civil law in a pluralistic society,'" was overshadowed during the election by that of high-ranking clerical opponents of Ferraro. Senator Patrick J. Leahy of Vermont voiced his concern over what single-issue politics was doing to the Catholic social jus-

lics who took pride in her candidacy, especially in view of the hierarachy's greater tolerance for ambiguity where male Catholic politicians with similar positions on abortion policy were concerned. Indeed, those with long memories were aware that Cardinal James Gibbons had spoken strongly against woman suffrage early in the century,[45] and that U.S. bishops had played a more subtle role in the defeat of the Equal Rights Amendment in the 1970s, despite clear teaching from the Second Vatican Council that "with respect to the fundamental rights of the person, every type of discrimination, whether social or cultural, whether based on sex, race, color, social condition, language or religion, is to be overcome and eradicated as contrary to God's intent" (*Gaudium et Spes* #29). Catholic women have felt the truth of these words, and they are no longer willing to leave political debates and activities to male authority figures.

The Challenges of Implementing Egalitarian-Feminist Values within Structures of Governance

Much feminist discussion of organizational life has simplified the opposition between the "pyramidal" structures of patriarchal governance and the "circular" model of feminist organization, at times confusing the value of respect for persons as equals with types of social organization that are functional only for relatively small groups in which frequent communication is a realistic possibility. Complex structures and organizational flow charts are not, however, inherently unjust in themselves. How they are designed and used is what determines whether or not they adequately respect and serve persons as individuals and groups. The greater the number and diversity of persons affili-

---

tice agenda in a 1984 article, "The Church We Love Is Being Used," reprinted in *Conscience* 8/4 (July/August 1987): 12–13. Declared Leahy: "If the right wing, through manipulation of single-issue politics, continues to defeat elected officials who support progressive steps, there will be no one left in government to shelter those broad values of compassion and justice the church has endorsed. Both as a Catholic and as a legislator, I hope many in the hierarchy of our church will soon reevaluate this course" (p. 13).

45. Citing the "Documents of the Catholic Bishops against Women's Suffrage, 1910–1920" from the Sophia Smith Collection at Smith College, Rosemary Radford Ruether quotes Gibbons from a 1911 interview: "I am unalterably opposed to woman's suffrage, always have been and always will be. . . . Why should a woman lower herself to sordid politics? . . . When a woman enters the political arena she goes outside the sphere for which she was intended." See Ruether, "Home and Work: Women's Roles and the Transformation of Values," *Theological Studies* 36 (1975): 653.

ated with an organization, the more challenging it is to ensure that the structure and manner of governance reflect the goals and ideals of the group.

It has been characteristic of Roman Catholicism to value and preserve structures of governance that seem most conducive for "universality," or global inclusiveness. Ordering the doctrine and discipline of a religious body that numbers nearly a billion human beings of diverse cultural, educational, and economic backgrounds is an immense task that requires a central authority. But the limitation that accompanies the strong central authority valued by the tradition is the ever-present danger of authoritarianism and excessive efforts to control that ultimately prove counterproductive.[46] Further complicating the picture in an age that affirms women's equality is the obsolete male exclusivity of church governance structures. Just as Roman intransigence in the sixteenth century led the scripture scholar Martin Luther to analyze abuses of church power in terms of a metaphor of the "Babylonian captivity" of the church to the interests of wealth and corruption, so in our time Catholics of egalitarian-feminist persuasion have reason to complain of Vatican "bullying" and the "inculturation of the gospel in patriarchy."[47] There is great scandal in the fact that a tradition calling itself "universal" is approaching the third millennium with women's dignity effectively denied in church law and sacramental practice.

CLASSIC WISDOM ON A CONTEMPORARY PROBLEM

My brief discussion of these two cases from the 1980s cannot do justice to their complexity, but I trust enough has been said to establish that both involve contrasting views of authority, obedience, and responsibility. They are also "hard cases," and part of their difficulty lies in the fact that they express deep spiritual conflicts that characterize the present epoch of change.

---

46. In August 1992 the eminent Brazilian Bishop Cândido Pandin described Vatican interference in the affairs of national episcopal conferences as an instance of "cultural colonialism." According to the *National Catholic Reporter* for October 2, 1992, Candin had stated in a letter to his episcopal colleagues that "[t]here is no respect for the ability of bishops to exercise their legitimate autonomy with regard to the way they organize their conferences, something that has nothing to do with the primatial function of the pope" (p. 11). Such problems could be prevented by Vatican policies that better reflected the wisdom of Pope Paul VI's encyclical *Octogesima Adveniens,* which rejects the search for universal solutions that disregard regional differences (#4).

47. I address the latter problem in Anne E. Patrick, "Inculturation, Catholicity, and Social Justice," *CTSA Proceedings* 45 (1990): 41–55.

It is for this reason that I turned at the conclusion of chapter 2 to historical moments that offer resources to aid reflection on why the present issues are so troublesome. There I recalled the first-century tension over observing Jewish law and the early-modern conflict over Copernicanism, noting that in both crises what was fundamentally at stake was the meaningful practice of religion, and not simply abstract ideas or political conflicts. Moreover, such struggles, past and present, involve deeply felt differences of opinion about what constitutes good behavior and good character. The contemporary women and men whom I described as saintly martyrs in chapter 3 are considered by some to have been sincere but unwise—not deserving of death but not particularly worthy of emulation either. Likewise there are conflicting interpretations about the merits of those I have praised as "truth tellers" and organizers of movements for social justice. Charles Curran and the Vatican 24 are such figures of controversy. Their visions of truth and justice have involved public confrontation with church officials the results of which are difficult to trace, but which surely include suffering on all sides because the opponents in the controversies feel betrayed and disrespected by those within the faith community itself.

This fact of suffering suggests that some light may be shed on these matters by the tragic narrative tradition. As I indicated at the beginning of chapter 3, historically such literature has functioned to show the limitations of a culture's dominant ideal of virtue when it has been pushed to a counterproductive extreme. Both the Curran case and the case of the Vatican 24 bring to mind the same issues that Sophocles explored in the tragedy *Antigone,* a work that classics scholar Martha Nussbaum analyzes brilliantly in her 1986 volume *The Fragility of Goodness.*

As Nussbaum points out, a tragic drama affords a richer source for ethical reflection than a "schematic philosophical example" because it does fuller justice to the complexity involved. A "whole tragic drama," she observes:

> is capable of tracing the history of a complex pattern of deliberation, showing its roots in a way of life and looking forward to its consequences in that life. As it does all of this, it lays open to view the complexity, the indeterminacy, the sheer difficulty of actual human deliberation.[48]

She goes on to indicate that part of the advantage of tragic literature is precisely its ability to encourage reflection that occurs through emotional

---

48. Martha C. Nussbaum, *The Fragility of Goodness: Luck and Ethics in Greek Tragedy and Philosophy* (Cambridge: Cambridge University Press, 1986), p. 14.

engagement: "We discover what we think about these events partly by noting how we feel; our investigation of our emotional geography is a major part of our search for self-knowledge." The compatability of her position with egalitarian-feminist values is evident in her indictment of the dominant philosophical tradition as expressed in John Locke's view that "the rhetorical and emotive elements of style are rather like a woman: amusing and even delightful when kept in their place, dangerous and corrupting if permitted to take control."[49] In contrast to this position, Nussbaum holds that we must recognize the very "*rationality* of the passions as they lead thought towards human understanding, and help to constitute this understanding." Indeed, by her account, "a contingent moral being . . . is neither a pure intellect nor a pure will; nor would he deliberate better in this world if he were."[50]

My sympathies lie predominantly with Curran and the Vatican 24 in these matters, much as they have always favored Antigone when I experience Sophocles' tragedy. But Nussbaum makes a good case for recognizing that Creon's concerns are not insignificant, although his perception of his duty as ruler leads him to act unwisely. Nevertheless, when one adds a feminist critique of patriarchal understandings of virtue to the analysis, what is clear is that the tragic action proves the futility of ideals of authority, obedience, and responsibility that center in control and are governed by fear of its loss. Such an analysis further suggests that *listening,* giving ear to difference, is a crucial quality in a leader, who is more effective when acknowledging that full truth and goodness transcend anyone's control, no matter how great his or her responsibilities.

Sophocles' tragedy opens with the daughters of Oedipus, Antigone and Ismene, confronting the fact that both of their brothers have been slain in battle. Their uncle Creon, ruler of Thebes, has declared that Eteocles, who defended the city, will be buried with full honors, but Polyneices, who led the attacking forces, will be left unburied. This is too much for Antigone, who defies her uncle's order and attempts to bury her brother out of respect for him and the will of the gods. Apprehended in this deed, she is led to Creon and condemned to death:

> Then go down there, if you must love, and love the dead. No woman rules me while I live. (lines 524–25)[51]

49. Ibid., p. 16.
50. Ibid., p. 47.
51. *Antigone*, trans. Elizabeth Wyckoff, in David Grene and Richard Lattimore, eds., *Sophocles: I* (New York: Modern Library, 1954), lines 524–25. Subsequent references are to this edition. Copyright, 1954, by The University of Chicago; quoted with permission.

Meanwhile Creon's son Haemon, who is engaged to marry Antigone, seeks to dissuade his father from this punishment, but Creon maintains that his duty to preserve order leaves him no alternative:

> If I allow disorder in my house
> I'd surely have to licence it abroad . . .
> The man the state has put in place must have
> obedient hearing to his least command
> when it is right, and even when it's not . . .
> There is no greater wrong than disobedience.
>
> (lines 659–72)

Creon continues, expressing the values of the patriarchal paradigm of virtue:

> . . . I must guard the men who yield to order,
> not let myself be beaten by a woman.
> Better, if it must happen, that a man
> should overset me.
> I won't be called weaker than womankind.
>
> (lines 676–80)

When a responsible patriarch speaks with such conviction, it is difficult to raise an objection, even if one is his only son. But Haemon is in a position to hear opinions that the powerful ruler has been shielded from facing, surrounded as he is by subordinates who fear his displeasure. And so Haemon makes bold to state that

> . . . the whole town is grieving for this girl,
> unjustly doomed, if ever woman was,
> to die in shame for glorious action done . . .
> This is the undercover speech in town.
>
> (lines 693–95, 700)

Haemon goes on to suggest that wisdom would urge some flexibility in the matter:

> And so the ship that will not slacken sail,
> the sheet drawn tight, unyielding, overturns.
>
> (lines 715–16)

But Creon remains unwilling to change his mind, and so he has Antigone walled up in a cave with just enough food to survive, but no hope of liberation. Later, when the blind prophet Teiresias declares that this course is unwise ("he's no fool / nor yet unfortunate, who gives up his stiffness / and cures the trouble he's fallen in" [lines 1024–26]), Creon at first dismisses the advice, but is finally moved to reconsider when the prophet foretells that the Furies will seek vengeance against him. By the time Creon repents, however, the tragedy is beyond stopping. Antigone has hanged herself, Haemon soon falls on his own sword, and Creon's wife Eurydice also kills herself. Creon's only option at the work's conclusion is exile, and unending sorrow.

Such a rich tale has multiple implications for the present impasse between Vatican authority and revisionist moral theology, between the male hierarchy and women possessed of deep religious convictions of their dignity and moral responsibility. The fact that the action ends with the deaths of so many characters testifies to the loss entailed when positions once taken for good reasons become hardened into absolutes. Creon's form of ruling is too harsh and inflexible; his downfall reveals the limits of the patriarchal mind-set that understands responsibility to require that total control be maintained over complex situations. Indeed, it is precisely because of his rigid efforts to preserve full control that Creon loses his authority altogether.

In her chapter on *Antigone* Nussbaum explains the connection between simplification and authoritarianism by showing that Creon's downfall is caused by his construction of

> a world into which tragedy cannot enter. Insoluble conflicts cannot arise, because there is only a single supreme good, and all other values are functions of that good. If I say to Creon, "Here is a conflict: on the one side, the demands of piety and love; on the other, the requirements of civic justice," he will reply that I have misdescribed the case.[52]

If one substitutes the term "church" for the word "city" in her analysis of Creon's failure, the similarities between his stance and that of the Vatican officials who disciplined Curran and the twenty-four nuns is remarkable:

> A plan that makes the city the supreme good cannot so easily deny the intrinsic value of the religious goods that are valued by the people who compose it. Only an impoverished conception of the city can have the simplicity which Creon requires.[53]

Nussbaum recognizes that Antigone too has oversimplified the issues, allowing one perceived duty to eclipse other values entirely, but it is clear that she does this in response to conditions established by her uncle as ruler. If Creon

---

52. Nussbaum, *Fragility of Goodness,* p. 58.
53. Ibid., p. 60.

had not insisted on an unreasonable edict, Antigone would not have disobeyed him. Creon, in fact, is a perfect example of the "ethic of control" that Sharon Welch has criticized so effectively in her study *A Feminist Ethic of Risk*. Welch observes that those who perceive their responsibility as a matter of ensuring a perfect realization of values tend to monopolize power and attempt a degree of control over the actions of others that is both immoral and unattainable. In the process they miss out on the considerable benefits of a different sort of power, namely, the power of influence. According to Welch, when responsible action is viewed as control, "the eager pursuit of the absolute good, of final solutions, often leads to impatience and intolerance with conflict of any sort, a dangerous tendency to see difference per se as a threat."[54]

In the egalitarian-feminist paradigm, by contrast, the role of leader does not carry this impossible burden of omnicompetence and full control. In this model, which seeks mutuality more than dominance, the roles are not defined so rigidly in terms of the superior commanding and the subject submitting, but rather both leader and follower practice the virtue of obedience in the sense of *listening* for all relevant clues to the truth and then pursuing as much good as seems reasonably attainable in the given circumstances. When leaders demonstrate their willingess to be influenced by aspects of truth beyond their original vantage, they gain the informed trust of their followers. Under such conditions, virtuous individuals are more likely to follow difficult requests for their cooperation, and even to sacrifice personal goods for shared objectives, precisely because they have reason to believe that such leaders have in fact gained a fuller picture of the situation than an individual can obtain.

What Welch calls the "ethic of risk" makes sense theologically in view of the Christian affirmation that ultimately God's care and God's mercy make up for what remains imperfect because of human limitations and the ambiguities of history. In the mind of patriarchy, it is a weakness for a leader to be influenced by a subordinate, to be seen in the process of reconsidering a position one has long maintained. But in fact this openness to data is a strength that makes for better governance as well as better science.

54. Sharon D. Welch, *A Feminist Ethic of Risk* (Minneapolis: Fortress, 1990), pp. 34–35.

CHAPTER FIVE

Seeking Truth
in a Complex World

[A]n honest effort to do justice to all aspects of a hard case, seeing and feeling it in all its conflicting many-sidedness, could enrich further deliberative efforts.
—Martha Nussbaum[1]

The two cases examined in the last chapter, that of Charles Curran and the Vatican 24, exemplify the tensions between revisionist moral theology and authoritarian, fundamentalist-leaning church leadership and between the egalitarian-feminist and patriarchal paradigms of virtue. The cases differ in many respects, however, including the length and manner of the investigative processes, the nature of the perceived offenses, the scope of the threatened sanctions, and the ecclesial support extended to those faced with punishments for actions taken conscientiously. In all of these differences the variable of gender is significant, although because the situations are complex the importance of this variable can only be gauged in approximate terms.

THE TRUTH OF POWER

Under patriarchal arrangements, the power of office is clear, and gender figures prominently in its distribution. Because of ancient misogynistic ideas and practices, women's roles in the church have been circumscribed and largely controlled by men since the first century. Thus, the structures that initially received Charles Curran and the Vatican 24 were quite different.

---

1. Martha C. Nussbaum, *The Fragility of Goodness: Luck and Ethics in Greek Tragedy and Philosophy* (Cambridge: Cambridge University Press, 1986), p. 45.

Whereas the young man devoting his life to a religious vocation could opt for a course of study leading to sacred orders and pastoral leadership in the Catholic community, the young women were destined to fill subordinate and nonsacramental roles. Whereas the financial resources of a diocese were available to support the education of a seminarian and priest, the proceeds of music lessons and general convent scrimping were required to educate the women, whose communities traditionally filled teaching and service positions for astonishingly low compensation.[2]

Although Curran originally ambitioned to be a simple parish priest, he was chosen for advanced study and sent to Roman universities at diocesan expense during his late twenties, at an age when a typical teaching sister of his generation was laboring full time, pursuing her bachelor's degree at Saturday and summer classes, and doing more housework daily than the average seminarian performed in a month.[3] Of the Vatican 24, some women had entered the convent after paying for their own college educations, and these were more likely to have obtained doctoral degrees than most sisters, who joined communities as secondary school students or graduates. In the case of the Vatican 24, educational level was not of primary importance (although many of the signers did possess advanced degrees), since the action that offended church officials did not involve scholarly writings, but rather a single statement affirmed in an effort to influence the U.S. election process. However, these background differences do testify to some disparities in allocation of

2. The financial difficulties of women religious are related to their subordinate status in the ecclesiastical system. As historian Jay P. Dolan observes in *The American Catholic Experience* (Garden City, N.Y.: Image, 1985), "By the early twentieth century, sisters generally received an annual salary of about two hundred dollars, or one third less than female public-school teachers and one half that received by teaching brothers. Many times, pastors failed to pay the full salary.... Compounding the [financial] problem was the status of sisters in the church. They were the Catholic serfs, having fewer rights and fewer options than priests, brothers, or lay people" (p. 289). A recent historical study by Annabelle Raiche and Ann Marie Biermaier reports the following of a representative parish school in Minnesota: "$300 remained the annual stipend for a teaching sister from 1920 through 1950. By 1965 the stipend had increased to $750 per year," and by 1971 the stipend was $1680. See *They Came to Teach* (St. Cloud, Minn.: North Star Press, 1994), pp. 99 and 130–31. Figures from another parish show significant increases in stipend and benefits over the period from 1965 to 1990 (from $750 plus housing in 1965 to $12,159 plus benefits of $2,341 along with housing and car in 1990), with the most substantial increases occurring in the 1980s (p. 131).

3. Curran's career is summarized in *Faithful Dissent*, pp. 3–49. For an incisive literary analysis of power differences between priests and sisters, see J. F. Powers, "The Lord's Day," in *The Prince of Darkness* (1947; New York: Doubleday Image, 1958), pp. 11–18.

church resources that made the financial situation of the women signers and their communities an important consideration during the years of threatened punishment. Women who had no personal property after decades of service as religious workers were faced with the possibility of losing not only the companionship of their communities but also the prospect of whatever retirement and healthcare support would otherwise have been theirs. Moreover, community leaders had reason to be concerned about the fate of all their members if matters escalated to a community-wide confrontation with Rome, since legally the community property is subject to hierarchical control.

Curran's perceived offenses included his involvement in the theologians' response to *Humanae Vitae* published as an advertisement in the *Washington Post* in 1968, but the actual items at issue during his confrontation with the Vatican in the 1980s were several opinions on sexual and medical questions that had been published in his scholarly writings. Among these were some tolerance for abortion, although only very rarely beyond two or three weeks after conception, and a willingness to live with *Roe v. Wade* as far as public policy was concerned.[4] His published work, in other words, went beyond the claims of the *New York Times* advertisement and was an instance of the "diversity of opinion" it said existed among Catholics. Curran's case was dealt with by the Congregation for the Doctrine of the Faith, and the sanction he faced involved a canonical requirement for teaching theology on a pontifical faculty, namely, the "official mandate" of his ecclesiastical superiors to do so. The process of his review was a lengthy one, and he received considerable support during this time. His bishop's testimony was quoted in the preceding chapter; beyond this, prestigious colleagues and several important organizations went on record in his behalf, including the Catholic Theological Society of America, the College Theology Society, and the Leadership Conference of Women Religious. Supporters helped him secure visiting professorships after he was dismissed from Catholic University, the American Association of University Professors censured his former employer, and eventually he obtained a tenured position elsewhere. His losses are still very great, and they are ecclesial as well as personal to Curran. No Catholic college or university enjoys sufficient academic freedom in this repressive climate to offer him a permanent

4. In a statement published in the *National Catholic Reporter* for March 21, 1986, Curran declares: "Truly individual human life begins at the time of individuation, which occurs between the 14th and 21st day after conception. One can be justified in taking truly individual life only for the sake of the life of the mother or for a value commensurate with life itself." He elaborates positions on abortion and related public policy in the final chapters of *Transition and Tradition in Moral Theology* (Notre Dame: University of Notre Dame Press, 1979), pp. 207–50.

position or even an honorary degree. And although other theologians who share his positions have not suffered such disciplinary action yet, their research and teaching have been affected, if only by prudent self-censorship. The words Martin Luther King, Jr., sent from the Birmingham jail in 1963 have considerable resonance still for moral theologians: "Injustice anywhere is a threat to justice everywhere. We are caught in an inescapable network of mutuality, tied in a single garment of destiny. Whatever affects one directly, affects all indirectly."[5]

But in the context of feminist explorations in Catholic moral theology it must be said that the injustices experienced by the Vatican 24 are yet more striking. To threaten these women with the loss of their religious families and their modest material security is quite disproportionate to their action and amounts to coercion against the exercise of political responsibility in a democratic society. Curran had been dealt with directly in correspondence from the Congregation for the Doctrine of the Faith; the Vatican 24 felt treated as nonpersons by the Congregation for Religious and Secular Institutes, since all correspondence was addressed to the officers of their communities and their own letters were effectively ignored. Public support for the signers was also considerably less than Curran received. No officer made a statement to the press praising the personal virtue of a signer the way Bishop Clark had done in behalf of Curran, nor did the Leadership Conference of Women Religious pass a resolution of support. Instead, for reasons that have much to do with gender-based power differences, LCWR elected a public posture of non-judgmental concern and a course of quiet diplomacy. They supported the officers of threatened communities with communications, meeting arrangements, and consultants. They proclaimed March 29, 1985, a "National Day of Prayer and Fasting" for women religious and others who wished to participate for the sake of "a just and peaceful resolution to the situation arising from the New York Times statement and the CRIS response to it."[6] They

---

5. Martin Luther King, Jr., "Letter from Birmingham Jail," in *On Being Responsible*, ed. James M. Gustafson and James T. Laney (New York: Harper & Row, 1968), p. 257.

6. LCWR announcement, March 1985. Also during March 1985 the LCWR Board recommended at hearings held by the U.S. bishops' committee seeking to draft a pastoral letter on women that the group "not issue a pastoral on women in society and in the church or alternatively that they defer writing for several years" ("LCWR Board Urges Change of Course," *Origins* 14 [March 21, 1985]: 655). Their testimony included the following statement: "Women religious have been profoundly alienated by experiences of highhandedness, lack of fair process, the imposition of male authority in 'problem' situations (as defined by males), and the trivialization and dismissal of authentic renewal in the approbation of community constitutions" (p. 654).

struggled behind the scenes to communicate to Vatican officials how American sisters felt about the situation and their belief that disastrous results would follow from an unsatisfactory outcome of the conflict. Former LCWR officials Lora Ann Quiñonez and Mary Daniel Turner describe this behind-the-scenes advocacy in their study *The Transformation of American Catholic Sisters:*

> Perhaps most critical of all, the women [LCWR executives in meetings with Vatican officials] underscored that key elements of the processes employed by church officials in this case were abhorrent to Americans—the presumption of guilt without an opportunity for self-defense, the preemptive determination of sanctions to be inflicted, and the bypassing of the individual sister and the legitimate community authority. . . . [T]hey explicitly put forward the thesis that personal and collective moral choices are made within the context of particular cultures and social traditions, not simply in relation to abstract laws and norms. Understanding and judging such choices must take into account cultural values and symbols. Dissent, for example, is not, in American culture, the heinous offense that church officials judge it to be.[7]

The approach taken by LCWR was chosen for various reasons, including the fact that avoidance of public confrontation had apparently been a factor in the successful resolution of tensions between the Vatican and the School Sisters of St. Francis of Milwaukee during the early 1970s, whereas two other communities, the Glenmary Sisters and the Immaculate Heart of Mary Sisters of Los Angeles, had previously suffered devastating losses from conflicts with church officials over reforms they had made following the Second Vatican Council. This history had influenced the Sisters of Mercy to back down from a confrontation over the issue of tubal ligation in 1982, as has been discussed in chapter 2, and it probably contributed to the decision of the officers of congregations affected by CRIS's response to the *New York Times* statement to maintain a closed circle of confidentiality about their meetings concerning the Vatican 24. This decision has been criticized by several signers and questioned by Marian McAvoy, who was President of the Sisters of Loretto at the time. She recalls in a recent essay:

> For me personally, one of the greatest difficulties was the constraint imposed by confidentiality. As the situation developed and because of differing attitudes toward the use of the media, confidentiality became increasingly important to the elected leaders. I found this limitation difficult for several reasons. Since the

7. Lora Ann Quiñonez and Mary Daniel Turner, *The Transformation of American Catholic Sisters* (Philadelphia: Temple University Press, 1992), pp. 137–38.

matters decided within the leaders' circle affected so personally the lives of the Loretto signers as well as other community members, my instinct was to share all pertinent information with them. Furthermore, Loretto people were accustomed to an openness which perhaps did not prevail so strongly in other groups. It was painful for me to tell the signers that I could not share with them what had taken place in the leaders' meeting. While I felt in a bind, I personally set a high value on the collaboration and camaraderie of the leaders' group and thought it important for Loretto's possible resolution. Therefore I respected meticulously the wishes of that group despite my misgivings.[8]

Among the sisters who signed there was objection not only to the silence of leaders about their meetings but also to their unwillingness to meet again with the laity involved in the statement after an initial gathering in December 1984. Political scientist Maureen Fiedler, a signer from the Loretto community, criticized this as a lost opportunity for shared power when she addressed the WomenChurch Convergence in Cincinnati in 1987:

> Both community leaders and signers felt battered by patriarchy and many reverted to old hierarchical modes of action. . . . Pressures for community loyalty cut across the solidarity the signers needed as a group. . . . These models carried over into relation with lay signers. The nun signers met with lay signers on several occasions, but we never incorporated them fully into strategy sessions. And with one exception, community leaders flatly refused to meet with them at all. Even though several lay signers were disinvited from Catholic institutions or suffered at their jobs because of the ad, we nun signers never organized for true "common cause" with them.[9]

Likewise, Ann Patrick Ware includes the idea of common meetings for lay and sister signers and community officers among the list of learnings from the experience she shared with other Loretto signers:

> We think it would not be wise in the future to have concerned religious leaders meet separately from their members who are involved. Likewise, it violates a basic understanding of church to have concerned laypeople separated off from religious, and one religious congregation separated off from another.[10]

8. Marian McAvoy, "The Only Way Available," in *Naming Our Truth*, ed. Ann Patrick Ware (Inverness, Calif.: Chardon Press, 1955), p. 148.

9. Maureen Fiedler, "Dissent Within the U.S. Church: The Case of the 'Vatican 24,'" in *Church Polity and American Politics: Issues in Contemporary American Catholicism*, ed. Mary C. Segers (New York: Garland, 1990), p. 309. Fiedler's imagery of battering helps to account for the very lack of a unified strategy that she criticizes.

10. Ann Patrick Ware, "A Case Study in Oppression: A Theological and Personal Analysis" (Chicago: National Coalition of American Nuns, 1993), p. 39.

Marian McAvoy felt the cogency of this line of thinking during the crisis, but her decision then was made in view of a practical judgment that she basically affirms today:

> I conceded that there could be better ways than the one we were following and ways that might point with greater hope toward a new church-in-the making. However, while the total group shared many of the same concerns, distinctions and divisions sprang primarily from differing roles and responsibilities.[11]

From an ethical perspective, these differences are crucial. Different responsibilities led not only to different interpretations of the situation calling for a response but also to different weightings of the values at stake, particularly justice, truth, and the survival of individual and community vocations. In short, women faced *prima facie* obligations of various sorts, and each had to estimate the prospective results of possible courses of action in light of the obligations she perceived. It is wise to acknowledge the room for error in these calculations, and to argue for and defend courses of action with allowance for the possibility of misjudgment. Under pressures and threats, however, such admissions may be dangerous vulnerabilities; moreover, the rhetoric of political activism does not lend itself to nuancing of this sort.

A significant point of difference among parties to this case concerned judgments about further use of secular media to promote resolution of the conflict. Some participants were convinced that the more media publicity the better and that the "second *New York Times* ad," the Declaration of Solidarity that appeared March 2, 1986, was an excellent strategy that ought not to have been so vehemently opposed by LCWR and the liberal Catholic press. Others judged the second advertisement to be counterproductive, or simply felt their time and money would be better spent in other ways. It may seem ironic that the idea of diversity of opinion so basic to the original statement was not always affirmed in published judgments of signers about other signers' decisions. What the discrepancy points to, of course, is the fact that individual decisions impinge on the common good, and judgments about the relative adequacy of courses of action are to be expected of moral and political subjects. It is the nature of political rhetoric to simplify matters, insisting that there is only one right thing to do; but life is more complicated than such rhetoric implies, and human action usually has mixed motives and results. To assert this is not to deny that some acts are more beneficial than others, but simply to say that a degree of humility, or recognition of the limits of fore-

11. McAvoy, "Only Way," p. 147.

sight in light of the complex causal processes of history, enhances the authority of those advocating actions to promote justice or other values.

A woman who had been an officer of a religious community published a powerful essay in the *National Catholic Reporter* for December 21, 1984, which helps to account for the officers' insistence on maintaining their closed circle of confidentiality as well as for the fact that apparently some of them "settled" matters with Rome in ways the women whose vocations were at stake found objectionable.[12] Under the headline "Nuns: The Battered Women of the Church," this author wrote anonymously because, "speaking publicly would only cause me and my order further anguish." Her experience appears not to have involved the *New York Times* statement, but difficulties she encountered during an arduous process of securing Vatican approval for the revised constitutions of the congregation she headed.

Her analysis recognizes that the analogy of "superiors of religious orders" as "battered women in the church" has differences as well as similarities with what women suffer in abusive marriages, but it does lift up some striking commonalities. Because the Vatican authorities have "unlimited power," the women have reason to fear "what might happen next," to themselves and to those who depend on their leadership. "Because they govern congregations whose members include sisters of diverse theological and cultural orientations, as well as many elderly sisters, religious superiors have to be concerned (or they think they have to be) about possible 'hurt' to the members of their orders." As the author points out, "A woman who is beaten by her husband knows what is going on but finds it very difficult to 'name it' to others" because of a legitimate fear that more harm will be the result. The solution calls for a process that first requires a safe space (analogous to a "women's shelter") where the realities can begin to be faced in a supportive context that allows a victim to gain strength and take practical steps toward changing her situation. Then, once this first step of "recognizing and naming the abuse" is under way, the victims of ecclesiastical injustice have the obligation to bring matters to the wider church:

12. The Dominican social justice activist Marge Tuite is quoted as voicing such a complaint in the account of Barbara Ferraro and Patricia Hussey, *No Turning Back: Two Nuns' Battle with the Vatican over Women's Right to Choose* (New York: Poseidon Press, 1990), p. 264. Another signer, School Sister of Notre Dame Jeannine Gramick, drew attention to the relevance of the anonymous *National Catholic Reporter* article to the case of the Vatican 24 in "The Vatican's Battered Wives," *The Christian Century* (January 1–8, 1986): 17–20.

A woman who thinks she is the only one being beaten is far more powerless than one who knows that her frightening reality is one she shares with other victims. As religious superiors increasingly share stories, there is an emerging awareness of what is going on and a recognition of a pattern. . . . They need to turn to the broader church to be understood, to have their pain taken seriously, and they need this broader church to be a part of that continuing conversion within the church that will mean for all people a church more faithful to the Gospel and, therefore, less violent, unjust and oppressive.

What this article suggests is that the crisis over the *New York Times* statement precipitated a need for intense work on many fronts among individuals with different levels of awareness of the problems they faced. In light of this analysis one can appreciate that some community officers needed the "safe space" of confidentiality and closed meetings, while also recognizing that other arrangements might have been more ideal.

Indeed, the fact that at least one participant has subsequently questioned the decision is significant. The entire episode of the *New York Times* advertisement and its aftermath involved many difficult choices on the part of many agents. It is notable that a number of the women involved have not only shared their experiences in print but also have been willing to critique their own decisions in light of subsequent learnings.[13] This models a maturity of moral agency that has not been usually been commended to Catholics, who so often are trained to think that all good people have the same correct moral opinions and no need to look back on deeds done in good faith.

From the brief analysis of these two cases it is clear that perceptions of truth and the exercise of power are at the base of the conflicts among theologians, sisters, and church officials. Curran and the Vatican 24 were essentially being asked by Rome to deny what they perceived as "true," to submit their judgments to those of church authorities on matters the Vatican has defined as "not true." In both instances, the individuals adopted the position advocated by St. Thomas Aquinas—"anyone upon whom the ecclesiastical authority, in ignorance of true facts, imposes a demand that offends against his clear conscience, should perish in excommunication rather than violate his conscience"—and accepted the consequences.[14] It will be for history to

---

13. Perhaps it is significant that the three women most willing to be self-critical in print—Maureen Fiedler, Marian McAvoy, and Ann Patrick Ware—all happen to be members of the Sisters of Loretto, the congregation with six signers, the largest number from any one group.

14. Quoted in Richard P. McBrien, *Catholicism* (Minneapolis: Winston Press, 1980), p. 1003.

judge who ultimately was in possession of "true facts," but Curran and the Vatican 24 have paid a substantial price for conscientiously living by their lights, and their willingness to suffer for their convictions has been encouraging for others. Considerable moral power enters the picture when individuals risk values and suffer losses on account of their beliefs, and this power is all the greater when there is reason to trust the basic goodness of those who take such stands.

Both cases warrant much fuller analysis, but for our purposes this will suffice. The ecclesiastical context has changed somewhat in the ensuing years, and it is to certain of these developments that we now turn. On the one hand, Vatican officials have sought to promote Catholic unity and doctrinal integrity by making several significant attempts to limit theological dissent. In February 1989 there appeared in *L'Osservatore Romano* a new Profession of Faith and Oath of Fidelity containing more extensive and rigorous definitions of the objects of faith than the traditional creed and extending the obligation to take the oath to several new groups, including "university teachers of disciplines dealing with faith or morals."[15] This document was later promulgated officially and has begun to be implemented despite the serious objections raised by theologians and experts in canon law.[16] There followed in 1990 a document seeking to regulate Catholic higher education, *Ex Corde*

---

15. "Doctrinal Congregation Publishes Faith Profession and Oath," *Origins* 18 (March 16, 1989): 661.

16. In 1990 the Catholic Theological Society of America published a 133-page report by its Committee on the Profession of Faith and the Oath of Fidelity, which analyzed various theological and canonical issues involved in the texts and their promulgation and concluded that serious ambiguities in both warrant further study. For this reason the committee suggested the appropriateness of bishops taking no action "against those who judge themselves in conscience unable to make this Profession of Faith or take the Oath of Fidelity in light of the problems surrounding them." Insofar as the Profession of Faith is concerned, one of these problems is that the new text adds three paragraphs to the Nicene-Constantinopolitan Creed, thereby attempting "to impose a view which two recent ecumenical councils have declined to teach explicitly, and whose meaning and extension is attended with a great deal of debate" (p. 116). The view in question is expressed in the following terms from the new Profession of Faith: "I also firmly accept and hold each and every thing (*omnia et singula*) that is proposed by that same church definitively (*definitive*) with regard to teaching concerning faith or morals. What is more, I adhere (*adhaereo*) with religious submission of will and intellect (*religioso voluntatis et intellectus obsequio*) to the teachings which either the Roman pontiff or the college of bishops enunciate when they exercise the authentic magisterium even if they proclaim those teachings in an act that is not definitive" (*Origins* 18 [March 16, 1989]: 663).

Ecclesiae, and in 1992 the *Catechism of the Catholic Church.*[17] The publication of the English version of this "universal catechism" was delayed in the United States, however, because the Vatican overruled the U.S. bishops on the question of employing inclusive language for humanity in this work. Thus, its release in June 1994 coincided with an apostolic letter of Pope John Paul II entitled "Ordinatio Sacerdotalis," which declared "that the church has no authority whatsoever to confer priestly ordination on women and that this judgment is to be definitively held by all the church's faithful," thereby compounding the sense of alienation felt by American Catholic feminists.[18] All these documents seek in various ways to ensure that those who teach in Catholic settings will not differ with official positions, even those that have not been defined as infallible. Most germane to the present study, however, is the encyclical on moral theology addressed to bishops throughout the world by Pope John Paul II in the fall of 1993, *Veritatis Splendor,* which will be discussed below.[19]

Meanwhile, on the other hand, Catholics influenced by egalitarian-feminist values have continued to grow in their appropriation of power and responsibility as moral agents. There are inevitable tensions between these two developments, and it would be simplistic to assume that all truth and virtue are on one side or the other. Ambiguity and complexity are evident in the thought and action of Vatican officials as well as in that of Catholic feminists, but because official juridical and sacramental power resides with Rome the problems in Vatican positions are, to my judgment, the more serious ones, especially when these encourage an idolatrous conflation of human with divine authority.

In the remaining pages of chapter 5 I shall first analyze the encyclical *Veritatis Splendor,* summarizing its contents and commenting on its strengths and limitations. Then, in a section called "The Enduring Voice of Haemon," I shall take note of how various bishops have articulated insights that counter the excessive

17. "The Apostolic Constitution on Catholic Universities," *Origins* 20 (October 4, 1990): 265–76. "Ordinances" for implementing *Ex Corde Ecclesiae* have subsequently been under discussion.

18. John Paul II, "Apostolic Letter on Ordination and Women," *Origins* 24 (June 9, 1994): 49, 51–52. In a column published June 17, 1994, in the *National Catholic Reporter,* Benedictine author Joan Chittester objected to both the letter and the sexist translation of the catechism, saying of the latter: "[W]omen should simply not buy, not read and not respond to the new catechism. It wasn't written for us. They have written only to themselves."

19. The text of the encyclical, followed by a brief official summary, is found in *Origins* 23 (October 14, 1993): 297–336.

patriarchalism of the Vatican, complicating the picture of magisterial teaching in ways that nurture hope among those influenced by egalitarian-feminist values.

VERITATIS SPLENDOR: AN EXERCISE OF PATRIARCHAL RESPONSIBILITY

Moral theologian John P. Boyle has observed that the 1993 encyclical, which mixes several genres of theological literature, could perhaps best be interpreted as a "*cri de coeur*" emanating from the heart of a pastor concerned for the well-being of his global congregation.[20] My own reading concurs with Boyle's judgment, for I see the encyclical as Pope John Paul II's effort to bring unity, focus, and leadership to a situation in moral theology he feels has been fragmented for too long. The encyclical is reminiscent of efforts made by Khasi religious leaders in northern India, who much earlier in this century sought to avert disaster by insisting on traditional taboos against taking wood from sacred groves. Meanwhile rationalists were calling their ancient wisdom nonsense and "proving" with their axes that "nothing bad will happen" to those who were taking the conveniently located trees. Indeed, the forest gods did not devour the modernizers on the spot, as ancient stories had threatened, and people harvested the once-forbidden trees without respect for the inter-connectedness of life or concern for future generations. The resulting desertification has been tragic for all concerned, including nonhuman creatures and the earth, and the entire episode has been a reminder that religious traditions sometimes possess wisdom that deserves respect even though it cannot be articulated in fully rational categories. Now, at the end of the century, there are ways to inspire care of the forest that do not require literal acceptance of ancient taboos, but decades ago this language was not available. The Khasi leaders may have operated out of fear of losing their hegemony; they may have sincerely believed the frightening myths; or they may have acted out of some combination of motives. What is important is not so much their motivation as the fact that their position had validity beyond what they were able to articulate at the time. Today this validity is acknowledged by scientists who note that ecological planning requires protecting trees in precisely those locations tradition had designated sacred.[21]

20. Boyle's unpublished remarks are summarized in Michael J. Schuck's report, "Moral Theology: *Veritatis Splendor* and Contemporary Moral Theology," *CTSA Proceedings* 49 (1994): 200.
21. This analogy provided the basis for the early response to "*Veritatis Splendor*" I published in *Commonweal* (October 22, 1993): 18.

This example seems an apt metaphor for papal efforts to stem human relational disaster by holding to classical sexual norms against the cultural tide of
relativism in this area, which is associated with such evils as the AIDS pandemic, the sexual misconduct scandals of the clergy, and the dismaying statistics on marriage survival rates. Although human sexuality is not the stated
theme of the encyclical, it is surely the subtext that occasioned and governs it,
since this is the area where disputes between the revisionists and the Vatican
are most pronounced. This situation differs from the Khasi example, however, in that the revisionist moral theologians are by no means siding with the
secularizers who would devastate human sexual ecology, but rather are advocating only modest changes in sexual teachings and not the wholesale defor-
estation of sexual and family values that everyone has reason to fear.

Veritatis Splendor is a lengthy document containing three chapters, framed
by an introductory discussion of "Jesus Christ, the true light that enlightens
everyone" and a concluding turn to "Mary, Mother of Mercy." The pastoral
intent of the document is made clear in its statement of purpose, which is to
"reflect on the whole of the Church's moral teaching with the precise goal of
recalling certain fundamental truths of Catholic doctrine which, in the present circumstances, risk being distorted or denied" (#4). Pope John Paul II
identifies a "genuine crisis" because of a "lack of harmony between the traditional response of the Church and certain theological positions." He seeks to
safeguard "sound teaching" in the moral sphere, as opposed to "a pluralism of
opinions and of kinds of behavior" that he deems problematic (#4). In short,
he aims "to set forth . . . the principles of a moral teaching based upon Sacred
Scripture and the living Apostolic Tradition, and at the same time to shed
light on the presuppositions and consequences of the dissent which that
teaching has met" (#5).

The first chapter of the encyclical, "Teacher, What Good Must I Do?" is
subtitled "Christ and the Answer to Questions about Morality." Here the
pope develops an extended meditation on the story of the rich young man in
chapter 19 of Matthew's Gospel, emphasizing the theme of obedience to the
law rather than the danger of riches usually stressed by interpreters of this
narrative. The analysis is not exclusively "deontological" or centered in duty
or obedience to principles, but has a purposive, value-oriented ("teleological") dimension as well, as the following observations make clear:[22]

---

22. The opposition between "deontological" and "teleological" approaches to morality is an
enduring tension in ethics, but ultimately methodologies that are adequate take account of both
poles of the dialectic, although their emphasis may be on one or the other. H. Richard Niebuhr

The commandments of which Jesus reminds the young man are meant to safeguard *the good* of the person, the image of God, by protecting his *goods*. "You shall not murder; You shall not commit adultery; You shall not steal; You shall not bear false witness" are moral rules formulated in terms of prohibitions. These negative precepts express with particular force the ever urgent need to protect human life, the communion of persons in marriage, private property, truthfulness and people's good name. (#13)

These points would basically be affirmed by revisionist moral theologians, as would the general observation that the task of interpreting traditional prescriptions has been "entrusted by Jesus to the Apostles and their successors, with the special assistance of the Spirit of truth" (#25). Where differences emerge is not on these fundamental claims but on the question of how theological dissent contributes to what the pope recognizes to be a developmental process of "authentic interpretation of the Lord's law" (#27).

There is a distinct difference in tone between the first chapter, which voices the personalist philosophy and spirituality of Pope John Paul II quite directly, and the second chapter, which is devoted to several rather technical topics in moral theology.[23] The title of chapter 2, from St. Paul's letter to the Romans 12:2, expresses the rigor of the pontiff's vision of the Christian life, "Do Not Be Conformed to this World," and its subtitle implies that theologians are in need of this advice: "The Church and the Discernment of Certain Tendencies in Present-Day Moral Theology."

An opening section on freedom and law objects to modernity's excessive valuing of autonomy, insists on the link between the created world and the orders of morality and salvation, and reiterates a long-standing claim that the

---

made an invaluable contribution to the discussion in *The Responsible Self* (New York: Harper & Row, 1963) by pointing out that different images of the moral agent are associated with the different emphases. Niebuhr suggests that deontological approaches stressing principles view the agent primarily under the metaphor of "citizen," while teleological approaches emphasizing consequences are governed by the metaphor of the agent as "maker." Niebuhr offered a third metaphor, that of the agent as "responder," in developing his own ethics of responsibility, at the same time acknowledging validity in the other images.

23. As Richard A. McCormick's review essay indicates, several authors have suggested that this technical chapter reflects the work of "other hands" besides the pope's. Ronald Modras finds material from the University of Lublin doctoral dissertation of Andrzej Szostek on *Norms and Exceptions,* and McCormick himself also detects the influence of John Finnis, an Oxford University lecturer in jurisprudence and member of the International Theological Commission (McCormick, "Some Early Reactions to *Veritatis Splendor,*" *Theological Studies* 55 [September 1994]: 485–86).

natural order requires the exceptionless prohibition of certain sexual acts: "contraception, direct sterilization, autoeroticism, pre-marital sexual relations, homosexual relations and artificial insemination" (#47). The pope also stresses the competence of the hierarchical magisterium to articulate moral norms and claims that "negative precepts of the natural law" (those prohibiting actions always and without exception) are "universally valid." He acknowledges, however, that "this truth of the moral law—like that of the 'deposit of faith'—unfolds down the centuries," which entails an ongoing need to discover "*the most adequate formulation* for universal and permanent moral norms in the light of different cultural contexts" (#53).

There follows a section entitled "Conscience and Truth," which argues that conscience is neither autonomous nor infallible. The theory of conscience developed here includes the idea of an inner conversation with God, imaged as a lawgiver whose law is inscribed on our hearts. Obedience is the ideal stressed: "whereas the natural law discloses the objective and universal demands of the moral good, conscience is the application of the law to a particular case; this application of the law thus becomes an inner dictate for the individual, a summons to do what is good in this particular situation" (#59).

A third section, "Fundamental Choice and Specific Kinds of Behavior," develops the claim that prohibitions of actions that are "intrinsically evil" allow for no exceptions; it insists also on the classic distinction between venial, or lesser, sins and those that are "mortal," namely, actions so "gravely disordered" as to cause loss of sanctifying grace (#68, 70).

The final section of the second chapter, "The Moral Act," takes aim directly at what the pope and his advisors regard as errors in contemporary moral theology: methodologies known as "consequentialism" and "proportionalism," which I shall discuss below, and the toleration of exceptions to certain prohibitions of acts held to be "intrinsically evil."

In the third chapter, "Lest the Cross of Christ Be Emptied of Its Power," Pope John Paul II returns to the spiritual vision that underlies his pastoral concern and also expresses the fear behind his efforts to control theological discussion. Subtitled "Moral Good for the Life of the Church and of the World," the chapter emphasizes the connection between truth and freedom, the need to oppose relativism and secularism, and the values of obedience, sacrifice, and martyrdom. The pontiff's discussion of martyrdom, which he describes as "the exaltation of the inviolable holiness of God's law" (#90), reflects the law-mysticism that characterizes his spirituality, and differs in emphasis from the view of contemporary martyrdom in chapter 3 of the present work. Some convergence of interests appears, however, in the following statement of his understanding of the practical import of his views on truth and obedience, which he quotes from his 1991 encyclical *Centesimus Annus:*

> If there is no transcendent truth, in obedience to which man achieves his full identity, then there is no sure principle for guaranteeing just relations between people. Their self-interest as a class, group or nation would inevitably set them in opposition to one another. If one does not acknowledge transcendent truth, then the force of power takes over, and each person tends to make full use of the means at his disposal in order to impose his own interests or his own opinion, with no regard for the rights of others. (#100)

He sees in democracy the danger of ethical relativism (#101) and reminds moral theologians (specifically those with an episcopal mandate to teach in Catholic seminaries and theological faculties) that their duty is "to set forth the Church's teaching and to give, in the exercise of their ministry, the example of a loyal assent, both internal and external, to the Magisterium's teaching in the areas of both dogma and morality" (#110). It is significant that the type of dissent explicitly condemned in *Veritatis Splendor* is defined quite narrowly:

> *Dissent,* in the form of carefully orchestrated protests and polemics carried on in the media, *is opposed to ecclesial communion and to a correct understanding of the hierarchical constitution of the People of God.*

However, because this paragraph continues by claiming that "[o]pposition to the teaching of the Church's Pastors cannot be seen as a legitimate expression either of Christian freedom or of the diversity of the Spirit's gifts," and by noting that bishops have the duty to insist "that *the right of the faithful* to receive Catholic doctrine in its purity and integrity must always be respected," the encyclical raises the possibility that dissent expressed in ways short of polemics in the media might also be grounds for ecclesiastical punishment (#113).

The chapter concludes with a reminder to the bishops of the seriousness involved in this "*reaffirmation of the universality and immutability of the moral commandments,* particularly those which prohibit always and without exception *intrinsically evil acts*" (#115) and of their own call to exercise vigilance over the teaching of faith and morals. It is theirs to grant or withdraw the designation "Catholic" where educational and healthcare institutions are concerned (#116), and the clear implication of the encyclical is that bishops should not tolerate dissent on the very matters most at issue today, such as contraception, abortion, sterilization, and homosexuality.

The pope's section entitled "Our Own Responsibilities as Pastors" is supported by a theological claim that there is an identification, apparently without remainder, between divine truth, goodness, and love, and the official teachings of the church:

> In the heart of every Christian, in the inmost depths of each person, there is always an echo of the question which the young man in the Gospel once asked Jesus: "Teacher, what good must I do to have eternal life?" (Mt. 19:16).... And when Christians ask [Jesus] the question which rises from their conscience, the Lord replies in the words of the New Covenant which have been entrusted to his Church. As the Apostle Paul said of himself, we have been sent "to preach the Gospel, and not with eloquent wisdom, lest the Cross of Christ be emptied of its power" (1 Cor. 1:17). The Church's answer to man's question contains the wisdom and power of Christ Crucified, the Truth which gives of itself.
>
> *When people ask the Church the questions raised by their consciences,* when the faithful in the Church turn to their Bishops and Pastors, *the Church's reply contains the voice of Jesus Christ, the voice of the truth about good and evil.* In the words spoken by the Church there resounds, in people's inmost being, the voice of God who "alone is good" (cf. Mt. 19:17), who alone "is love" (1 Jn 4:8, 16).

I have quoted this section from paragraph #117 at length because its rhetoric warrants close scrutiny. Not only does the passage unify the encyclical by reminding readers of the themes of the first and third chapters, which are based on the story of the rich young man and the doctrine of the power of the cross, but it subtly recommends substituting for awe at the mystery of God's truth and saving power an attitude counter to Catholicism's esteem for the balance of faith and reason, namely, fideistic submission to authoritative definitions of right and wrong behavior. Note how the quotation from St. Paul is used to suggest that the very lack of "eloquent wisdom" in Vatican arguments on the points disputed by revisionist moral theologians is to become the basis for assenting to them, "lest the cross be emptied of its power." This comes close to saying, "Believe in the intrinsic evil of contraception *because* our reasons are not convincing; adopt the ancient motto, *credo quia absurdum*—'I believe because it is absurd'—and all will be well." The text itself does not go quite so far, but its authoritarian emphasis lends itself to such interpretation.

The themes of submission to what is not understood and obedience to suffering imposed by God are reinforced in the final paragraph (#120), which commends Mary as "the radiant sign and inviting model of the moral life." Here the pope lifts her words from the context of the story of the miracle at Cana—"Do whatever he tells you" (John 2:5)—and offers them to present-day readers of the encyclical, who have earlier been encouraged to associate the divine "voice" with that of the hierarchical magisterium. *Veritatis Splendor* concludes with a prayer to "Mary, Mother of Mercy," which affirms that hope should not rest in our own moral efforts but in "God who is rich in mercy" (#120).

UBI VERITAS, DEUS IBI EST:
FURTHER REFLECTIONS ON *VERITATIS SPLENDOR*

This encyclical is one pope's contribution to a centuries-long effort on the part of church leaders to articulate moral teaching that is both faithful to the Christian tradition and reasonable in the light of contemporary knowledge and experience. Pope John Paul II is surely right to recognize that our era is a critical one for the church and for humanity more generally. Indeed, such developments as critical philosophy, historical consciousness, Marxism, transnational and computerized capitalism, developments in science and technology, and the liberation movements among various oppressed groups have all put pressures on classical Catholicism, even as Aristotelianism and Copernicanism did during earlier times of crisis.

Beyond the concern for authority in changing times is another feature of the contemporary situation that bears directly on the dispute between the Vatican and revisionist moral theology concerning sexual questions. If the official teaching in this area is not fully convincing to present-day believers, one may still pose some challenging questions to the revisionists: Are the modes of moral reasoning that allow conscientious couples to elect artificial contraception and medically indicated sterilization readily distinguishable from the rationalizations that accompany an irresponsible approach to sexual activity, marital commitment, or parenthood?[24] Is a departure from the clas-

24. Of particular concern to the hierarchy are the scandals involving the clergy, a problem by no means limited to Catholicism. Although those guilty of criminal sexual misconduct comprise a small percentage of priests and religious brothers (and, much more rarely, sisters), the cases of abuse have harmed victims irreparably, and in combination with the inadequate responses of religious superiors and bishops have cost the U.S. church as much as half a billion dollars in recent years. These factors have also caused injustice to the majority of clergy and religious, whose ministries are adversely affected by the climate of distrust created by the scandals. The pope makes no mention of this problem in the encyclical, but he undoubtedly felt pressure to exert control over any factors he judged to be contributing to its causes. Using data available in 1993 about Chicago priests, Andrew M. Greeley concluded "that an estimate of one out of ten priests as sexual abusers might be too high and an estimate of one out of twenty might be too low." See Greeley, "How Serious Is the Problem of Sexual Abuse by the Clergy?" *America* (March 20, 1993): 7. According to a *Washington Post* story by Christopher B. Daly (cited here from the *St. Paul Pioneer Press* for November 6, 1994), lawyers for plaintiffs in one

sic "venereal pleasure principle" (which holds that all deliberately chosen sexual pleasure is seriously sinful except when it is the result of genital intercourse between lawfully wedded spouses that is not artificially closed to procreation) a factor contributing to the distressing rates of HIV infection and induced abortion throughout the world?[25] Revisionists have already developed good ways to answer these questions and will perform a valuable service by devoting even more attention to the pastoral and educational aspects of implementing a revised sexual ethic grounded in the principles of justice and respect for persons. The dilemma posed by this encyclical and by other church practices controlling dissent is that theologians are inhibited from engaging the disputed questions, and thus their ideas for addressing these vexing pastoral problems are hardly allowed a hearing because adherence to the classic formulas on sexual questions has come to symbolize loyalty to the church.

Rumors preceding the release of the encyclical conveyed the possibility that not only was the pope going to hold the line on sexual questions, but he was also likely to elevate the most controverted teaching in recent Catholic history, the ban on all forms of artificial contraception as expressed in *Humanae Vitae,* to the status of an "infallible" doctrine, something Pope Paul VI had deliberately avoided doing in 1968. It is to Pope John Paul II's credit that he chose not to do this and instead was content to say that conscience is *not* infallible.

On this point, as on other fundamental claims of the encyclical, the pope and the revisionist moral theologians are in substantial agreement. For example, those who favor a "proportionalist" method of moral reasoning, including Richard McCormick and Charles Curran, wholeheartedly endorse the tradi-

---

major suit estimated in 1994 that U.S. bishops had already paid in excess of $500 million and the cost could go as high as $1 billion "within a few years." Because cases are settled on a diocese-by-diocese basis, exact figures have not been available. Columnist Clark Morphew observed in the *St. Paul Pioneer Press* for November 13, 1994, that estimates of damages paid to victims to date ranged from $200 to $500 million, adding that the secrecy of out-of-court settlements made it impossible to know exact figures.

25. This phrasing of the principle reflects the contemporary situation in official teaching, which approves of "natural" forms of family planning not acceptable in the first half of the century. A representative articulation of the principle from a college textbook widely used before the Second Vatican Council is as follows: "Deliberately to accept and enjoy venereal pleasure outside marriage is grievously sinful. Whether that pleasure has been intentionally procured or has risen spontaneously, yielding to it is in both cases gravely sinful." Quoted here from Edwin F. Healy, *Moral Guidance,* revised by James F. Meara (Chicago: Loyola University Press, 1960), p. 175.

tion's insistence on such matters as human dignity, the existence of an objective moral order, and the fact that freedom is not an absolute value. In opposing the contrary opinions, the pontiff is arguing with the secular culture rather than with revisionist theologians, who deplore relativism and subjectivism as much as he does. Another point of agreement, and a strength of the encyclical, is its stress on the unity of spirituality and ethics in the Christian life. The pope's generosity in sharing his scripturally inspired vision of the Christian life and its demands, which is inevitably colored by the particularities of his own experiences, can inspire all members of the church to attend more deeply to the mystery of God's Spirit present in their lives.

With respect to the encyclical's limitations, there are several that warrant attention here. These include sexist language, a questionable interpretation of natural law, vague and inaccurate criticisms of moral theologians, highly selective readings of scripture in support of legalism and fideism, and an uncritical theory of truth that risks promoting an idolatrous form of faith through confusion of the judgments of religious authority figures with the transcendent Divine Source of life, meaning, and value.

Sexist Language

The maintaining of sexist language, and particularly the use of "man" in contexts where gender-fairness would require "humanity" or "human beings," has in recent years mutated from an unconscious manifestation of a patriarchal mentality to a deliberate defense against any inroads of feminism. Whereas prior to the 1980s religious authorities could plead ignorance of the effect that sexist translations of Roman documents had on many American readers, the moral arguments in favor of gender-inclusive language had gained such a purchase in this culture by 1993 that Vatican intransigence on the matter created an unnecessary scandal for the church in this country. In the case of the encyclical, theologian Lisa Sowle Cahill observes:

> Many Catholic feminists, and not only so-called "radical feminists," view the church as singularly unresponsive to women's viewpoints and experiences in defining the human goods of sexuality, parenthood, marriage, and gender-related ecclesial and social roles. This encyclical insists repeatedly that there must be norms prohibiting "intrinsically evil acts," especially in sexual behavior. Yet its stubbornly noninclusive language confirms that such norms are still being defined within a male-oriented mind-set.[26]

26. Lisa Sowle Cahill, "Veritatis Splendor," *Commonweal* (October 22, 1993): 16. After

Understanding of Natural Law

A distinctive feature of Roman Catholic ethics has been that its arguments are based on scripture *and* natural law, in contrast to the *sola scriptura* basis of sectarian Christian groups. The meaning of "natural law" is not a simple matter, however, for the phrase has been employed differently by thinkers over the centuries. In a widely used textbook, moral theologian Timothy O'Connell stresses that natural law theory in general is opposed to both subjectivism and legalism, for it is a realistic theory holding that "the formulation of the *ought* is contained in the reality of *is*." In other words, "what makes things right and wrong is precisely and solely the fact that they truly help or hurt the human persons that inhabit this world."[27]

The concept is believed to have originated with the ancient Stoic philosophers, and St. Paul used it when speaking of the Gentiles in his letter to the Romans: "For when the Gentiles who do not have the law by nature observe the prescriptions of the law, they are a law for themselves even though they do not have the law. They show that the demands of the law are written in their hearts" (Rom. 2:14–15). This usage expresses one of the great advantages of the approach, namely, its recognition that all human beings have moral obligations, which are in principle communicable across cultural differences. As O'Connell notes, "natural law" theory entails the elements of "nature" and "reason," and different schools have emphasized one or the other. The Vatican has favored interpreting natural law with emphasis on "nature," so that the obligation to follow natural law entails conforming to what nature is thought to require, particularly where sexual questions are concerned. Revisionists have designated this a "physicalist" view of natural law, objecting to its uncritical understanding of "nature" and noting that historically this view led to such problematic notions as the idea that masturbation is worse than heterosexual rape, because the former is "unnatural" while the latter involves

---

two embarrassing experiences of being overruled by the Vatican on the matter of using inclusive language for humanity in official publications (first in 1993, when the publication of the universal catechism was delayed, and again in 1994, when approval for liturgies using the inclusive New Revised Standard Version of the Bible was peremptorily withdrawn), the U.S. bishops went on record at their November 1994 meeting in favor of inclusive language. Writing in the *St. Paul Pioneer Press* for November 17, 1994, columnist Clark Morphew correctly interpreted this as a polite but firm way of protesting Vatican interference with their pastoral judgment.

27. Timothy O'Connell, *Principles for a Catholic Morality* (New York: Seabury, 1978), pp. 150, 144.

an act conforming to the "natural" (that is, procreative) purpose of the sexual organs.[28]

By contrast, revisionists have favored an understanding of natural law that stresses the *rationality* of human nature rather than the "nature" of physical processes. This approach allows for more flexibility in interpreting obligations, because it is open to arguments about the harmful or beneficial effects of various actions in assessing their rightness or wrongness. It is precisely this emphasis on "reason" that allows for the judgment that some previously forbidden sexual actions may be morally right under certain circumstances.

Both sides of the contemporary debate claim the authority of St. Thomas Aquinas, whose *Summa Theologiae* has been so influential in the development of Catholic moral thought. On the basis of the knowledge of reproductive biology available in the thirteenth century, St. Thomas did hold that masturbation and consensual homosexuality were more grievously wrong than heterosexual rape or incest, and he used the "unnatural/natural" distinction to reach this judgment.[29] However, revisionists argue that such "physicalism" is not central to his understanding of natural law, which is articulated most clearly thus:

> Since all things are regulated and measured by Eternal Law, as we have seen, it is evident that all somehow share in it, in that their tendencies to their own proper acts and ends are from its impression.
>
> Among them intelligent creatures are ranked under divine Providence the more nobly because they take part in Providence by their own providing for themselves and others. Thus they join in and make their own the Eternal Reason through which they have their natural aptitudes for their due activity and purpose. Now this sharing in the Eternal Law by intelligent creatures is what we call "natural law."
>
> . . . [T]he light of natural reason by which we discern what is good and what evil is nothing but the impression of divine light on us.[30]

---

28. Particularly useful discussions of natural law are found in Joseph T. C. Arntz, "Natural Law and Its History," in Franz Böckle, ed., *Moral Problems and Christian Personalism* (New York: Paulist, 1965), pp. 39–57; Richard M. Gula, *Reason Informed by Faith: Foundations of Catholic Morality* (New York: Paulist, 1989), pp. 220–49; and Charles E. Curran and Richard A. McCormick, eds., *Readings in Moral Theology No. 7: Natural Law and Theology* (New York: Paulist, 1991). Curran's essay in this volume, "Natural Law in Moral Theology," discusses "physicalism" and "naturalism" in the encyclical *Humanae Vitae* (pp. 247–95). See also Cynthia S. W. Crysdale, "Revisioning Natural Law: From the Classicist Paradigm to Emergent Probability," *Theological Studies* 56 (1995): 464–84.

29. *Summa Theologiae*, IIaIIae, Q.154 a.12.

30. *Summa Theologiae*, IaIIae, Q.91 a.2. Quoted here from the Blackfriars edition, vol. 28 (New York: McGraw-Hill, 1964), p. 23.

For this reason Lisa Sowle Cahill argues that St. Thomas is inconsistent in his assessments of sexual actions, noting also that these judgments reflect a patriarchal mind-set:

> Aquinas here neglects his own principle that the human faculties of reason and freedom are higher and more distinctive than physical characteristics and processes, for if the distinctively personal aspects of sex were recognized (over and above what humans have in common with animals), then certainly rape and incest would be recognized as greater sins against human dignity than contraception, masturbation, and consensual homosexuality. Moreover, this narrow adherence to a physicalist norm of "the natural" in sexual matters would hardly have been possible in a culture which respected the dignity of women as well as men, and which recognized that incest and rape are usually crimes perpetrated against females by males.[31]

Veritatis Splendor does not rank various sexual sins, but it grounds its assertion that "contraception, direct sterilization, autoeroticism, pre-marital sexual relations, homosexual relations and artificial insemination" (#47) are all intrinsically evil on magisterial statements that have been developed on the basis of such classicist judgments about what is "natural." For this reason the encyclical's stated disavowal of "physicalism" and "naturalism" in the paragraph listing the above actions is not convincing, although the prohibitions are defended by claims about the human meaning of these behaviors (as defined by church authorities) rather than their physical characteristics.

On a more general note, the Dominican theologian Herbert McCabe accuses the encyclical of misreading St. Thomas when it says that his *Summa Theologiae* taught that the ten commandments "contain the whole natural law" (*Veritatis Splendor* #79), because for St. Thomas the natural law was "nothing but the exercise of practical reasoning," and therefore "concerns any and every kind of specifically human activity." McCabe continues:

> Thus the use of artificial contraceptives, say, or homosexual acts or masturbation or *in vitro* fertilisation, none of which are mentioned in the decalogue, come within the scope of natural law simply because we can reason practically about them. On the other hand, perhaps in their case, since they are not *revealed* to us as prohibited, we should be chary about speaking of "mortal sin" in their connection.[32]

---

31. Lisa Sowle Cahill, *Women and Sexuality* (New York: Paulist, 1992), p. 10.
32. Herbert McCabe, "Manuals and Rule Books," *The Tablet* [London], December 18, 1993, p. 1650.

For McCabe, such prohibitions are better understood as part of a "flexible" training manual to be assessed and revised in light of its effectiveness for education to virtue. Reason, informed by the presence of God's Spirit, can be trusted to guide this process of revision. The disappointing feature of the encyclical in McCabe's opinion is that it seeks "to *base* an account of Christian morality on the ten commandments, and this can only lead to a sterile polarisation of 'legalism' or 'liberalism.'" The example of St. Thomas, McCabe maintains, should have encouraged transcendence of such a "post-Renaissance" preoccupation in favor of seeing "human life as the movement towards our real selves and towards God guided by the New Law which, as he insists, is no written code but nothing other than the presence in us of the Holy Spirit."[33]

Criticisms of Moral Theologians

A third difficulty with the encyclical is the way it confuses revisionist moral theologians with secular advocates of unbridled subjectivism and relativism. The thinkers criticized are not named, and indeed their actual positions are not recognizable in what is said about them, but accusations against "proportionalism," "teleologism," and "consequentialism" have rendered suspect a substantial school of European and North American scholars, including Bernard Häring, Joseph Fuchs, Peter Knauer, Charles Curran, and Richard McCormick. These theologians have all published responses to *Veritatis Splendor;* McCormick's survey of a wide range of reactions, including those of journalists, bishops, philosophers, and theologians on both sides of the debate, is particularly useful for our purposes.[34]

McCormick identifies the central issue as that of defining the meaning of the "object" of a human action, what the behavior itself "intends" irrespective of the agent's motive for performing it. He notes that the encyclical accuses revisionist moral theologians of saying that a good motive justifies a wrong action, and he emphatically denies this:

> In brief, the encyclical repeatedly and inaccurately states of proportionalism that it attempts to justify *morally wrong actions* by a good intention. This, I regret to say, is a misrepresentation, . . . a caricature. If an act is morally wrong, nothing can justify it.[35]

33. Ibid.
34. McCormick, "Some Early Reactions," pp. 481–506.
35. Ibid., p. 491.

Proportionalism is a name given to the approach to moral reasoning characteristic of revisionists who employ the long-established criterion of "proportionate reason" in ways that extend its use beyond areas typical of past moral theology. It is not a self-chosen designation but a term first used by those who opposed the flexibility the approach allows with respect to behaviors already designated by the magisterium as "intrinsically evil," such as contraception or sterilization.

Notre Dame theologian Jean Porter traces the origins of the movement to the efforts of German Jesuit Peter Knauer to overcome certain limitations of the principle of the "double effect," by arguing that the valid aspects of its several criteria were essentially contained in the concept of "proportionate reason."[36] This principle holds that when an action will have results that are both good and bad, the action is morally justified only when several criteria are satisfied:

> (1) The good effect and not the evil effect is *directly intended;* (2) the action itself is good, or at least indifferent; (3) the good effect is not produced *by means of* the evil effect; and (4) there is a proportionate reason for permitting the foreseen evil effect to occur.[37]

As traditionally employed, this principle has allowed for such actions as, for example, the amputation of a cancerous leg, which involves the "evil" of loss of bodily integrity and mobility, but also offers the "good" of a reasonable hope that the person's life will be extended significantly. Both revisionists and their opponents would agree that the amputation is allowable, but technical discussions of recent decades have altered the extent to which they would employ all of the classical criteria. Basically the revisionists, influenced by such factors as the philosophical insights discussed in chapter 2 of the present work, have discerned that the only useful criterion is that of "proportionate reason," while their opponents judge it essential to maintain more of the traditional criteria, especially the second, which they understand to entail accepting past magisterial definitions of which actions are good or indifferent and which are "intrinsically evil."

This difference on what may seem a merely technical point of methodology cashes out in opposite positions on such practical questions as artificial insemination by the husband to overcome infertility in marriage. Typically a

36. Quoted in William C. Spohn, "Forum—Proportionalism: Method or Menace?" *CTSA Proceedings* 46 (1991): 159. See also James F. Keenan, "The Function of the Principle of Double Effect," *Theological Studies* 54 (June 1993): 294–315.

37. Healy, *Moral Guidance,* pp. 18–19.

revisionist would argue that whatever lack of goodness may be involved in the man's self-stimulation to obtain sperm for the procedure is offset by the "proportionate reason" of marital fecundity. By contrast, the official Catholic teaching is that "masturbation" is intrinsically evil and therefore cannot be done for any reason. What the proportionalists would say to this argument is that the judgment about "intrinsic evil" in this case represents a formula arrived at centuries ago on the basis of a claim that self-stimulation causes evil without a proportionate reason. The historically inclined would also point out that ancient taboos concerning bodily fluids as well as beliefs that miniature human beings were contained in the male "seed" contributed to this judgment.[38] It is also worth noting that although the magisterium eschews "teleologism" and "consequentialism" where all sexual activity is concerned, one may regard its insistence that something stronger than "results" must govern decision making in this area as actually based on unacknowledged teleological thinking. Indeed, its adherence to strict "deontological" absolutes on all sexual questions is maintained at considerable cost precisely because the *results* of alternative approaches are so greatly feared.

The above discussion hardly does justice to the details of a debate that has gone on for decades, but it should provide sufficient background for appreciating why revisionists have been misrepresented in the encyclical. Their claim is that when defining an action as "intrinsically evil" in the past, what theologians and church authorities have in fact been doing is indicating that some behavior causes harm without a proportionate reason. The phrase "intrinsically evil," in short, is an evaluative one that presumes the evidence of disproportionality even when it does not articulate it. The premature introduction of the judgment of "intrinsically evil" short-circuits the reasoning process about a given action and is especially questionable when arguments are based on authority rather than on the foreseen results of the action.

Proportionalists have pointed to an inconsistency in that most Catholic moral theology has been teleological in its emphasis—reasoning about the moral quality of an action from its anticipated effects—whereas sexual matters have been treated deontologically, with absolutes defended as unqualified duty, regardless of lack of empirical verification that disproportionate harm is caused by allowing exceptions to classic norms. To a great extent the debate centers on what counts as an intellectually adequate *description* of an action, and some way beyond the impasse may eventually be found by developing a

---

38. See Philip Keane, *Sexual Morality: A Catholic Perspective* (New York: Paulist, 1977), pp. 60–61.

more complex vocabulary for certain behaviors traditionally lumped in the "intrinsically evil" category. Indeed, the pope's acknowledgment that there is an "ongoing need to discover *the most adequate formulation* for universal and permanent moral norms in the light of different cultural contexts" (#53) is promising, as are efforts by theologians to provide new terminology for various morally distinguishable actions.[39] To enhance the climate for the reception of new terminology, revisionists will do well, after denying the mistaken accusations of subjectivism and relativism, to develop arguments for change that address the implicitly teleological fears behind official intransigence on questions of sexual morality.[40]

Selective Readings of Scripture

The dialectic between freedom and law is an ancient one in Christianity, and this pope has come down heavily on the side of law, culling from the Bible texts that support making obedience (in the reductive sense of conformity to authoritative teaching) the chief expression of love for God and neighbor and the only authentic way of exercising authentic human freedom. One will find in the New Testament, however, many ideas to complement the encyclical, which combines the love mysticism of John and the law emphasis of Matthew with little regard for the teachings of Jesus and Paul on the dangers of legalism. It should also be noted that the encyclical's focal story from Matthew 19 about the rich young man who went away sad because his wealth kept him from following Jesus is primarily about "the danger of riches" and only secondarily about the value of observing the law. Indeed, reading that story in the context of Jesus' arguments with the Pharisees might suggest that the Matthean concern over the danger of riches could apply to wealth and power beyond the material order. Here Matthew's rendering of the parable of the buried and invested talents in chapter 25 is instructive. There seems to be an analogy between the fearful servant who buries his talent and the unwillingness of the Vatican to allow the natural law tradition to be invested on the open market of intellectual exchange.

39. McCormick mentions vocabulary distinctions and invites further attention to diverse experiences as a step toward advancing thought ("Some Early Reactions").

40. An example of a work that addresses such fears on the part of Catholics and Protestants alike is Patricia Beattie Jung and Ralph F. Smith's study *Heterosexism: An Ethical Challenge* (Albany: SUNY Press, 1993).

Feminists, moreover, will point out that "rich young men" have long served as paradigms of moral agency and will argue that although some powerful persons may require strict rules to prevent harm to others, it is a mistake to overgeneralize from their experience. In addition, a Lucan corrective to the encyclical's Matthean emphasis on "poverty of spirit" would insist that any moral teaching in Jesus' name must mean good news for the materially poor and oppressed, especially women and children. Finally, a Lucan text that speaks directly to the present controversy over Catholic moral theology addressed by the encyclical is absent from *Veritatis Splendor.* This is the passage from Acts 10 already mentioned at the conclusion of chapter 2 above, concerning the vision that allows the apostle Peter to abandon his hard-line position on observing the law. Peter does not believe what he hears at first and objects to the voice instructing him to change his sense of what God's requires: "But Peter said, 'By no means, Lord; for I have never eaten anything that is profane or unclean.' The voice said to him again, a second time, 'What God has made clean, you must not call profane'" (Acts 10:14–15 NRSV). As I stated earlier, the complex questions raised by new knowledge of human sexuality and new technological powers are putting in question some long-held beliefs about God's will where sexual aspects of human existence are concerned. Peter has reason to object to the wholesale rejection of a sexual ethic that has functioned relatively well for centuries, but it is also possible that God is inviting him to regard some behaviors in a new, more complex way. Most scholars would agree that this narrative of Peter's vision is a symbolic description of a momentous change in Christian understanding of God's will, which followed a period of intense argument not unlike today's dispute between revisionists and fundamentalist-leaning church officials and scholars. Although *Veritatis Splendor* would limit moral theologians to explaining and defending norms as articulated by the hierarchical magisterium, God's Spirit may well be requiring them to invite Peter "a second time" to appreciate God's freedom to ask new things of God's people.

Uncritical Theory of Truth

The most serious limitation of this encyclical that would celebrate "The Splendor of Truth" is a theological one. Repeatedly the document conflates the transcendent Truth associated with the Deity with the pronouncements of the hierarchical magisterium. Here one sees the practical import of the philosophical developments discussed above in chapter 2, developments that require a more critical and historically conscious reading of scripture and tradition than *Veritatis Splendor* promotes. Indeed, the encyclical's pervasive bias toward ecclesiastical fundamentalism invites misinterpretation of claims that are basically valid in themselves, such as the following passage that the pope quotes from his earlier encyclical *Centesimus Annus:*

> If there is no transcendent truth, in obedience to which man achieves his full identity, then there is no sure principle for guaranteeing just relations between people. Their self-interest as a class, group or nation would inevitably set them in opposition to one another. If one does not acknowledge transcendent truth, then the force of power takes over, and each person tends to make full use of the means at his disposal in order to impose his own interests or his own opinion, with no regard for the rights of others." (*Veritatis Splendor* #100)

In the context of the encyclical, these words serve to obscure the crucial distinction between "transcendent truth" and magisterial pronouncements. The revisionists who question the validity of some magisterial interpretations of "natural law" are actually *defending* the transcendence of truth over any human formulations of moral obligation. The failure to acknowledge the *transcendence* of truth lies on the other side of the argument, insofar as magisterial claims encourage the near-divinization of classic statements about "intrinsically evil actions" by implying that official interpretations of the biblical commandments should be regarded as "transcendent truth" by loyal Catholics. The extent of this legalism is apparent in the passage that reminds bishops of the seriousness involved in the "*reaffirmation of the universality and immutability of the moral commandments,* particularly those which prohibit always and without exception *intrinsically evil acts*" (#115). The word "immutability" here reflects a classic attribute of the Deity, one typical of theologies influenced by Neoplatonism. The freedom of the Deity to ask new things of human beings is denied in this apotheosis of Vatican understandings of moral obligation.

"Truth," however, is not a static object possessed by church authorities; as a transcendent reality, it represents a goal toward which all must strive. As the conciliar *Declaration on Religious Freedom* (*Dignitatis Humanae*) recognizes:

> On their part, all men are bound to seek the truth, especially in what concerns God and His Church, and to embrace the truth they come to know, and to hold fast to it.
>
> This sacred Synod likewise professes its belief that it is upon the human conscience that these obligations fall and exert their binding force. The truth cannot impose itself except by virtue of its own truth, as it makes its entrance into the mind at once quietly and with power. (#1)

There is some irony in the fact that an encyclical focused on the transcendent "splendor of truth" discourages the very quality that could lead to more convincing magisterial teaching on disputed moral questions. If the goal is truth, the path would seem to require honesty, but this is precisely the virtue being placed at risk when conformity to others' accounts of reality is made the hallmark of loyalty to the church.

MOVING BEYOND THE IMPASSE

Despite these several limitations, the encyclical remains important, especially for its emphasis on an objective approach to morality, its critique of individualism and the absolutization of autonomy, and its insistence on the unity of the spiritual and the moral life. Moreover, particularly in the disputed area of human sexuality, the pastoral *cri de coeur* ringing through *Veritatis Splendor* deserves a thoughtful response.

The fear implicit in the Vatican's holding the line on "intrinsically evil actions" seems partly a concern for protecting traditional authority by leaving official teachings on sexuality unquestioned. But it also stems from a conviction that human welfare requires a very clear and very restrictive sexual code. Catholics will do well to let go of the first concern, not only because of love of transcendent truth and trust in God's mercy but also out of a practical recognition that, at least in modern cultures, authority gains when it is willing to change in light of new data and suffers when it shows intransigence in the face of new evidence and changed circumstances.

As to the second concern, the best course is to translate the *cri de coeur* into an agenda for honest, extensive research: What are the human needs where guidelines for sexual behavior are concerned? Is it possible that these vary over the course of a lifetime? Could they be different for females and for males? For those whose attraction is primarily for the same sex and for those attracted primarily to the opposite sex? For those with more complex sorts of erotic feelings than persons who claim a basically homosexual or heterosexual orientation and female or male identity? For those with a history of childhood abuse or sexual addiction and those whose lives have been relatively free of such patterns?

To open up such a line of questioning when one has placed confidence in a tradition whose legitimate authorities have long claimed full knowledge of God's will in this area requires a profound conversion. It means turning from excessive dependence on past judgments and authority figures toward the wisdom and mercy of God, a move quite compatible with the conclusion of *Veritatis Splendor*, although not made explicit there. The encyclical ends with this prayer:

> O Mary,
> Mother of Mercy,
> watch over all people,
> that the Cross of Christ
> may not be emptied of its power,
> that man may not stray
> from the path of the good
> or become blind to sin,
> but may put his hope ever more fully in God
> who is "rich in mercy" (Eph 2:4).
> May he carry out the good works prepared
> by God beforehand (cf. Eph 2:10)
> and so live completely
> "for the praise of his glory" (Eph 1:12).

Placing hope "ever more fully in God" is precisely what is required today, and a first step is to renounce the lenses of sexism and heterosexism, which distort the picture of reality that has influenced the tradition's development. If our vision can thus grow clearer, we may see new meaning in what St. Paul wrote a few lines later in the same letter to the Ephesians. He was addressing the first-century tension between Jewish and Gentile Christians, but his insights apply also to the current controversy between "classicists" and "revisionists" on sexual questions:

> It is [Christ Jesus] who is our peace, and who made the two of us one by break-ing down the barrier of hostility that kept us apart. In his own flesh he abol-ished the law with its commands and precepts, to create in himself one new man from us who had been two and to make peace, reconciling both of us to God in one body through his cross, which put that enmity to death. (Eph. 2:14–16)

Such a change of heart was impossible for the tragic figure Creon, who had come to believe that disaster would occur if even a quiet, unceremonious burial outside the city were provided for Polyneices. But it is not too late for Peter to put to rest past claims of possessing full and certain knowledge of God's will regarding all aspects of human sexuality. It is the absolutism and universality of the claims about the meaning of sex and details of sexual behavior that are problematic, and if this can be surrendered, the classic sexual ethic still has a great deal to teach women and men who are living at the end-times of patriarchy and the dawning of an age of egalitarian-feminist values.

I have suggested in earlier chapters that the traditional sexual ethic has served a complex social, moral, and religious agenda. Here I would add the judgment that this rigorous ethic has functioned as a way of both *maintaining* and *coping with* the patriarchal social order that has characterized Christianity for most of its history. New guidelines must be developed for the post-patriarchal era, and undoubtedly pluralism will be required because human sexual reality is far more complex than past moral theology recognized. The insight with which John Mahoney concludes his history of Catholic moral theology bears repeating here: "It is the mystery of God which earths all theology and at the same time makes theological pluralism unavoidable."[41]

Human existence, which occurs in the presence of Divine Mystery, has itself been recognized as a mystery by the magisterium, but only incompletely so. "Man is a mystery to himself," the magisterium asserts, but then goes on to claim that the meaning and purpose of women and of human sexuality are quite evident, not mysterious at all, despite mystifying rhetoric on marriage, women, and family. The restoration of an *authentic* sense of mystery to the Christian moral life, especially where sex is concerned, is long overdue. Moral theologian Christine Gudorf has made this point explicitly in writing about the need for Catholic and Protestant churches alike to overcome a history of complicity in various types of sexual oppression. The churches would do well, she suggests, to learn from the attitude of awe in the face of creation manifested by those scientists who see their efforts to understand biological processes and reduce human suffering as participating in the very mystery of God. This appreciation for the mystery of creation invites an attitude of humility that can ground openness to new discoveries about the sexual dimensions of existence. Writes Gudorf:

> This is the place to begin sex education, with an appreciation of sexuality, with an understanding of its complexity and variation. Once we understand it better from biological, behavioral, psychological, and relational perspectives, then we can begin to probe sexual behavior with a focus on morality, instead of trying to conform our knowledge of sexuality to the behavioral rules we inherit, which is what too many in the churches have been doing.

Such an approach, she believes, would both reduce the number of victims

41. John Mahoney, *The Making of Moral Theology: A Study of the Roman Catholic Tradition* (Oxford: Clarendon Press, 1987), p. 337.

and "free up tremendous amounts of energy and resources to deal with other obstacles to the promotion of the kingdom."[42]

Two sorts of openness are crucial as we develop guidelines that respect the mystery, complexity, and variety of human sexuality. In the first place, there is need to be open to as full a range of scientific knowledge and human experience as possible, which will require that women's experience in various cultural situations be taken into account and that sexual differences among men be regarded with new respect. In the second place, there is need to be open to the possibility that God may "will" in our time something analogous to the acceptance of diversity that Peter came to endorse in the first century. The encyclical itself does not express such openness, but in view of the tradition's long history of accepting a plurality of styles of prayer and spiritual discipline, there is the possibility of some such development where sexual ethics is concerned latent in Pope John Paul II's emphasis on the unity of the spiritual and moral dimensions of Christian life.

THE ENDURING VOICE OF HAEMON

The above analysis affirms the validity of several main concerns of *Veritatis Splendor* but differs in the understanding of truth, moral obligation, and authority brought to these matters. The pastoral concern expressed in this encyclical tends to be of the "controlling" variety, with the authority figure seeing his task as setting up a system that will obviate disciplinary problems with theologians and at the same time reinforce a simplistic ethic of obedience to official teaching among Catholics in general. Pastoral concern, however, can express itself differently than in this authoritarian fashion, and indeed various members of the hierarchy have offered an approach to the tensions behind the encyclical that is more promising.

Bishop Kenneth Untener of Saginaw, for example, has suggested that the problems over *Humanae Vitae* provide an occasion for bishops to ask themselves some challenging questions, since "[i]n the eyes of many people, the teaching church has committed a teacher's cardinal sin: it has become more concerned about itself than about truth." He offers the analogy of maps

---

42. Christine E. Gudorf, *Victimization: Examining Christian Complicity* (Philadelphia: Trinity Press International, 1992), p. 111.

drawn by early explorers to illustrate the problem of defending ideas no longer supported by evidence:

> Picture early maps drawn by explorers of North America. You can recognize Florida, the Great Lakes, the outline of both coasts. The contours are real, not figments of their imagination, for they walked the terrain, climbed the hills, sailed the lakes and rivers. Gradually the maps changed. The terrain didn't. The maps did.
>
> They changed because others also walked the land and sailed the waters, and because new technology gave us additional data. It was the same continent, but now we knew it differently. If in the face of all this, early mapmakers insisted on the correctness of their original map and refused to listen to the cumulative experience of others who had walked the land, or refused to accept the new information provided by technology, we would begin to suspect their motives. They would appear to be more concerned about defending their map than the truth of the terrain.[43]

Other bishops have in recent years given evidence of a similar trust that it is an appropriate exercise of authority to listen to others and be affected by what they relate. Such men as Thomas Gumbleton, Rembert Weakland, Raymond Lucker, and Frank Murphy, to mention a few, have conveyed a willingness to acknowledge that certain questions must remain open despite a Vatican preference for considering them settled. Bishop Gumbleton, a leader in the peace movement, has also promoted the church's reconsideration of homosexuality, and Archbishop Weakland has voiced his willingness to ask the pope's permission to ordain a married man to the priesthood if the needs of a eucharistic community would otherwise be unmet.[44] Weakland also showed a courageous approach to episcopal leadership by listening to a variety of women's positions on abortion during six sessions in Milwaukee in the spring of 1990. He continued to affirm official teaching on this topic, but acknowledged that his way of presenting this doctrine would be affected by what he had learned.[45] Prior to the 1994 papal letter officially banning discussion of

43. Bishop Kenneth Untener, *"Humanae Vitae:* What Has It Done to Us?" *Commonweal* (June 18, 1994): 12.

44. Gumbleton's interest in this matter developed as the result of a question posed by his mother: Would his brother be damned because of homosexuality? (Reported by Tom Roberts in the *National Catholic Reporter,* November 4, 1994). Weakland's pastoral position was reported by Peter Steinfels in the *New York Times,* January 9, 1991.

45. Findings from these sessions were published in the archdiocesan newspaper as well as *Origins* 20 (May 31, 1990): 33–39.

women's ordination, both Bishop Lucker and Bishop Murphy had published articles dealing with this question. Lucker outlined a challenging reform agenda in a 1991 article entitled "Justice in the Church," pointing to the need to overcome institutionalized racism and sexism and calling the fact that women's ordination cannot be discussed "a sign of injustice."[46] The following year Murphy advocated the scholarly study of this issue as well as reconsideration of the ban on artificial contraception. He also went on record as "personally in favor of the ordination of women into a renewed priestly ministry," adding that "[w]omen's calls, as well as men's should be tested. Justice demands it. The pastoral needs of the church require it."[47]

These bishops are deeply loyal to the church and to their episcopal vocation, which they recognize is one of promoting unity and teaching authentically. Instead of seeing uniformity as the essence of unity or conformity as the hallmark of loyalty, however, they understand their pastoral duties in more complex ways. None would deny the primacy and authority of the Petrine office, but neither would they confuse papal opinion with the transcendent will of God nor abdicate their collegial duty to express their own views on what is true and good for the church.

In an eloquent address to the Catholic Theological Society of America in 1989, the late archbishop of St. Louis, John L. May, identified the spiritual problem that inhibits love, trust, and honesty in the church:

> I think there is too much fear in the church today. Nameless accusations and ungrounded suspicions threaten to divide bishops from theologians and theologians from bishops, debilitating our attempts to support one another in our specific ministries for the good of the church. This climate of fear could come to stifle our collaborative initiatives under a pall of anxiety that will not dissipate —unless we determine that we have had enough of it.[48]

Such a determination is evinced in the words Untener addressed to his episcopal colleagues in 1990, when commenting on some proposed guidelines for teaching about sexuality and birth control:

46. Raymond A. Lucker, "Justice in the Church: The Church as an Example," in *One Hundred Years of Catholic Social Thought,* ed. John A. Coleman (Maryknoll, N.Y.: Orbis, 1991), p. 100.

47. P. Francis Murphy, "Let's Start Over: A Bishop Appraises the Pastoral," *Commonweal* (September 25, 1992): 14.

48. Archbishop John L. May, "Address of Welcome," *CTSA Proceedings* 44 (1989): 191.

We also say, "it is our earnest belief that God's Spirit is acting through the mag-isterium . . . in developing this doctrine." This is true, but it is not the entire truth. It is also the earnest belief of our church that the Spirit acts through the entire people of God in developing doctrine. . . . Do we have adequate struc-tures and procedures to listen to the *sensus fidelium*, particularly on this issue? . . . [W]e call for those who dissent to study and pray over their position. Could they not say to us, "We will, if you will . . . and let's do it together?" Would such a process weaken the authority of bishops, or would it in fact strengthen it?[49]

One hopes that, unlike Creon, Vatican authorities will come to acknowl-edge that dissent among so many faithful Catholics is not a problem to be controlled but a reality to be respected

49. Untener, "*Humanae Vitae*," p. 14.

CHAPTER SIX

Toward Liberating Conscience:
Spirituality and
Moral Responsibility

> If I attend properly I will have no choices, and this is the ultimate condition to be aimed at. . . . By the time the moment of choice has arrived the quality of attention has probably determined the nature of the act."
>
> —Iris Murdoch[1]

Despite the difficulties with certain aspects of Pope John Paul II's encyclical *Veritatis Splendor*, the document's pastoral insights remain important. Paramount among these are, first, the recognition that much harm in our world is traceable to the uncritical celebration of individual liberty in modern society, and, second, the insistence that true fulfillment comes not from unbridled subjectivism but rather from the commitment to express one's freedom in a transcendent and relational context. As a pastoral document, the encyclical seeks to inspire moral seriousness and a life of loving discipleship. To avoid the reductive legalism it unfortunately promotes, a good strategy is to interpret its discussions of "law" less literally than the text itself tends to do, at the same time distinguishing two broad types of norms that are conflated in the encyclical.

The Oxford theologian Herbert McCabe offers a helpful metaphor for thinking about these things in his article on *Veritatis Splendor,* "Manuals and Rule Books," which was treated briefly in the last chapter and warrants further attention here. Building on an analogy between human life and games

---

1. Iris Murdoch, *The Sovereignty of Good* (New York: Schocken Books, 1971), pp. 40, 67. My use of these sentences was suggested by Martin Price's treatment of Murdoch in *Forms of Life: Character and Moral Imagination in the Novel* (New Haven: Yale University Press, 1983), p. 153.

such as football, McCabe points out that a *rule book* is necessary to set the norms for what the game entails, while a quite different sort of text, a *training manual*, offers instruction designed to help one learn to play the game well:

> Like a game, [human life] is difficult and challenging, involves successful and unsuccessful play; and like a game, it has boundaries, to transgress which means playing some other game which is not what human life is about; and these boundaries and transgressions can be set forth as rules. But human living demands, above all, skills transmitted through education, especially those called virtues: skills in doing all things as befits a good human being. . . . [V]irtues have to be acquired by our learning from each other or the Holy Spirit or both.[2]

This distinction between a rule book that establishes basic norms for what counts as properly human behavior and a training manual that offers disciplines designed to strengthen virtue is useful for moral theology because it balances concern for maintaining universal principles with concern for respecting the differences among individuals. Whereas such general principles as "do not commit rape or murder" apply to everyone, guidelines for developing good habits of character will vary according to the needs of persons. In other words, just as training in a sport involves drills that address weaknesses of specific individuals, so moral advice corrects dispositions and traits that impede an individual's practice of justice and charity.

At this point it is useful to approach the issues with the aid of an additional metaphor. If we appreciate the "law" (or basic rule book) as a symbol of the claims that the reality transcending each individual makes upon that individual, we may regard the "training manual" as functioning like a set of corrective lenses, which we require to offset the visual distortions inhibiting our ability to "read" the situations that call for response on our part.[3] This imaginative strategy also accommodates pluralism, for nobody assumes that the same strength of eyeglasses is helpful for an entire population. The analogy has limits, of course, but it can help us understand why the detailed codes that evolved over

2. Herbert McCabe, "Manuals and Rule Books," *The Tablet* [London], December 18, 1993, p. 1649.

3. Citing the influence of William F. May, Richard A. McCormick has entitled a recent book, *Corrective Vision: Explorations in Moral Theology* (Kansas City, Mo.: Sheed & Ward, 1994). McCormick declares in the introduction that "opening people's eyes to dimensions of reality they may have missed" is an essential purpose of moral theology (p. vii). My development of the concept takes the metaphor in a somewhat different direction but may well have been influenced by McCormick's title.

centuries of experience with the human heart need to be assessed in light of their effectiveness in guiding diverse persons along a path of virtue.

As soon as we recognize the need for different "training programs" or "eyeglasses," we are entering the realm of ethical guidance rather than universal moral teaching. Indeed, the need for such a move suggests that the Catholic tradition may be coming full circle to the practice that gave rise to the discipline of moral theology in the first place. Historians agree that moral theology arose in response to the practice of individual confession, which itself developed out of the monastic tradition of mentoring the spiritual growth of individuals.[4] Interestingly enough, the recent decline in frequency of sacramental confession among Catholics has been accompanied by an increase in the practice of seeking and providing spiritual direction. The practice is far from universal, however, and tends to be linked with the educated classes, and especially persons with ties to communities of vowed religious. Because access to competent spiritual guidance is presently so limited, one can appreciate why church officials hesitate to announce a tolerance for pluralism in disputed moral areas, particularly sexual ethics. The stakes are high, and the secular culture's sexual permissiveness has not contributed to much growth in virtue in our time. The more permissive cultural situation has, however, contributed to considerable growth in *knowledge,* since the ability of twentieth-century scientists to study sexuality and report their research to the public has made available data that were not known in the past. This new knowledge has put in question some long-standing beliefs and has increased pressures for adjustment in Catholic sexual teachings, leading to the developments in moral theology that occasioned the encyclical's reassertion of official authority and traditional norms.

In light of these developments, in this chapter I first discuss how a renewed spirituality can offer a way beyond the impasse between conscience and authority that *Veritatis Splendor* tends to reinforce. Then, after suggesting that a liberationist spirituality can help overcome the passivity fostered by authoritarian moral training, I next invite reconsideration of the notion of moral responsibility itself, giving particular attention to the findings of research about the socialization of women. There follows a description of the several elements involved in the moral life of Christians, which are mapped and analyzed with the concerns of a spirituality of justice in mind. Finally, these

4. John Mahoney reviews this history in *The Making of Moral Theology: A Study of the Roman Catholic Tradition* (Oxford: Clarendon Press, 1987), pp. 1-36. See also John A. Gallagher, *Time Past, Time Future* (New York: Paulist, 1990).

themes are drawn together in a discussion of attentiveness and solidarity with victims, which concludes with a close look at the significance of biblical references to Rachel, a woman who laments her losses and longs for a message of hope.

ETHICS, SPIRITUALITY, AND RELIGIOUS TRANSFORMATION

Is there a way beyond the "sterile polarisation of 'legalism' and 'liberalism'" that McCabe finds reinforced in *Veritatis Splendor?* The words with which he concludes his critique suggest an answer:

> You cannot fit the virtues into a legal structure without reducing them to dispositions to follow the rules. You can, however, fit law and obedience to law into a comfortable, though minor niche in the project of growing up in the rich and variegated life of virtue. It is a pity that a major attempt to restate Christian morality should not have tapped the resources of a more ancient Aristotelian tradition, such as St. Thomas inherited and transformed, which sees human life as the movement towards our real selves and towards God guided by the New Law which, as he insists, is no written code but nothing other than the presence in us of the Holy Spirit.[5]

The theological affirmation that our guide to goodness is not in the end a list of commandments or objectively wrong behaviors but "the presence in us of the Holy Spirit" provides the answer to the problems of legalism and obsession with proving the universal validity of classical rules for sexual conduct, as well as the safeguard against relativism and subjectivism. The belief that God's Spirit dwells in us grounds our hope that openness to new data and the cautious revision of sexual ethics it requires will not lead to disaster, but simply to a new stage on our pilgrimage through history. Indeed, this affirmation of "the presence in us of the Holy Spirit" also highlights a recognition shared by *Veritatis Splendor,* the *Catechism of the Catholic Church,* revisionist moral theologians, and many feminists from diverse traditions—namely, that spirituality and ethics are intimately connected. As the new catechism succinctly states, "the moral life is spiritual worship" (#2047). In fact, spirituality is foundational to both theology and morality, for it constitutes, as Anne E. Carr puts it, "the experience out of which both derive as a human response."[6]

---

5. McCabe, "Manuals and Rule Books," p. 1650.

6. Anne E. Carr, *Transforming Grace: Christian Tradition and Women's Experience* (San Francisco: Harper & Row, 1988), p. 202.

Although this point may seem merely a truism, it carries important implications for the project of reconstructing moral theology. As I have mentioned, the tradition's respect for pluralism where the spiritual life is concerned offers a basis for recognizing some diversity in morality as well. Moreover, much recent literature on spirituality expresses the paradigm shift from patriarchal to egalitarian-feminist understandings of goodness, as well as newer interpretations of crucial religious doctrines such as grace and salvation. These developments affect moral theology quite directly, for a spiritual vision is what inspires and sustains ethical behavior among religious persons.

For various reasons, separate disciplines of moral and spiritual theology arose in Catholic contexts, with the latter taking on remarkably new contours in recent decades. In fact, so dramatic have been the post-Vatican II developments in the area once called spiritual theology that it has evolved into something of a new discipline, now called "spirituality."[7] Among ordinary Catholics, spirituality has been a most attractive subject, as the popularity of publications, conferences, and study programs in this area testifies. As theologian Joann Wolski Conn has noted, "[r]eligious publishers are selling more books about spirituality than any other kind."[8] In contrast to other theological disciplines, spirituality (and to some extent its predecessor, spiritual theology) has functioned to create a space where religious experience is free to interpret and express itself. Its tolerance for pluralism is evident in our speech, which has long distinguished, for example, Ignatian, Franciscan, and Benedictine forms of spirituality without ranking their acceptability. One never hears, by contrast, of Norbertine morality or Dominican ethics, for pluralism has *not* been tolerated in this arena. In the realm of doctrine (studied by dogmatic or systematic theology) and morals (studied by moral theology or ethics) the magisterium has insisted on uniformity, but in matters of spirituality we have enjoyed some liberty to search, experiment, and discern without pressure to be "correct" at every juncture. It is this feature of the discipline

7. Important recent discussions of these matters include Walter H. Principe, "Toward Defining Spirituality," *Studies in Religion/Sciences Religieuses* 12 (1983): 127–41; Sandra M. Schneiders, "Spirituality in the Academy," *Theological Studies* 50 (1989): 676–97; and Joann Wolski Conn, "Toward Spiritual Maturity," in *Freeing Theology: The Essentials of Theology in Feminist Perspective*, ed. Catherine LaCugna (San Francisco: HarperSanFrancisco, 1993), pp. 235–59. See also Michael Downey, ed., *The New Dictionary of Catholic Spirituality* (Collegeville, Minn.: Liturgical Press, 1993), especially s.vv. "Feminist Spirituality," by Sandra M. Schneiders; "Spirituality, Christian," by Walter H. Principe; and "Spirituality, Christian (Catholic), History of," by Richard Woods.

8. Conn, "Toward Spiritual Maturity," p. 235.

that makes spirituality so appealing to persons who have experienced religious authority as overly controlling in some aspects of life.

Another factor contributing to widespread interest in spirituality is that this area reflects the religious paradigm shift now in progress in Western Christian culture. In addition to what has been said in the second and third chapters about this development, I would stress here the growing sense of historical consciousness that has affected Catholics in our day. As we have come to realize that even long-standing institutions and doctrines are products of human culture that did not always exist in their present forms, our interest in social justice (always part of the tradition, but particularly stressed in modern papal encyclicals beginning with *Rerum Novarum* in 1891) has gained new impetus.[9] Once we appreciate how much change has occurred in the past, we find it easier to dream of alternative futures, or utopias, and to take action to realize the values of these ideal visions within present circumstances. In this century we have seen the effects of historical consciousness not only in the many struggles for liberation from colonial oppression around the globe but also in the movements for racial justice, equal rights for women, and care of the environment. Just as Ptolemaic astronomy eventually gave way to a more adequate model for understanding the solar system, so also a paradigm for Christian living that stressed an otherworldly, elitist, and individualistic form of spirituality is yielding in our day to a more integral vision of what authentic discipleship requires. The eclipse of the former paradigm by the newer model is by no means complete, but it is clear from the literature of contemporary spirituality that very different interpretations of God and the Christian life are now widely accepted.[10]

Spirituality is coming to be seen as concerned not only with prayer and pious practices but with the whole of the Christian religious life. Moreover, the latter is understood not merely as the vowed "state of perfection," but as

9. I probe these matters in "Ethics and Spirituality: The Social Justice Connection," *The Way* (Supplement 63, 1988): 103–16.

10. Joann Wolski Conn describes the shift in terms of a transition "from individualism, hierarchy, and male centeredness to a new paradigm of interdependence, mutuality, and inclusiveness" ("Toward Spiritual Maturity," p. 253). Elsewhere she lists these characteristics of contemporary work in spirituality: "sustained attention to feminist issues, concern for the link between prayer and social justice, reliance on classical sources for answers to current questions, recognition of the value of developmental psychology and its understanding of the 'self,' and agreement that experience is the most appropriate starting point" (*Spirituality and Personal Maturity* [New York: Paulist, 1989], p. 31).

the graced reality of all the baptized. In addition, since the Second Vatican Council, Catholics have come to appreciate the spiritualities of other religious traditions, as well as those of persons whose spirituality takes a "nonreligious" form, for example, secular feminists or peace activists. In sum, the compass of what counts under the heading of spirituality has grown considerably in recent decades, and there has been greater affirmation of worldly values and appreciation for pluralism of experience and perspective.

Whereas the pre–Vatican II view was more otherworldly and stressed the relationship between an individual's soul and God, the newer view emphasizes that God is immanent in all relationships and expresses a much greater esteem for the earth and for human embodiment and sexuality. As African-American liberation theologian Toinette Eugene has observed, "Spirituality is no longer identified simply with asceticism, mysticism, the practice of virtue, and methods of prayer. Spirituality, i.e., the human capacity to be self-transcending, relational, and freely committed, encompasses all of life, including our human sexuality."[11] This trend is evident in recent works such as Joan Timmerman's *Sexuality and Spiritual Growth* and Christine Gudorf's *Body, Sex, and Pleasure.* Timmerman describes the relation between spirituality and sexuality as sacramental and observes that "a lifestyle conducive to spiritual growth will be characterized by a number of qualities, including progress toward personal freedom, increased capacity for intimacy, and an environment in which ecstasy is possible."[12] Gudorf's book, which seeks to reconstruct Christian sexual ethics on the basis of a radically incarnational theology that rejects body/soul dualism, concludes with a chapter entitled "Regrounding Spirituality in Embodiment."[13]

11. Toinette Eugene, "While Love Is Unfashionable: An Exploration of Black Spirituality and Sexuality," in *Women's Consciousness, Women's Conscience,* ed. Barbara Hilkert Andolsen et al. (Minneapolis: Winston Press, 1985), p. 124. Similarly, at the conclusion of her 1989 study of the medieval mystics Hildegard of Bingen and Hadewijch of Antwerp, historical theologian Elizabeth Dreyer argues that the contemporary task is to transcend the Neoplatonic tendency to see matter, embodiment, and sex as antagonistic to the spiritual life and "to look toward sexuality as an important locus and model for our spiritual lives" (*Passionate Women: Two Medieval Mystics* [New York: Paulist, 1989], p. 73).

12. Joan H. Timmerman, *Sexuality and Spiritual Growth* (New York: Crossroad, 1992), p. 34.

13. Christine E. Gudorf, *Body, Sex, and Pleasure: Reconstructing Christian Sexual Ethics* (Cleveland, Oh.: Pilgrim, 1994). For historical studies related to these concerns, see Elizabeth Dreyer, *Passionate Women;* and Margaret R. Miles, *Practicing Christianity: Critical Perspectives for an Embodied Spirituality* (New York: Crossroad, 1988).

For these and many other contemporary thinkers, God's relation to creation is seen not primarily as one of domination and control but as one of energizing and nurturance. In *She Who Is,* Elizabeth Johnson objects to the classical depiction of the divine in terms of "dominating power" thus:

> Is this idea of God not the reflection of patriarchal imagination, which prizes nothing more than unopposed power-over and unquestioned loyalty? Is not the transcendent, omnipotent, impassible symbol of God the quintessential embodiment of the solitary ruling male ego, above the fray, perfectly happy in himself, filled with power in the face of the obstreperousness of others?[14]

Reflection on women's experiences of power leads Johnson to offer a "resymbolization of divine power not as dominative or controlling power, nor as dialectical power in weakness, nor simply as persuasive power, but as the liberating power of connectedness that is effective in compassionate love."[15]

Although operating out of a different context, systematic theologian Matthew Lamb similarly rejects images of divine domination:

> The creative act of Infinite Intelligence-Love is not that of a dominating engineer or of a manipulating imperial bureaucrat imposing order upon all of creation in spite of itself. Rather . . . [t]he infinitely free creative act of God informs all spatio-temporal events—the concrete whole of the created universe—with orientations toward the freedom of intelligence, truth, responsibility, and compassionate love. Such a consciousness of God gives an ultimate meaning and value to the human drama in which we all participate.[16]

According to this approach, God's valuing of our earthly existence fills history with intrinsic meaning. This carries implications for Christian life quite different from those obtaining when earthly existence was regarded mainly as a testing period preliminary to "real" fulfillment in the afterlife.

Our understanding of grace is likewise being transformed. Instead of tending to image grace in concrete, reified terms as some sort of "thing" needed for admittance into heaven, we are coming to understand grace in personal terms, through images of presence and empowerment. Roger Haight, in fact,

---

14. Elizabeth A. Johnson, *She Who Is: The Mystery of God in Feminist Theological Discourse* (New York: Crossroad, 1992), p. 21.

15. Ibid., p. 270.

16. Matthew Lamb, "Christian Spirituality and Social Justice," *Horizons* 10 (1983): 37. This essay, developed out of concern over the arms race and the threat of nuclear destruction, objects to the "privatized" spirituality of modern culture, which relegated spirituality to "an ethereal type of private mysticism, while social justice was left to pressure-group politics" (p. 34).

makes a convincing case for regarding grace as simply another name for the "Spirit of God." The latter term, he points out, is "the biblical symbol for God's power immanent in the universe":

> [The Spirit of God] is the power of life in the Old Testament and applies especially to God's power as it is manifest in human beings. In Christian tradition, the Spirit is the immanent power of God working in human beings, inspiring, turning one to God, providing the basic energy for one's faith and movement toward God.[17]

FROM OTHERWORLDLINESS TO HISTORICAL AFFIRMATION

Accompanying the newer understandings of God and grace are the changes in ideals for Christian life discussed in chapter 3. Whereas the spirituality of otherworldliness reinforced individualism and implicitly supplied a rationale for avoiding concern for justice and ecology, the newer approach considers these matters to be at the heart of discipleship. This is reflected in the various ways of describing this spirituality, including "creation-centered," "liberationist," "womanist," "*mujerista*," "feminist," and "ecofeminist." There are, of course, important differences among thinkers who claim these designations, but all share an appreciation for history and embodiment that contrasts markedly with the approach to spirituality dominant in the first half of this century.

In a chapter on spirituality in his volume *An Alternative Vision: An Interpretation of Liberation Theology,* Roger Haight perceptively distinguishes this newer spirituality from "one-sided" forms that tend to affirm one half of a polar tension at the expense of the other, whereas liberationist spirituality affirms both poles of the tension at once. Thus, preconciliar spirituality stressed the divine transcendence at the expense of God's immanence, affirmed the spiritual by denigrating the physical and material, favored contemplation over action, and emphasized the individual without due regard for social context. Liberationist spirituality, by contrast, "insists that contact

---

17. Roger Haight, *An Alternative Vision: An Interpretation of Liberation Theology* (New York: Paulist, 1985), p. 141. Here Haight is building on Karl Rahner's theology of the Holy Spirit, which is discussed in the latter's *Foundations of Christian Faith* (1976; trans. William Dych; New York: Seabury, 1978), pp. 316–18.

with the transcendent God in prayer and other cultic activity does not 'leave the world behind' but rather bestows an absolute depth and seriousness precisely to our life in this world." Second, the liberationist approach rejects residual body-soul dualism, and regards spirituality itself as "living a corporeal and bodily existence in the world according to the Spirit of God."[18] As the Dominican writer Richard Woods has observed, despite the way Christians have been slow to accept their bodiliness, the fact is that according to Matthew's Gospel (Matt. 25:31–46),

> final judgment on our discipleship will not be based on orthodoxy of belief or even regular attendance at religious services, but on how we treated one another's bodies—especially those of the poor. Things like adequate food, clothing, shelter and medicine are not merely expedient. They matter. There is no access to the minds and souls of people—or to the kingdom of heaven— except through bodies. Outside the flesh, there is no salvation.[19]

Finally, with respect to the third and fourth polarities, Haight observes that liberation spirituality insists on the "formula of contemplation in action" and rejects "privatization and individualism by stressing the social constitution of the person and the social dimension of human freedom."[20]

Undoubtedly there have been saints and scholars in the past who affirmed all of these tensions, but their influence was considerably offset by the dominant strain of anti-body sentiment in Western Christian thought. As historical theologian Margaret R. Miles observes:

> The nuclear world is at least partly the product of a tradition in which human bodies have not been sufficiently valued in spite of doctrines of creation, Incarnation, and resurrection of the body that would seem to affirm human body-selves. Oddly, these central tenets of Christian faith do not seem as characteristic of Christianity as centuries of practical advice to deny, despise, and even to damage one's body in harsh ascetic practices. The notion of human transcendence over the material conditions of human life has created some endemic problems in Christian tradition, problems that perhaps have only become fully visible and urgently pressing in the contemporary world.[21]

18. Haight, *Alternative Vision*, pp. 237–38.

19. Richard Woods, "If God Wanted Us To Be Angels, He Wouldn't Have Clipped Our Wings," *National Catholic Reporter* (July 29, 1988): 12–13. For a survey of literature dealing with attitudes on embodiment at various historical stages, see James F. Keenan, "Christian Perspectives on the Human Body," *Theological Studies* 55 (1994): 330–46.

20. Haight, *Alternative Vision*, pp. 238–39.

21. Miles, *Practicing Christianity*, p. 13.

Although the current shift from what may be called an otherworldly spirituality of *Pilgrim's Progress* to a this-worldly spirituality of historical affirmation is neither complete nor proceeding without controversy, a consensus is growing in favor of the new model. Spirituality is no longer relegated to the cloister, and matters of ecology and economic justice are increasingly seen as central to Christian discipleship.

As these emphases are affirmed, it will be important to keep in mind the ideal of *balance,* so well expressed by Haight's imagery of polar tensions. Otherwise we will fall into an oversimplified notion of progress that fails to do justice to the positive aspects of past configurations of the Christian life. It will not be wise, for example, to celebrate material and worldly values to the point where a transcendent dimension to history is lost from sight, which would effectively deny the central affirmation of faith that our inevitable suffering and death are not grounds for despair but passages into the mystery of risen life in Christ. An adequate spirituality requires a vista beyond the present world as well as the passionate affirmation of creation. Like earlier efforts, the new model of spirituality remains finite; however much an improvement over the recent past, and however necessary for our era, this model can never do complete justice to the realities it tries to convey. There will remain an ongoing need to revise the best efforts of feminists and other liberation theologians to articulate a model for the Christian life.

IMPLICATIONS FOR MORAL THEOLOGY

The surge of popular interest in spirituality and the burgeoning of this transformed academic field are of great relevance to the renewal of moral theology called for by the Second Vatican Council. The conciliar "Decree on Priestly Formation," *Optatem Totius* (#16), states:

> Special attention needs to be given to the development of moral theology. Its scientific exposition should be more thoroughly nourished by scriptural teaching. It should show the nobility of the Christian vocation of the faithful, and their obligation to bring forth fruit in charity for the life of the world.

This mandate's emphasis on scriptural nourishment and Christian vocation suggests that a renewed moral theology will make its connections with spirituality more evident, which entails a high level of collaboration between experts in both disciplines.[22] Moreover, the delineation of obligation in terms

22. Many scholars have called for greater collaboration between experts in spirituality and moral theology. Denise Lardner Carmody, for example, observes in *Virtuous Woman: Reflec-*

of practical benefit to the world invites spirituality and ethics both to go beyond concentration on subjective states and experiences to the *effects* of our attitudes and choices on others. This shift of emphasis parallels the more general trend in Christian ethics, already mentioned in chapter 3, to interpret matters more in terms of "responsibility" than in terms of "obedience." Indeed, a liberationist form of the ethics of responsibility holds great promise for integrating the domains of personal and social transformation, a task often neglected in the past. Noting that today's global concerns require that we overcome our cultural conditioning to passivity, Miles perceptively declares, "A life before God in our time requires a degree of social responsibility far greater than that recognized by most historical Christian writers."[23]

A 1995 incident in Minnesota exemplifies this need for greater social responsibility. On Sunday morning, May 7, David DeMatthew boarded a city bus carrying a loaded assault rifle and rode to the Minneapolis-St. Paul airport, where he recklessly fired forty-three rounds of ammunition in the baggage claim area. He was subdued by police before anyone was injured, but the incident might have ended disastrously. Two items in the *St. Paul Pioneer Press* for May 9 comment on the episode in ways that are instructive for moral theology.

The first response was an editorial that asked how a man with such a troubled psychological history could have obtained an assault weapon, and how the bus passengers could have failed to notify authorities about the danger he presented. The second was a cartoon that shed considerable light on the case. It depicted a young man on a shooting rampage near a luggage carousel, with two older men off to the side preoccupied with their own conversation. One of these wore the logo of the National Rifle Association on his cap and declared through his tears to the other, "I always get misty-eyed watching someone exercise their 2nd amendment rights."[24]

---

tions on Christian Feminist Ethics (Maryknoll, N.Y.: Orbis, 1992), that "moralists would be wise to join forces with ascetical and mystical theologians to clarify the processes through which people's consciousnesses become converted, enlightened, sanctified" (p. 106). Psychologist Sidney Callahan has contributed a valuable resource for such collaboration in her study *In Good Conscience: Reason and Emotion in Moral Decision Making* (San Francisco: HarperSanFrancisco, 1991).

23. Miles, *Practicing Christianity,* p. 3.

24. In an editorial column following up on this cartoon, it was noted that Kirk Anderson's cartoon had received "more calls from angry readers" than any in the last thirteen years (*St. Paul Pioneer Press,* May 14, 1995). Many callers claimed membership in the National Rifle Association.

The editorial commented on why the bus passengers had not done anything about the man carrying an unconcealed assault rifle, opining that perhaps they had not thought to call the police because they were uncertain whether or not DeMatthew was breaking the law:

> All anyone would have had to do would have been to exit the bus, pick up a phone and call 911. Has the law become so confused as to what is legal and illegal about carrying and displaying guns that the public is paralyzed?
>
> Let there be no mistake, no confusion. It is illegal in this state to carry a rifle or shotgun in a public place unless it is unloaded and covered in a gun case. Fellow passengers on the bus ride with DeMatthew Sunday said he made no effort to conceal the rifle.
>
> Luck, fast reactions and professional cool by airport police kept this from being a mass murder of unthinkable proportions. Would that others had acted more responsibly earlier. (page 8-A)

This incident, which came within weeks of the bombing of the federal building in Oklahoma City that took 168 lives on April 19, 1995, is of significance for moral theology for two reasons. In the first place, it dramatically calls attention to the permissiveness of our society where weapons are concerned, in the process implying that citizens and religious leaders who ought to know better have been complicit in allowing such situations to develop. Sadly, despite clear teaching on the dignity and value of human life, Catholics share in this complicity. Our theologians and church leaders have made some efforts to address the moral and policy issues of gun control, but these are remarkably weak compared to the attention given for decades to the policy issues surrounding abortion and, more recently, euthanasia.[25]

In the second place, the incident shows that theoretical positions about the nature of moral responsibility have very practical implications for our lives. As the *Pioneer Press* editorial concludes, citizens ought to have acted "more responsibly." But what does that mean? If acting responsibly means keeping the law and fulfilling the duties of their state in life, people can hardly be faulted for riding peacefully on a bus to church, work, or the shopping mall. There is no law on the books stipulating that citizens must know the regulations concerning guns and notify police when they see someone in violation of these regulations. Nor have catechetical materials prepared people to recognize such situations as instances where God is enabling and requiring them

---

25. In November 1994 the U.S. bishops called for Catholics to "reorganize our priorities and recommit our resources to confront the violence in our midst" ("Confronting a Culture of Violence," *Origins* 24 [December 1, 1994]: 425).

to act for the benefit of others. Indeed, a legalistic approach to the Christian moral life inspires no action in this case, and this is the problem with laying so much stress on the commandments and definitions of "intrinsically evil" actions that a whole range of significant behaviors is excluded from attention.

Many factors beyond Christian moral training could have contributed to the passivity of these passengers, who may have come from various religious and secular backgrounds. Nevertheless, their inaction illustrates the passivity that legalistic moral training of any sort cultivates so well. Moreover, since the population of Minnesota is predominantly Christian, it is reasonable to assume that some passengers knew the parable of the Good Samaritan, but they failed to apply its lesson to their situation. In this case, taking action to prevent injury to strangers was the moral ideal for a disciple, or for any human being, but no one approached this ideal.

What are we to think of this incident? Why did the persons who might have prevented great harm make no effort to do so? To answer this question by simply pointing to the weakness and sinfulness of human nature—"People are just naturally selfish and unwilling to get involved"—is to cut off hope for improving things. A better approach is to probe for more precise reasons, ones that may suggest some remedies. It will prove useful, for instance, to look closely at the way the term "responsibility" functions in moral thought, for we shall discover here a complexity not apparent at first glance.

RETHINKING RESPONSIBILITY

Although the term "responsibility" was used only occasionally and in limited contexts by ethicists prior to World War II, it has risen to great prominence in moral discourse in the latter half of the twentieth century. Indeed, to some extent it has eclipsed the emphasis on duty and obedience that dominated ethical reflection before ex-Nazis attempted to defend their atrocities on the grounds of "following orders." Thus, the concept of responsibility came into favor among theorists of the moral life, functioning as the central category in the ethics of such influential Christian thinkers as Dietrich Bonhoeffer, H. Richard Niebuhr, and Bernard Häring.[26] Nevertheless, despite

26. For a discussion of this development, see Albert R. Jonsen, *Responsibility in Modern Religious Ethics* (Washington, D.C.: Corpus Books, 1968). In *Free and Faithful in Christ* (New York: Seabury, 1978), Bernard Häring discusses explicit links between "creative liberty" and "fidelity in responsibility" (1:59–103).

this shift in terminology, until there are changes in society and in the socialization of women and men, responsibility language can itself be problematic.
Theorists may have one thing in mind when they employ the language of
responsibility, but those who hear the term will interpret it according to their
own experience. Humorist Garrison Keillor's naming of the Catholic church
in the mythical town of Lake Wobegon "Our Lady of Perpetual Responsibility" reflects this general situation, and research in several fields attests to particular difficulties where women are concerned. To help close the gap
between new terminology and new ways of being and behaving, I suggest that
we may profitably distinguish two basic types of responsibility—passive and
creative.

Passive responsibility involves being dutiful and living up to the demands
of one's roles. Creative responsibility looks beyond the predefined role
descriptions of the "good Catholic," "the good homemaker," and the like and
sees a myriad of needs and possibilities for action—indeed, a world calling for
transformation. Creative responsibility involves being conscientious in pre-
venting harm and promoting good through realistic appraisal of the likely
consequences of our decisions, and it entails the willingness to act without
absolute assurance of being right. Instead of relying entirely on others' formulas for behavior, one does one's own interpreting of what is going on and one's
own analysis of how to prevent or minimize harm and contribute to the
betterment of life for oneself and one's neighbors. This by no means rules out
benefiting from the wisdom of others, but it does rule out abdicating one's
judgment to outside authorities. The price of creative responsibility is substantial. One risks being mistaken, being criticized, losing approval and
status. But the rewards are high, including an enhanced sense of self-esteem
that comes from using one's powers, and a sense of being a full adult participant in life rather than a minor who is only marginally involved in shaping
one's self and the contexts of one's life. In addition, the larger society also
stands to gain when the creative energies of individuals are available for the
concerns of the common good.

Both types of responsibility have their usefulness, like the white keys and
the black keys on the piano. The problem is that our socialization has
equipped us too well for the one, and very poorly for the other. Women and
men alike have been damaged by forms of moral training that deny or minimize the agent's role in recognizing obligations and in balancing obligations
that are experienced as being in conflict. Women, however, face particular
problems because of the socialization typically provided females in this culture, which fosters passivity and stifles growth toward exercising power and

creative responsibility. Thinkers from a range of disciplines have analyzed this problematic situation, and the research of three representative scholars will illustrate its dimensions. These include sociologist Virginia Sapiro, philosopher Madonna Kolbenschlag, and psychologist Carol Gilligan.

WOMEN'S SOCIALIZATION AND RESPONSIBILITY

In a 1983 study entitled *The Political Integration of Women,* sociologist Virginia Sapiro set out to discover why, more than sixty years after gaining the vote in this country, women were still so marginal to American political life.[27] She had administered questionnaires to girls in school and to adult women and compared the results. Her finding was that the girls felt very knowledgeable and self-confident about politics and their potential for affecting the world, but the women had lost this sense of capability. Why? The hypothesis providing the best answer to this question was that the *responsibilities* associated with women's adult roles—wife, mother, homemaker—contribute directly to our political marginality. Sapiro's research suggests a variation on the Sleeping Beauty motif. It is as if young girls are energetic and active but tend to be enchanted into passivity and powerlessness as they approach the roles of adult women. Because they *know* that women are not supposed to be president or bishop, they begin to lose self-esteem and lower their aspirations. Why are there so few women in the U.S. Senate? Why are there none running for president? Sapiro's research into the reasons why women's political involvement continues to be so small compared to our numbers points to one key culprit, which she terms "privatization." Privatization involves the mindset that women are intended to center their lives on traditionally "feminine" concerns, mainly domestic and nurturing ones, with the result that we are perceived and we see ourselves as not really capable of effective action on broader matters.

It is obvious that Sapiro is talking about the passive type of responsibility when she says such things as, "adult norms become internalized in a desire to be a 'good parent,' 'good wife,' 'good worker,' or 'good citizen.' Adult responsibility means knowing what is expected of one and fulfilling that expectation."[28] She finds that efforts to conform to the norms and ideals associated with "feminine" roles—efforts to be docile, passive, supportive of men, and

---

27. Virginia Sapiro, *The Political Integration of Women: Roles, Socialization, and Politics* (Urbana: University of Illinois Press, 1983).

28. Ibid., p. 47.

so on—result in low self-esteem and low estimates of our own power, qualities that inhibit our full participation in a democratic society. *Women's adult
roles,* Sapiro concludes, reduce our self-esteem as well as our understanding of
politics and our political efficacy. In short, the orientations fostered by being
a "responsible" woman in the passive sense, "form a clear picture of the acqui-
escent member of a political community."[29] This passivity, moreover, extends
beyond the political realm studied by Sapiro and affects other dimensions of
life as well. And so women wait for a liturgy that nourishes our spirits, we
wait for a meaningful work situation or supportive living environment, we
wait for justice in the church and in the world.

The image of waiting is prominent in Madonna Kolbenschlag's study *Kiss
Sleeping Beauty Goodbye,* which examines several fairy tales as "parables of
feminine socialization" and shows how cultural myths succeed in dwarfing
our spiritual and ethical capacities. In the chapter "Sleeping Beauty at Seventeen," she describes how young women are conditioned to wait for that magic
kiss that will awaken them to existence, meanwhile allowing their own spiritual powers to atrophy. Typical of this attitude of waiting is what she calls "the
desire to live for another." Observes Kolbenschlag:

> This role will school [the young woman] in self-forgetfulness, service and sacri-
> fice, in nurturing rather than initiating behaviors. Above all, it will teach her to
> "sleep"—to wait, forever if necessary, for the expected other who will make her
> life meaningful and fulfilled. She will give up everything when the expected one
> comes, even the right of creating her own self. Whether it is a husband, a reli-
> gion or a revolution, she is ready to live outside of herself, to abdicate responsi-
> bility for herself in favor of something or someone else.[30]

Women who have been drugged by our cultural myths will seek fulfillment
through others and, while waiting for this vicarious fulfillment, will tend to
see themselves as persons "that things happen to," rather than as agents who
make things happen.[31]

Carol Gilligan makes a similar point in her influential study of psychological theory and women's development, *In a Different Voice.* She speaks of the
perceived conflict between "selfishness" and "responsibility" that leads in
many instances to what she calls the "mysterious disappearance of the female
self in adolescence," when an underground world is mapped out and "kept

---

29. Ibid., p. 106.

30. Madonna Kolbenschlag, *Kiss Sleeping Beauty Goodbye: Breaking the Spell of Feminine
Myths and Models* (1979; reprint, New York: Bantam Books, 1981), p. 10.

31. Ibid., p. 15.

secret because it is branded by others as selfish and wrong."[32] Influenced by cultural pressures that expect women to epitomize "the morality of self-sacrifice," a woman may live and suffer under the mistaken assumption that "she is responsible for the actions of others while others are responsible for the choices she makes."[33] Such women may be very responsible in the passive sense. They will pour out vast energy into conforming to others' expectations, but in a deeper sense they remain morally asleep. As Kolbenschlag puts it, "The possibility of shaping their existence, their environment, their self never occurs to them."[34]

The poignancy of this situation for anyone is well captured in a quotation from the character Monica in *The Three Marias: New Portuguese Letters:* "In the end, what difference can my absence from this world make to you, if all I gave you was my absence from myself...."[35] All in all, Kolbenschlag's investigation of feminine myths and models leads to a finding remarkably similar to that of sociologist Sapiro:

> The passivity and privatization of women in our society are the most serious obstacles to their own autonomy and personal growth, and also to the transformation and redemption of the entire social structure.[36]

32. Carol Gilligan, *In a Different Voice: Psychological Theory and Women's Development* (Cambridge, Mass.: Harvard University Press, 1982), p. 51. Although Gilligan's research sample is limited and her findings controversial, her influence is considerable. Her claim that girls and boys tend to "hear" responsibility language differently is particularly interesting for ethical theory, at least as a hypothesis for reflection if not as a demonstrated generalization. Two typical eleven-year-olds expressed this difference. For Jake, responsibility "pertains to a limitation of action, a restraint of aggression, guided by the recognition that his actions can have effects on others" (p. 37). By contrast, Amy sees responsibility more as an extension of action than a limit on action. For her, responsibility "connotes an act of care rather than the restraint of aggression" (p. 38). Gilligan concludes: "To Jake, responsibility means *not doing* what he wants because he is thinking of others: to Amy, it means *doing* what others are counting on her to do regardless of what she herself wants" (p. 38). In Gilligan's view, Amy must learn that "responsiveness to self and responsiveness to others are connected rather than opposed" (p. 61), and that the morality of an action should be judged "not on the basis of its appearance in the eyes of others, but in terms of the realities of its intention and consequence" (p. 83). For a recent assessment of Gilligan's contributions, see Cynthia S. W. Crysdale, "Gilligan and the Ethics of Care: An Update," *Religious Studies Review* 20/1 (January 1994): 21–28.

33. Gilligan, *In A Different Voice*, p. 82.

34. Kolbenschlag, *Kiss Sleeping Beauty Goodbye*, p. 16.

35. Quoted in Kolbenschlag, p. 27, from Maria Isabel Barreno, Maria Teresa Horta, and Maria Velho da Costa, *The Three Marias: New Portuguese Letters*, trans. Helen R. Lane (1973; New York: Bantam, 1976), p. 232.

36. Sapiro, *Political Integration*, p. 78.

Such socialization, which has its parallels in the lives of some men, can set individuals on a tragic, misguided quest for innocence, which confuses goodness with not taking action under ambiguous circumstances. Playing into this dynamic is a spirituality that lacks trust in God's daily forgiveness and in God's supportive presence in our process of making choices in situations where innocence is hardly possible, given the ambiguities of real-life situations. Jesus seems to have known about such ambiguities—why else would he have stressed the need for daily forgiveness in the prayer he taught his disciples?—but in subsequent centuries the ready accessibility of divine forgiveness has been forgotten by many Catholics. What we need is a sense of God's enabling power and presence, along with a reconstituted vision of what authentic moral responsibility requires.[37]

Such a vision understands life as experienced in the presence of the Other who has so identified with the situation of humanity that our tradition speaks of the mystery of Divine Incarnation and witnesses in its sacred texts to the fact that ultimately the success or failure of our lives depends on how we have employed our talents in our relationships with our neighbors, especially those who suffer from the lack of what human dignity requires. This religious vision entails, in the first place, that we *attend* to those others and see our own well-being as bound up with theirs.

A MAP OF THE MORAL LIFE

To appreciate how one may develop the sort of attentiveness that facilitates creative responsibility and leads to actions that are of practical benefit to our neighbors, it is useful to consider the chief elements involved in the moral life. From James Gustafson's lectures in Christian ethics I have learned to think in terms of a "map" of the moral life that comprises four interrelated elements: God, the ultimate power grounding our lives and their possibilities; the moral agent; the context or situation calling for a moral response; and the principles and values influencing that response.[38] To these I have found it

---

37. In *En la Lucha: A Hispanic Women's Liberation Theology* (Minneapolis: Fortress, 1993), Ada María Isasi-Díaz discusses interviews with various women that illustrate both the exercise of "creative responsibility" and the sense of God's supportive presence. See especially her chapters "In Their Own Words: Latinas as Moral Agents," and "Conscience, Conscientization, and Moral Agency in Mujerista Theology" (pp. 86–165).

38. Divinity School, The University of Chicago, Autumn 1973.

useful to add a fifth component, that of the persons who mediate or interpret for the agent the other factors. This model is simple, but it illustrates well three ideas basic to the approach to moral theology taken here: the interrelatedness of the spiritual and ethical dimensions of life; the highly social nature of the experience of conscience; and the diversity of ways that different persons will understand and weight the elements, depending on their backgrounds and interpretive frameworks.

God

How individuals image and understand Divine Reality is crucial, for there is a correlation between styles of faith and styles of ethics. If our image of God is primarily that of the controlling, punishing patriarchal judge, it is likely that fear, shame, and guilt will dominate our lives.[39] Our moral energies will be spent on efforts to keep secure by keeping the rules, with the result that our fundamental trust is placed in the rules and in those who set and interpret the rules in our Christian communities. We will feel betrayed if the rules change, for they have been the focus of our life decisions.

On the other hand, if we tend to think of Divine Reality as sustaining and empowering our lives, aspects associated with the Sophia tradition being developed in our time by such thinkers as Elisabeth Schüssler Fiorenza and Elizabeth A. Johnson, our trust will be placed in the compassionate God who relieves us of the burden of always having to be perfectly correct and innocent in relation to the rules.[40] Salvation is experienced as a gift, not as something we must achieve by navigating a moral obstacle course. With such a God-image one appreciates rules as relatively important and useful, at the same

---

39. My critique of *patriarchal* notions of divine judgment is made with the understanding that a more adequate interpretation of this symbol remains crucial for Christian ethics. I concur with Elizabeth A. Johnson that whereas patriarchy opposes justice and compassion, "[i]n the transformative gestalt of a feminist paradigm, the justice orientation of God as creative mother does not stand in contrast to her compassion but is rather an indispensable expression of it" (*She Who Is*, p. 185).

40. See Elisabeth Schüssler Fiorenza, *In Memory of Her: A Feminist Theological Reconstruction of Christian Origins* (New York: Crossroad, 1983); eadem, *Jesus: Miriam's Child, Sophia's Prophet* (New York: Continuum, 1994); and Johnson, *She Who Is*. Although not legalistic, the Sophia tradition is morally demanding. Observes Johnson: "Sophia, whose paths are justice and peace, shows that the passion of God is clearly directed toward the lifting of oppression and the establishing of right relations. . . . What is needed is to listen to the loud cries of Jesus-Sophia resounding in the cries of the poor, violated, and desperate, and to ally our lives as the wisdom community to the divine creative, redeeming work in the world" (p. 166).

time recognizing that they are limited, fallible indicators of where goodness may lie. God's liberty to ask new things and, as it were, change the rules is preserved under this model, for it emphasizes that we can safely trust the creator and sustainer of our being to guide and support us as we discern what we ought to do. Indeed, God has entrusted us with what we need for our living and has enjoined us to use our powers of reason and imagination to promote on earth the values of love, truth, and justice.

Agent

Classical moral theology has recognized that differences of age, commitments, and responsibilities affect the ethical quality of human actions. Thus, children "below the age of reason" are considered incapable of serious sin; married persons have rights (and duties) to sexual activities that are considered wrong for others; and civil authorities may cause violence that ordinary citizens are forbidden to initiate. As the term "agent" (derived from the Latin *agere,* "to act" or "to do") suggests, the focus has been on the decision-making and acting side of the moral life rather than on the dispositional side, with special emphasis on the factors that affect culpability, namely, knowledge and freedom. Indeed, in the past, attention to attitudes and virtues has been left more to ascetical theology, a discipline that was mainly associated with the "life of perfection" aspired to by those in religious vows. Edwin Healy's widely studied college textbook *Moral Guidance,* for example, devotes most of its chapters to the decalogue and awards a scant dozen pages to consideration of the moral and theological virtues.[41]

More recently moral theology is reflecting two new and related developments: the factor of gender is being seen as morally significant, and matters of character and virtue are receiving much more attention. Both trends are evident in the fact that women have been asking whether our tradition's emphasis on humility, submissiveness, and self-sacrifice is the best thing for those who live on the subordinate end of unjust power relationships. It makes sense to recommend humility and self-sacrifice to those for whom pride and the

41. Edwin F. Healy, *Moral Guidance,* revised by James F. Meara (Chicago: Loyola University Press, 1960). The sexist language with which Healy introduces this section is worth noting. He observes that "virtue" is among the theological terms that have lost significance for modern readers; indeed, it suffers from "the connotation of prudishness and lack of virility." To offset this perception, Healy reminds readers that "the word itself means power and implies manliness, strength, and courage" (*Moral Guidance,* p. 33).

"will to power" are major temptations, but as Valerie Saiving pointed out in 1960, most women have different temptations and require different corrective virtues. Literary scholar Carolyn Heilbrun has expressed the contrasting experiences of self beneath these differences in brief quotations from two poets: male exuberance as seen in Walt Whitman's "I celebrate myself and sing myself; and what I assume you shall assume," and female diminishment as expressed in Emily Dickinson's "I'm nobody."[42]

Of course it would be a mistake to overgeneralize, but to some extent the self-images of most women have been damaged by patriarchy, and there is validity to Saiving's claim that the besetting temptations of women in our culture tend to involve not pride and self-aggrandizement but rather failure to have a centered self. Given our subordinate status, the tendencies we must guard against include such things as "triviality, distractibility, and diffuseness; lack of an organizing center or focus; dependence on others for one's own self-definition—in short, underdevelopment or negation of self."[43] For many women, efforts to stress humility and self-sacrifice are misplaced because they exacerbate a tendency to drift through life without really taking responsibility for their choices and the impact of their lives on the world. The "cult of true womanhood" expected females to be passive and deferential to male authority, maternally nurturing but otherwise as asexual as possible, concerned with the needs of others and forgetful of their own. This Victorian ideal of womanhood, epitomized in the phrase of the poet Coventry Patmore, "The Angel in the House,"[44] lingers on in the romantic praise of "women's special gifts" by patriarchs who refuse to share power justly. It also exists in a transmuted form in the exaggerated claims of some contemporary feminists, often inclined to separatism, who espouse a dualistic anthropology that assigns superiority to the female sex.

Principles and Values

These are the factors that govern our moral responses. They include broad *rules or norms* (such as "One ought to tell the truth") and *goods* that one hopes

42. Carolyn G. Heilbrun, "Presidential Address 1984," *PMLA* 100 (May 1985): 281–82.

43. Valerie Saiving [Goldstein], "The Human Situation: A Feminine View," originally published in *The Journal of Religion* (1960); cited here from *Womanspirit Rising*, ed. Carol P. Christ and Judith Plaskow (New York: Harper & Row, 1979), p. 37.

44. For a discussion of the tendency to view women as either angels or monsters, see Sandra M. Gilbert and Susan Gubar, *The Madwoman in the Attic: The Woman Writer and the Nineteenth-Century Literary Imagination* (New Haven: Yale University Press, 1979), pp. 20–36.

to preserve or promote (such as health or life). What makes the moral life such a challenge is that rules and values are often experienced as being in conflict with each other. Consider, for example, the values of peace and justice. The tensions between them become apparent when we contrast the slogans "Peace at any price" and "Justice at all costs." At times it is impossible, given the limits of human existence, to realize both values fully, and in such cases the ethical task involves discerning a course of action that preserves as much as possible of both competing values.[45] In these difficult instances it makes an enormous difference whether one or more values—such as truth or life—are seen as *absolute and never to be compromised* or as *relative to God*, which means the task of moral discernment will require us to prioritize in difficult cases and, for example, sometimes allow the reluctant taking of life. Moreover, agents whose imaginative capacities are well developed have an advantage in these conflict situations because the best solutions often involve envisioning a third alternative beyond the stark either/or of the dilemma as initially perceived.[46]

Circumstances and Events

These constitute the situation that calls for a response and requires a moral decision. What is crucial to recognize here is how important the process of interpreting a situation can be for ethics. Depending on one's experiences and perspective, the same objective data will have different meanings for different agents. A bias of gender, race, class, or nationality will make some features of a situation leap to attention, while others are dismissed as irrelevant. Consider how different property rights look to the owner of a large estate and to a starving peasant, or how much one's view of pregnancy can be colored by experiences of gender, parenting, economic benefits, and social relationships. If Christians are serious about doing good in the world, it is essential that we somehow compensate for the biases inherent in our social location and strive for the sharpest possible analysis of our local and global situations.

Doing this analysis requires an asceticism whose chief characteristic is the habit of attending to the actual situation of those whose lives are affected by ours, especially the victims of injustice whom the privileged so easily forget. Compensating for the biases of our social location also requires that in assess-

---

45. Philosopher W. D. Ross offers useful ways of thinking about such dilemmas in *The Right and the Good* (Oxford: Clarendon Press, 1930).

46. A pioneering contribution on this topic is Philip S. Keane, *Christian Ethics and Imagination: A Theological Inquiry* (New York: Paulist, 1984).

ing moral dilemmas we should use the findings of all the relevant sciences. Clearly these ideals are ones we can never achieve in their fullness, and this fact has the merit of returning even the most conscientious moral agents to awareness of their constant need for God's mercy and support.

Intermediaries

The fifth factor in this map of the moral life involves the people who interpret and communicate the other elements to the agent. Our sense of God, our values and principles, our way of regarding ourselves and the situations we face are all mediated to us by others. The importance of mediators where morality is concerned is particularly strong in Catholicism because for centuries the practice of sacramental confession has been a significant aspect of our piety. The close connection between moral theology and confession, in fact, is a major reason for differences in the ways Catholics and Protestants approach ethics.[47] In the past, the ethical writings of Protestants have been more pedagogical, while Catholic moral theology has been more juridical, because it was developed to prepare future priests for their role in the confessional. This role was essentially that of a judge who heard the self-accusation, consulted the law, rendered the verdict, and assigned the penalty. This juridical emphasis led naturally to a great emphasis on *rules,* with less attention to education in discernment of situations and in weighing conflicts of values and principles. As a result, many Catholics grew up confident that there was a simple method to assure correct moral discernment: find out what "the Church" teaches about a moral question and follow it. The only decision seemed to be whether or not to keep the rules; the goal was to have no transgressions to confess.

Catholics today are still affected by moral training that overemphasized the judgments of the experts; but increasingly they are recognizing that it is a mistake to think that others have certain knowledge of our moral obligations and it is immature to abdicate total responsibility for our lives to external authorities. But these insights are negative ones; the needed correctives are less widely acknowledged. These include instruction that will render moral agents both competent and confident in their skills of moral reasoning, guidance in the cultivation of their powers of imagination and creativity, and,

47. For a discussion of these differences, see James M. Gustafson, *Protestant and Roman Catholic Ethics: Prospects for Rapprochement* (Chicago: University of Chicago Press, 1978), pp. 1–29.

above all, encouragement in the spiritual discipline of attending preferentially to the situation of the suffering and oppressed. Is it not the victims of history whose lives mediate most clearly and urgently what God is enabling and requiring us to be and to do?

ATTENTIVENESS AND SOLIDARITY WITH VICTIMS

Surely there is need to study anew the Gospel stories of Jesus breaking rules for the sake of his neighbor's welfare and proclaiming that a person's need can preempt even important obligations of religious law. Jesus' opposition to narrow legalism is as instructive today as it was in the past, for however well intentioned, such legalism fosters a one-dimensional caricature of the moral life. The authoritarian moral agent lives on the surface and misses the joy that accompanies deep trust in God's saving grace as one employs the powers of imagination and creative thought for the sake of increasing the well-being of all God's creatures. The way toward this moral maturity, as Jesus has shown us, requires attending deeply to the realities of our lives and seeing more than first meets the eye.

The twentieth-century philosopher and mystic Simone Weil has written eloquently of these matters:

> In the first legend of the Grail, it is said that the Grail (the miraculous vessel that satisfies all hunger by virtue of the consecrated Host) belongs to the first comer who asks the guardian of the vessel, a king three-quarters paralyzed by the most painful wound, "What are you going through?"
>
> The love of neighbor in all its fulness simply means being able to say to him: "What are you going through?" It is a recognition that the sufferer exists, not only as a unit in a collection, or a specimen from the social category labeled "unfortunate," but as a man, exactly like us, who was one day stamped with a special mark by affliction. For this reason it is enough, but it is indispensable, to know how to look at him in a certain way.
>
> This way of looking is first of all attentive. The soul empties itself of its own contents in order to receive into itself the being it is looking at, just as he is, in all his truth.
>
> Only he who is capable of attention can do this.[48]

Weil further insists that this quality of attention is linked with love: "The

---

48. Simone Weil, *Waiting for God*, trans. Emma Craufurd (1951; New York: Harper & Row, 1973), p. 115.

poet produces the beautiful by fixing his attention on something real. It is the same with the act of love. To know that this man who is hungry and thirsty really exists as much as I do—that is enough, the rest follows of itself."[49]

This knowledge of equivalent existence is indeed a first step, but whether or not "the rest follows of itself" would seem to depend on the agent's willingness to stay with and act out of this insight. Spiritual discipline is surely required for one to follow through in ways that actually benefit the suffering neighbor. Weil implies as much in her imagery, which suggests that attentiveness has both visual and aural dimensions that continue in a temporal process. Not only must one see the neighbor; one must also ask "What are you going through?" and then *listen* with openness to whatever this neighbor will say. The ideal of solidarity does not presume that the suffering neighbor has the exact formula for what one must do, but it does entail that this person's answer to the question What are you going through? provides crucial data about the context in which decisions will be made. How else are we likely to be in the position of those to whom the Lord will say, "I was hungry and you gave me food, I was thirsty and you gave me drink" (Matt. 25:35), if our eyes and ears are not focused on the lives of history's victims?

What the liberationist and feminist perspectives add to the traditional Christian concern for those in need is the recognition that to a great extent their sufferings are caused by *systemic* injustice. This means that the gift of "food" and "drink" should not be limited to the alleviation of immediate symptoms; we must also address the root causes of the unjust distribution of what is needed for our neighbors to flourish. Thus, from a feminist-liberationist perspective, there will be a priority of attention given to those whose lives are most harmed by racism, sexism, violence, and economic injustice. As Elizabeth Johnson puts it, the goal to keep in view is the "flourishing of poor women of color in violent situations."[50]

THE RACHEL PRINCIPLE

An ethic of responsibility built on this insight will address the question What are you going through? in the first place to the poor and oppressed, and it will go on from there to develop a praxis of solidarity with them. As

49. Simone Weil, *Gravity and Grace*, trans. Arthur Wills (New York: G. P. Putnam's Sons, 1952), p. 173.

50. Johnson, *She Who Is*, p. 11.

mujerista theologian Ada María Isasi-Díaz has expressed it, "Solidarity is the appropriate present-day expression of the gospel demand that we love our neighbor."[51] She goes on to insist that solidarity is a matter of effective, cohesive struggle governed by an understanding of interconnected issues; it goes well beyond mere agreement with and support of a people's cause. Solidarity requires mutuality as well as praxis, and its "goal is not the participation of the oppressed in present social structures but rather the replacement of those structures by ones in which full participation of the oppressed is possible."[52]

Biblical support for this way of approaching the moral life is plentiful. Indeed, the scriptures offer something that can be called "the Rachel principle" to remind us of this priority and keep the challenges of solidarity in the forefront of conscience. Rachel is one of the original "mothers of the disappeared." Her voice comes wailing out of Matthew's Gospel just before John's voice is heard crying for repentance because God's reign is near:

> A voice was heard in Ramah,
>   sobbing and loud lamentation;
> Rachel weeping for her children,
>   and she would not be consoled,
>   since they are no more.
>   (Matt. 2:18)

Rachel is everywoman, mourning every loss from violence and injustice. The Rachel principle suggests that if we hear that anguish into speech, the questions of action will be addressed much more adequately than if we limit our attention to traditional rules of conduct.[53] Asking Rachel what she is going through will invite a whole range of activity designed to allow Rachel to know that there is hope for her future, which is what God assures Rachel in the prophecy that Matthew recalls in his quotation:

> In Ramah is heard the sound of moaning,
>   of bitter weeping!

---

51. Ada María Isasi-Díaz, "Solidarity: Love of Neighbor in the 1980s," in *Lift Every Voice: Constructing Christian Theologies from the Underside,* Susan Brooks Thistlethwaite and Mary Potter Engel, eds. (San Francisco: Harper & Row, 1990), p. 32.

52. Ibid., p. 35.

53. Nelle Morton's phrase "hearing to speech" is discussed in her *The Journey is Home* (Boston: Beacon, 1985), pp. 202–10. My discussion of "the Rachel Principle" here is based on remarks prepared for the College Theology Society in 1994 and published as "From Hearing to Collaboration: Steps for the Privileged Toward a Praxis of Solidarity," in *Women and Theology,* Mary Ann Hinsdale and Phyllis H. Kaminski (Maryknoll, N.Y.: Orbis, 1995), pp. 105–8.

> Rachel mourns her children,
>   she refuses to be consoled
>   because her children are no more.
>   Thus says the Lord:
> Cease your cries of mourning,
>   wipe the tears from your eyes.
> The sorrow you have known shall have its reward,
>   says the Lord,
>   they shall return from the enemy's land.
> There is hope for your future, says the Lord.
>   (Jer. 31:15–17)

How to support this hope is something we must figure out together, Rachel and we, and on occasion, Rachel in others and Rachel in us.

Something to notice here is that a scandal of particularity is associated with Rachel. She is one of four women who bore Jacob's children in the Genesis narrative, and because she is the one most favored by patriarchy, her losses are recalled by Jeremiah and lifted up by Matthew. This privilege does not invalidate the Rachel principle, but it does suggest that we will do well to remember that for every Rachel we encounter, there is a Leah and a Zilpah and a Bilhah, a less-favored sister and a pair of female slaves. Being attuned to all these voices, then, is the first step toward a praxis of solidarity—hearing them not as a disembodied sound track but, insofar as possible contextually, in a way that connects with the human richness and complex relatedness of the speakers.[54] Collaborating on common projects is an excellent way to promote this contextual hearing.

Internalizing the voices of the victims of injustice is the second step toward a praxis of solidarity, which means hearing them regularly in one's own self-talk. This may in fact be a distinguishing characteristic of that elusive entity we call a "properly formed conscience"—one that hears the voices of those adversely affected by the systems we live by, as well as by what we choose to do and what we never get around to doing.[55]

---

54. Isasi-Díaz models such contextual hearing in *En la Lucha* (see n. 37 above) as well as in the book she co-authored earlier with Yolanda Tarango, *Hispanic Women: Prophetic Voice in the Church* (San Francisco: Harper & Row, 1988; reprint, Minneapolis: Fortress, 1992).

55. H. Richard Niebuhr discusses the conversational character of conscience in "The Ego-Alter Dialectic and the Conscience," *Journal of Philosophy* 42 (1945): 352–59. His conclusion offers a useful set of distinctions: "The choice does not lie between the good conscience of a self which has kept all its laws and the bad conscience of the transgressor, but between the dull con-

Because the praxis of solidarity is so idealistic and so demanding, I would recommend as a third step something on the order of harmonizing the voices. This image is meant to suggest not a classical blend of "easy listening" but rather a mode of hearing that allows us to retain inner peace as much as possible. Perhaps a better way of expressing what I have in mind is this: to allow the challenging protests and demands to play over a ground alto of God's healing and empowering and justice-making love for us all.

The story of the rich young man that governs the encyclical *Veritatis Splendor* contains the injunction, "sell what you have and give to the poor" (Matt. 19:21). What this means for moral theology, I believe, is that in addition to requiring corrective lenses, we also need hearing aids. "The Lord hears the cry of the poor" is a refrain Catholics sometimes sing at our liturgies.[56]

It invites further questions: Do *we* hear these cries? Do we trace the connections between our culture's obsession with individual freedom and the starving, suffering victims of corporate greed? Between our nation's tolerance of easily available guns and the routine violence in our cities? Between our society's obsession with "property rights" and ecological devastation?

As I implied in chapter 2, the task of liberating conscience is a lifelong one, entailing an agenda for spiritual growth that is completed only with one's final breath. This is so because the liberation we need in order to love God, neighbor, and self requires being freed from the individualism, shame, and guilt of religious authoritarianism as well as from the isolation, despair, and indecisiveness of secular liberalism. A fully liberated conscience has transcended perfectionism as well as indifference, and its basis for joy and confidence is God's mercy rather than its own record of "right" choices.

There can be no impenetrable boundaries between the theological disciplines of spirituality and Christian ethics, for both concern the vision of what human well-being and authentic discipleship involve. Spirituality supplies the vision and the motivation, the context within which ethics matters. Its long-standing interest in the cultivation of virtue constitutes a natural bridge with morality, whose interests involve character as much as action. Christian ethics draws from the wisdom of the religious tradition as well as that of secular disciplines, including philosophy and the sciences, to provide data about

---

science which does not discern the greatness of the other and the loftiness of [God's] demands, the agonized conscience of the awakened, and the consoled conscience of one who in the company of the Spirit seeks to fulfill the infinite demands of the infinite other" (p. 359).

56. "Psalm 34," paraphrased by John B. Foley, S.J.; copyright 1978 North American Liturgy Resources.

the likely effects of various choices as well as clarity about ways of discerning value and making moral judgments. The relationship between these two theological disciplines is reciprocal and complementary, and both are accountable to the same biblical norm that has been modeled so definitively in Jesus: "What does the Lord require of you but to do justice, and to love kindness, and to walk humbly with your God?" (Micah 6:8 NRSV).

We have long been aware that the biblical term for human holiness is "justice." What the newer religious paradigm and the liberation theology perspective are providing is the awareness that no life is holy if it ignores the material circumstances of other persons. As Matthew Lamb has observed, "Basic human and social rights are . . . constitutive elements of the human common good which defines both the moral virtue of justice and essential elements of our justification by God's redemptive love in Christ." The cries of history's victims, he goes on to say, "are the voice of the living God."[57] If it is the task of spirituality to sensitize us so that we are capable of hearing that voice, it is the function of Christian ethics to help us discern what will be the wisest, the most humanly effective response. As Elizabeth Johnson reminds us, "mutuality in relation with God calls forth human responsibility for the good of the world."[58]

57. Lamb, "Christian Spirituality and Social Justice," pp. 43, 49.
58. Johnson, *She Who Is*, p. 244.

CHAPTER SEVEN

Conscience as Process:
Choosing Our Common Good

> I think we best make decisions of conscience through an integrated, recursive process in which we direct and focus attention back and forth, within and without, activating, mutually testing, and monitoring all our human capacities of thinking, feeling, and self-consciousness.
>
> —Sidney Callahan[1]

Discerning what is the right thing to do and then acting according to this decision—this ideal is at the heart of ethics. When the right deed happens also to be enjoyable, things are easy enough, but when it entails difficulty or sacrifice, then why should we bother?

This is a question that ethics as such cannot answer. As the philosopher Henry David Aiken pointed out some decades ago, when moral discourse reaches the level of probing our reasons for caring about the enterprise itself, we are on a different plane entirely. This new plane of discourse, which he designated "post-ethical" or "human," involves the grounds for caring about morality at all.[2] We may also call this dimension religious, in the broad sense of having to do with one's "ultimate concern," to use the phrase of Paul Tillich, or one's "center of value," as H. Richard Niebuhr expressed it. These theologians employed such general language in order to account for the fact that even those who deny traditional forms of religious faith are implicitly building their lives around the functional equivalent of what theists call

---

1. Sidney Callahan, *In Good Conscience: Reason and Emotion in Moral Decision-Making* (San Francisco: HarperCollins, 1991), p. 115.

2. Henry David Aiken, "Levels of Moral Discourse," *Ethics* 62 (1952): 235–48. Reprinted in Aiken, *Reason and Conduct* (New York: Knopf, 1962).

"God," despite the fact that they may consider themselves atheists or agnostics. As Martin Luther recognized, "Trust and faith of the heart alone make both God and idol. . . . Whatever then thy heart clings to . . . and relies upon, that is properly thy God."[3]

Christians, of course, are quick to claim that God has much to do with their efforts to lead moral lives but slower to account for just why this is the case. In fact, the reasons are complex: they vary with stages of psychological development, and they reflect the tensions between conflicting religious paradigms we have been considering in this volume. This last factor may be seen by noting a subtle change in the wording of a widely used prayer.

The Act of Contrition has long been taught in catechism classes to prepare students for the sacrament of Penance. In the early decades of this century the text approved for use in the United States went as follows:

> O my God! I am heartily sorry for having offended Thee, and I detest my sins, *because I dread the loss of heaven and the pains of hell,* but most of all because they offend Thee, my God, who art all-good and deserving of all my love. I firmly resolve, with the help of Thy grace, to confess my sins, to do penance, and to amend my life.[4]

This version expresses quite clearly the individualistic, otherworldly spirituality that prevailed in the pre–Vatican II era. It continued to be taught well into the 1940s, although a rewording of certain lines introduced in 1941 eventually became standard for reciting in confession. The revision reads:

> O my God! I am heartily sorry for having offended Thee, and I detest all my sins, *because of Thy just punishments,* but most of all because they offend Thee my God, who art all-good and deserving of all my love. I firmly resolve, with the help of thy grace, to sin no more and to avoid the near occasions of sin.[5]

I have italicized some crucial lines in these prayers to bring out how the change allows for both precritical and postcritical understandings of what may be termed the ultimate sanctions for our moral choices. A believer who takes the symbols of heaven, hell, and purgatory literally will probably have

3. Quoted by H. Richard Niebuhr in *Radical Monotheism and Western Culture* (New York: Harper & Row, 1960), p. 119; see also Paul Tillich, *Dynamics of Faith* (New York: Harper & Row, 1957).

4. Quoted here from Rev. M. Philipps, *The Baltimore Catechism No. 2* (Minneapolis, 1911), p. 128.

5. Quoted here from Rev. Michael A. McGuire, *The New Baltimore Catechism and Mass, No. 2* (1941; New York: Benziger Brothers, 1949), p. 5.

them in mind when mentioning his fear of "Thy just punishments," whereas another who understands these realities more symbolically may have other things in mind, including the injury her behavior has done to another person. Thus, the remorse and practical difficulties she suffers as a result are accepted as aspects of "God's punishments," while the imagery of otherworldly sanctions serves mainly as a reminder that our lives do end and the effects of our living extend beyond death. Indeed, the imagery reinforces the idea that our "fundamental option"—the basic orientation of our choices in life—is forever fixed once we have drawn our last breath.[6]

In the post–Vatican II period there has been considerable variety in the celebration of Penance, with much less standardization evident in prayers of contrition used by penitents. Furthermore, it is interesting that all references to punishments have been omitted from the version featured in some contemporary catechetical materials, which is taken from a 1974 translation of the Revised Rite of Penance:

> My God, I am sorry for my sins with all my heart. In choosing to do wrong and failing to do good, I have sinned against you whom I should love above all things. I firmly intend, with your help, to do penance, to sin no more, and to avoid whatever leads me to sin. Our Savior Jesus Christ suffered and died for us. In his name, my God, have mercy.[7]

This prayer focuses the contrition on one's relation with God in the present, surely a central aspect of the believer's repentance and motivation for leading

---

6. The idea of setting one's life direction appears in biblical and classical sources, such as Augustine. In this century theologians including Karl Rahner and Bernard Häring have developed the concept of "fundamental option" to offset the mentality that interprets the moral life too rigidly as a pattern of frequent shifts from the state of sin to the state of grace, caused by mortal sins and their confession in the sacrament of penance. In *Veritatis Splendor* Pope John Paul II objects to an interpretation of fundamental option that is not held by the moral theologians who employ the concept; he suggests they would dissociate particular choices from a person's basic religious orientation and thereby deny the serious implications of concrete actions. But as Brian V. Johnstone observes, the notion functions otherwise in the work of moral theology: "As a corrective to a legalistic, act-centered image of the moral life, punctuated by frequently alternating choices for and against God, the idea of fundamental orientation presents that life as a unified dynamic process. It points to an enduring stance, beneath more peripheral choices. However, all would agree that the fundamental option is not a once and for all choice; it can be changed, deepened or reversed." See Johnstone, "Fundamental Option," in *The New Dictionary of Theology*, ed. Joseph A. Komonchak, Mary Collins, and Dermot Lane (Collegeville, Minn.: Liturgical Press, 1991), p. 407.

7. Quoted here from Christiane Brusselmans and Brian A. Haggerty, *We Celebrate Reconciliation: The Lord Forgives* (Morristown, N.J.: Silver Burdett & Ginn, 1990), p. 53.

a moral life. It retains the individualism of preconciliar forms, however, and this may contribute to a trend that some confessors have noted, namely, the utilization by penitents of improvised or unofficial prayers of contrition, some of which express sorrow for having injured other persons as well as for offending God.

This chapter, entitled "Conscience as Process: Choosing Our Common Good," will take these small but significant developments in the ritual practice of Catholics as a point of departure for probing some possibilities for growth that underlie our present tensions. I first deepen this discussion of the religious motivation for pursuing the moral life, giving particular attention to the changing status of symbols of otherworldly rewards and punishments in Catholicism. I next offer a method for the exercise of individual conscience, a four-step process of moral reasoning in faith. I then suggest that there is value in extending the process of self-scrutiny to the discipline of moral theology itself, selecting the problem of racism as particularly appropriate for an examination of professional conscience by moral theologians in this country. Finally, I return to the religious basis of these ethical considerations by affirming the transcendence of the ideal of the common good toward which all our human moral efforts are directed as well as the power and presence of the Divine Spirit guiding these limited efforts toward the perfection of justice and charity, symbolized as the reign of God.

WHY BE MORAL?

Magisterial literature has continued to employ the symbols of the eschatological realities (or "last things," as they have been called) straightforwardly, but many Catholics have been affected by the critical probing of these matters done in modern times by secular and religious thinkers. These critiques have been so powerful because they include moral as well as intellectual grounds for questioning whether the Deity actually created human beings mainly to test their obedience on earth and then reward or punish them in the afterlife. This is the worldview implied in the pre–World War II catechism version of the act of contrition and expressed much more fully in a variation published in 1945 in *The Sodality Manual*, a spiritual guidebook for members of the Jesuit-led movement for laity once popular on Catholic campuses and still strong in many parishes:

> O my God, I am heartily sorry for my sins. I am deeply sorry, because *mortal sin means the loss of my soul and the eternal pains of hell.* O my God, never let me

know the terrifying pains of being lost forever and condemned to the torturing flames of hell. I know that because of mortal sin one loses all right to heaven, *the real purpose of life,* and the joys that you have prepared for those who love you. I am sorry for my serious sins, and I promise that I shall never again be guilty of sin.

O my God, I am sorry for my venial sins, since because of them *I shall deserve long imprisonment in purgatory* and thus be deprived of the sight of you and kept from the joys of heaven.[8] (emphasis added)

Here we see a very explicit elaboration of classic imagery of the afterlife as well as a strong expression of otherworldly spirituality. But does this provide an adequate basis for morality? Even the prayer itself suggests it does not, for after laying out the fiery imagery it goes on to say:

But this time, dear Lord, I am sorry . . . because serious sin nailed you to the cross, and . . . venial sins helped make your Passion so terrible and so filled with pain and rejection.[9]

However, this second strand of motivation, based on personal attachment to Jesus, continues to reinforce the individualism characteristic of preconciliar piety. It remains vulnerable to the charge that attention is focused primarily on the agent's fears and feelings and not on the effects the deeds so regretted may have had on the lives of other persons.

The slight shift from explicit mention of heaven and hell to the vaguer "just punishments" in the two editions of the *Baltimore Catechism* occurred within a wider culture that had for some time been wrestling with the issue of articulating the grounds for morality to educated modern persons. Notions of heaven and hell were easier to accept on a literal level in earlier times, but with the advent of modernity, the existence of these "places" came into question.[10] There was also objection to the self-interest so prominent in a morality centered on personal rewards and punishments in the afterlife.

Among the secular critics of otherworldly motivation for morality was the British thinker Mary Ann Evans. In an essay published in January 1857, just

8. Daniel A. Lord, ed. *The Sodality Manual* (St. Louis: The Queen's Work, 1945), pp. 377–78. It is perhaps significant that in the "short form" of the "examination of conscience" the editor includes an Act of Contrition that seeks to discount the very imagery stressed earlier: "O my God, I am sorry for my sins now, not through the loss of heaven or the pains of hell, but because they nailed you to the cross. You are so good, so generous, and so loveable" (p. 379).

9. Ibid., p. 379.

10. See, for example, Thomas Pickering Walker, *The Decline of Hell* (Chicago: University of Chicago Press, 1964).

as she was beginning to write fiction and shortly before she assumed the pseudonym George Eliot, she eloquently contested the idea that other-worldly sanctions should provide the basis for right living. The essay is a polemic directed at the poet Edward Young, whose mid-eighteenth-century work *Night Thoughts on Life, Death, and Immortality* was widely praised in her time. Eliot's challenge to Young is scathing:

> If it were not for the prospect of immortality, he considers, it would be wise and agreeable to be indecent, or to murder one's father; and, heaven apart, it would be extremely irrational in any man not to be a knave.[11]

Contrary to popular opinion, which esteemed the poet as a sublime religious and moral teacher, Eliot objected to Young's poetry because it "substitutes interested obedience for sympathetic emotion, and baptizes egoism as religion."[12] She judged it false and insincere, utterly lacking in genuine emotion, and proposed in place of Young's otherworldly morality a this-worldly ethic of sympathy that has found considerable resonance among other modern thinkers:

> We can imagine the man who "denies his soul immortal," replying [to Young], "It is quite possible that *you* would be a knave, and love yourself alone, if it were not for your belief in immortality; but you are not to force upon me what would result from your own utter want of moral emotion. I am just and honest, not because I expect to live in another world, but because, having felt the pain of injustice and dishonesty towards myself, I have a fellow-feeling with other men, who would suffer the same pain if I were unjust or dishonest towards them.[13]

These debates have been repeated in various forms often in the last two centuries, but since they tended to involve secular humanists and Protestants, Catholics could initially ignore them, protected as they were by a cloud of antimodernist sentiment fostered by the Vatican.

By the mid-twentieth century, however, various historical and cultural factors increased the pressure on traditional views of eschatology, even for Catholics. While only a few were exposed to the ways systematic theology was

---

11. Mary Ann Evans [George Eliot], "Worldliness and Other-Worldliness: The Poet Young," in *Essays of George Eliot,* ed. Thomas Pinney (New York: Columbia University Press, 1963), pp. 338-39. Young's work of some ten thousand lines of blank verse was published in nine volumes during 1742–45 under the title "The Complaint, or Night Thoughts on Life, Death, and Immortality."

12. Evans [Eliot], "Worldliness," p. 358.

13. Ibid., p. 373.

beginning to open up these questions, many were affected by literary works that explored eschatological themes. Prominent among the writers who invited reexamination of these topics was the novelist Graham Greene, who tested the limits of literal understandings of heaven, hell, and purgatory in several works from the 1940s and 1950s, including *The Power and the Glory, The Heart of the Matter*, and *The End of the Affair*. Greene exposed the difficulties of literalistic eschatological thinking in such powerfully dramatic ways that a thoughtful reader was bound to ask whether the religious system appropriated in childhood was quite so neat as the catechism had suggested.

Greene put the case most effectively in *The Power and the Glory*, the story of an alcoholic priest in postrevolutionary Mexico of the 1930s, who is hunted down and shot by a Marxist police lieutenant in an effort to rid the province of Tabasco of the last vestiges of Catholic ritual. It is difficult for a reader to follow the anguish of this man without questioning the simple calculus for determining eternal destiny learned at school. Besides drinking, the priest's sins include fathering an illegitimate daughter, and he is unable to muster what he considers proper contrition for this act of drunken lust because he feels such affection for the child. Nor is there anyone to whom he can turn to make a confession and receive absolution. Nevertheless, he offers mass for the people even though he is sure this is an act of sacrilege that will mean damnation if he dies without confession. His own wrestling with textbook eschatology is depicted as he speaks to the people during this ritual:

> "The police watching you, the soldiers gathering taxes, the beating you always get from the jefe because you are too poor to pay, smallpox and fever, hunger ... that is all part of heaven—the preparation. ... And what is heaven?" Literary phrases from what seemed now to be another life altogether—the strict quiet life of the seminary—became confused on his tongue: the names of precious stones: Jerusalem the golden. But these people had never seen gold.
>
> He went rather stumblingly on: "Heaven is where there is no jefe, no unjust laws, no taxes, no soldiers, and no hunger. Your children do not die in heaven. ... Oh, it is easy to say all the things that there will not be in heaven: what is there is God. That is more difficult. Our words are made to describe what we know with our senses."[14]

In such passages Greene invites readers not only to realize that the language of the afterlife is symbolic but also to transcend understandings of salvation that are too individualistic and otherworldly in favor of ones that include communal and this-worldly dimensions. As the priest comes to risk his phys-

14. Graham Greene, *The Power and the Glory* (1940; New York: Viking, 1962), pp. 94–96.

ical and spiritual safety for the sake of the people he was called to serve, he recognizes that his eternal destiny is bound up with theirs. "[I]f there's ever been a single man in this state damned, then I'll be damned too," he thinks at one point, expressing an insight with some validity despite the exaggerated nature of his judgment. In the end he is captured because his sense of duty leads him to answer an outlaw's request for the last sacraments, even though he realizes the man is luring him across the border into a trap. As he faces execution, the priest judges his life a failure, although readers are convinced he has earned a place among the martyrs.

> Tears poured down his face: he was not at the moment afraid of damnation— even the fear of pain was in the background. He felt only an immense disappointment because he had to go to God empty-handed, with nothing done at all.[15]

After the priest is shot, Greene's narrative shows that this shabby man with the "funny smell" has won the respect of the people, while his antagonist, the self-disciplined, dedicated Marxist police lieutenant, has lost it. In the process the story helps complicate the reader's sense of eschatology in ways that were articulated officially by the Second Vatican Council a quarter century after the novel was published. As Dermot A. Lane has noted, conciliar teaching on eschatology is "remarkable for the way it overcomes the separation of individual and social eschatology, links the present and the future, and establishes a unity between the earthly and the heavenly."[16]

One of Greene's last works of fiction, *The Honorary Consul* (1973), reinforces these theological developments through several characters involved in a contemporary Argentinian setting of social injustice and revolutionary efforts.[17] In this novel Greene represents the priestly ideal by combining the strengths of two characters, the secular physician Eduardo Plarr and the priest-turned-revolutionary Léon Rivas, who together stumble their way toward a faith that seeks to do justice. Despite their flaws, these men are admirable in ways the "archbishop's priest," portrayed as someone who relates only to the wealthy, is not. The latter's preoccupation with the souls in purgatory, Greene's narrative makes clear, is quite problematic, since it is accompanied by such a scandalous lack of concern for the bodies in the *barrio*.

15. Ibid., p. 284.
16. Dermot A. Lane, "Eschatology," in *The New Dictionary of Theology*, ed. Komonchak et al., p. 337. See also Peter C. Phan, "Contemporary Contexts and Issues in Eschatology," *Theological Studies* 55 (September 1994): 507–36.
17. Graham Greene, *The Honorary Consul* (New York: Simon & Schuster, 1973).

A METHOD OF MORAL DISCERNMENT

The crucial insight to hold on to amidst the shifting interpretations of eschatological symbols is the necessity of interpreting our lives in an ultimate context that presumes our ongoing relatedness with the Creator and other creatures. What we choose matters, and it matters beyond our individual selves and families as well as beyond our own deaths. The ultimate context is Mystery, but we have seen its human face in the life, death, and resurrection of Jesus, and we have come to know something of its intentions in our regard from the biblical record of its saving activity on our behalf. We are called to lead morally serious lives that express in deeds our disposition to love God and neighbor as ourselves. We have reason to know that we can never succeed fully, which would be grounds for discouragement were it not for the balancing truth that God's mercy makes up for what we lack. This mercy is not "cheap grace" but a form of healing and empowerment that, depending patiently on our cooperation and willingness to change, transforms our lives and enables them to bear fruit for eternity, that is, well beyond our ability to reckon.

Paralleling the deepening of eschatological understanding in our day has been a renewed emphasis on character and virtue in ethics, which some have termed "dispositional ethics."[18] Both trends have the potential to restore a balance upset by our religious culture's excessively legalistic emphasis on obeying moral rules. A core insight of dispositional ethics is that our choices and our selves are interdependent realities, mutually influencing each other. For this reason I have stressed the import of consciously relating the spiritual vision that guides and governs a moral agent in the ethical task of making decisions about action. Vision alone will not suffice, however; we must also grow more confident and competent in the skills of practical moral reasoning and acting.

As we consider this topic of how to make good moral decisions, it will be useful for each reader to recall a significant choice from his or her own life, one where much was at stake and where there were good reasons for going either way. What influences or pressures did you feel? What were your feelings about yourself and God as you tried to discern what course was best, or least harmful? How do you feel about the decision now?

Such an exercise raises many questions, including the basic question of

---

18. D. M. Yeager provides rich insight on this topic in "On Making the Tree Good: An Apology for a Dispositional Ethics," *Journal of Religious Ethics* 10/1 (Spring 1982): 103–20.

what actually constitutes a "moral" decision. Is it one that involves rules, or can other choices be considered moral as well? There is a well-cultivated tendency to think in terms of tensions over traditional moral rules, but many other decisions also have ethical significance. The choice of what to own and how to use it, which friendships to develop, which sorts of employment and leisure activities to pursue—all these items bear on the ultimate fruitfulness of our lives in relation to our vocation to advance the values of God's reign. Thus, it is meaningful to regard any important decision as a moral one, at least in a fundamental sense.

Although a rule-centered form of moral training tends to create the impression that "moral decisions" are quite different from other decisions, in fact the boundaries drawn between the types are more flexible and permeable than we might at first suppose. The matter of smoking cigarettes provides a good example of a decision once considered nonmoral, at least for adults with a bit of discretionary money, and now recognized as having great ethical significance because of the harm the practice causes for individuals and society.[19] Another set of examples involves decisions about purchasing food and household products and disposing of their packaging. Convenience and cost were formerly the main factors we considered as we wheeled our shopping carts around the stores, hardly giving a thought to what went into the trash. But ecological sensitivity has complicated this picture, and new knowledge has created a new sense of obligation in the area of household purchasing and waste disposal that is most properly seen as ethical. Likewise, the duty to be in solidarity with unjustly compensated farmworkers has led to another set of moral considerations where grocery shopping is concerned. These everyday examples are among many that could be advanced to show how traditional lists of rules cover only part of the scope of our moral lives.

It is of course possible at a certain level of abstraction to distinguish "moral" decisions from "aesthetic" or "practical" ones, but in life our choices usually have more than one dimension, and when significant values are involved, they are inevitably moral to some extent. As the *Catechism of the*

---

19. Citing the *American Medical News* for June 6, 1994, *Second Opinion* observes: "About $16 billion of $87 billion spent this year on inpatient care will be for treatment of conditions attributable to smoking. Smoking-related illness is the single largest drain on Medicare's trust fund, expected to consume $800 billion over the next 20 years" (October 1994): 104. A World Health Organization report has characterized smoking as "the leading cause of premature death in the industrialized world," and its spokesman, Dr. Alan Lopez, has voiced concern over a future "'tidal wave of mortality' due to smoking in developing countries" (quoted from *Chicago Tribune,* September 20, 1994, in *Second Opinion* [January 1995]: 82).

Catholic Church declares, "Human acts, that is, acts that are freely chosen in consequence of a judgment of conscience, can be morally evaluated" (#1749). Some readers were surprised that this position was developed later on in the *Catechism* with detailed mention of matters not generally associated with the decalogue, including tax evasion, "work poorly done" (#2409), and mistreatment of animals or spending "money on them that should as a priority go to the relief of human misery" (#2418). But such extensions of the scope of moral judgment are warranted because ethics is concerned with the *effects* of human attitudes, choices, and actions as well as with their motives and intentions.

Reflection on our past experience also leads to the realization that the process of decision making is complex and not always fully conscious. Choices may be reached in stages, and they sometimes seem to "make themselves" because the overriding factors have converged while we were attending to other aspects of life. Nonetheless, from the decisions we affirm as well as those we regret there comes a recognition that we can increase the likelihood that our choices will be relatively good ones. Most basically, the willingness to give time to a prayerful process of discernment is essential. One example of such a process is offered below.

Step 1: FOCUS THE QUESTION. What is going on here? What is this act or decision really about? What is it I must decide? Take time prayerfully to get the question right—for now—and trust that the answer will be given. When a genuine dilemma is present, creative imagination will be required for a breakthrough, and this cannot be forced. Experience will show that stating the question, seeking advice, attempting to figure out a solution—all these active and conscious steps—are often insufficient to reach an answer. Also needed is "down time," the willingness to leave a problem alone and trust that a reasonably adequate answer, if not a fully satisfactory solution, will present itself.

Step 2: TOUCH BASE WITH YOURSELF. Why am I inclined to do this or that? What are my motives? What do I fear? What do I hope? What do I care about? Which previous decisions of mine have contributed to the situation? What have I learned from past experience that may be helpful here? How would someone I greatly admire be likely to respond to this dilemma? It is here that the long-standing tradition of *imitatio Christi* has bearing, as well as the practice of contemplating the lives of the saints.

Step 3: DO THE WORK OF ETHICS IN CONSULTATION WITH OTHERS. What is likely to happen if I choose one way or the other, and also if I delay my decision? Whose interests am I mainly thinking about when I imagine these effects? What moral norms and principles have bearing on this situation? What values are to be realized, disvalues to be minimized? What are the viable alternatives? Can I *imagine* a way to act that allows for competing values to be respected? When the matter is serious, such questions should be posed not only within one's own mind but also in conversation with trusted others. This is where religious authority and community have a crucial role to play, and where the individual agent has much to gain from being open to guidance from the wisdom of the tradition. No one has perfectly certain knowledge of what God is enabling and requiring us to be and to do, but the very fallibility of our individual consciences points to the need to gain perspective and insight from beyond ourselves.

Step 4: MAKE YOUR OWN CHOICE AND ACT ON IT IN PEACE AND TRUST. The techniques for discernment of spirits worked out by religious guides can prove useful here. One process involves preparing a four-column listing of the reasons for and against both choosing to do the act in question and choosing not to do it. At first it may seem redundant to itemize the reasons *for doing something* and also the reasons *against not doing it,* along with those *in favor of not doing it* and *against doing it,* but it does not take long to discover that very different feelings and insights can emerge when the question is posed in slightly different forms. The point of the exercise is not to come up with a mathematical proof that one decision is perfectly right, but rather to give ourselves time to attend to as many relevant considerations as possible and to be instructed by the patterns that take shape. Sometimes there will be a long list in one column, but a single factor in another will prove more decisive.

At a point only the agent can detect, time is judged to have run out; some decision, even if only provisional, needs to be made. It is then that the prayerful attention to principles and consequences can yield to an overarching sense of God's support for our efforts. After bearing the burden of the ethical, it becomes time to accept the consolation of the religious.[20] The Christian who has sought in this process to "put on the mind of Christ Jesus" will have employed a set of principles reflecting the values of God's reign—a realm of justice, truth, peace, and love. Anticipated consequences will have been assessed on a wide scale, not with the myopic lens of self-interest or group-

---

20. Although I employ the phrase "the burden of the ethical" in a different way here, my use is inspired by James M. Gustafson's 1970 address to the Society of Christian Ethics, "The Burden of the Ethical: Reflections on Disinterestedness and Involvement," published in his *Theology and Christian Ethics* (Philadelphia: Pilgrim Press, 1974), pp. 33–46.

interest narrowly conceived. Agents who give time to this process will not always emerge with a clear sense of God's will, but they usually can proceed with some confidence that although they cannot control all the variables at play in the situation, the option that has been judged best can be followed with a peaceful heart because our limitations repose on a sea of Divine Mercy.

THE ETHICS OF DOING ETHICS

The need to maintain a balance between bearing the burden of the ethical and accepting the consolation of the religious suggests another matter for attention as these explorations in Catholic moral theology are brought to a close. This is the fact that ethics itself should not be immune from moral scrutiny. After all, the decision to define this or that as an ethical problem, the choice to focus an article or a lecture on a particular topic, the design of a syllabus or a curriculum—all of these are human actions, with consequences in this world. Our professional decisions may lack the life-and-death drama of medical or military ones, and our power for good or harm may seem small compared to that of engineers or corporation executives, but there is reason to examine the practice of doing ethics in light of moral concerns from time to time.[21] If one's point of view is feminist and liberationist, prominent among these concerns will be the question: What seems to have happened to the victims of systemic injustice as the result of the way we are going about our work? Or, more positively: How might we do more toward promoting the values of God's reign?

Clearly in light of such standards we will discover many ambiguities, and even downright sins of omission and commission, in our professional lives. In an ecclesiastical situation where authorities are quick to chastise moral theologians who dissent from official teaching, there is some danger that instincts for self-preservation may make us less self-critical than we ought to be, but scrutinizing the effects of our scholarly activities is essential if we are to make greater progress toward the ideals for moral theology mandated by the Second Vatican Council. Listening to those who object to injustice is especially required if our discipline is to help Catholics "bring forth fruit in charity for the life of the world" (*Optatem Totius* #16).

The case of racism is an excellent topic for an examination of professional conscience by white moral theologians. In his challenging essay "The African

---

21. These concerns are discussed more fully in Anne E. Patrick, "Ethics for Church Professionals," *New Catholic World* (January–February 1983): 21–24.

American Experience and U.S. Roman Catholic Ethics: 'Strangers and Aliens No Longer?'" seminary professor Bryan Massingale reviews decades of literature in moral theology and concludes that there is a lack of sustained attention to matters of racial justice in the two most prominent records of U.S. Catholic reflection in the field, the "Notes on Moral Theology" in *Theological Studies* and the reports from the ongoing seminar in moral theology from the *Proceedings of the Catholic Theological Society of America* (CTSA).[22]

The "Notes on Moral Theology" are review essays on topics in the discipline, based primarily on journal literature and published once or twice a year in the Jesuit-edited quarterly *Theological Studies*. Massingale finds that a few instances of sustained attention to racial justice were evident in the 1940s and 1950s, but that "[a]fter 1963, with the exception of [Robert H.] Springer's appeal in 1970 that Catholic ethicists pay more attention to this subject, the theme of racial justice all but disappears from this moral survey."[23] It does not disappear entirely, however, and the sort of treatment it receives is worth noting. Richard A. McCormick, who authored "Notes on Moral Theology" surveys during 1965–1987, lists racism prominently among major issues of the day on a few occasions, but apparently there was very little journal literature for him to analyze. In a 1977 discussion of Christian faith and moral reasoning, for example, McCormick mentions racism first in a discussion of "major moral problems of our time," followed by "poverty, deprivation of civil rights, warfare, [and] violence."[24] Scrutiny of the indexes for subsequent surveys, however, turns up only two more references to racism, neither of which is treated in connection with a publication on that topic.[25] It must be noted, however, that McCormick develops his ideas on addressing racism elsewhere, particularly the structural racism affecting healthcare facilities.[26]

---

22. Bryan N. Massingale, "The African American Experience and U.S. Roman Catholic Ethics: 'Strangers and Aliens No Longer?'" forthcoming in *Black and Catholic: The Challenge and Gift of Black Folk: Contributions of African American Experience and World View to Catholic Theology,* ed. Jamie T. Phelps (Milwaukee: Marquette University Press, forthcoming). Cited here from Massingale's typescript.

23. Ibid., p. 7.

24. Richard A. McCormick, *Notes on Moral Theology 1965 Through 1980* (Washington, D.C.: University Press of America, 1981), p. 630. A similar mention of "the problem of racial justice" occurs in the survey for January–June 1967 (ibid., p. 117).

25. Richard A. McCormick, *Notes on Moral Theology 1981 Through 1984* (Washington, D.C.: University Press of America, 1984), pp. 127, 150.

26. Richard A. McCormick, *Health and Medicine in the Catholic Tradition* (New York: Crossroad, 1984), pp. 81–82.

Massingale's analysis of the *CTSA Proceedings* discovers two "extensive examinations of the American race question" during the period from 1946 to 1972, followed by the first documented presentation by an African-American member to the CTSA in 1974, Joseph Nearon's "Preliminary Report: Research Committee for Black Theology," in 1974.[27] In this report Nearon forthrightly named the racism affecting theology and observed:

> If this fact can be blamed on the cultural situation, if it is more the result of omission and inattention than [due] to conscious commission it is still a fact. There is an insensitivity here which can only remain blameless until it is pointed out and I serve notice to you, my colleagues, that I am now pointing it out. I hasten to add that I do this not to condemn but to awaken.[28]

Massingale indicates that the CTSA "*as a whole* has made conspicuous efforts in recent years to be attentive to the African American experience." He faults its ongoing seminar in moral theology, however, for not focusing on racial topics in any of its meetings since the seminar was reorganized in 1982.[29]

Massingale's indictment of late-twentieth-century U.S. moral theology is offered in the hope that naming the problem of inattention to racism is an essential step toward improving things. Because his interests are more constructive than critical, however, his statement of the problematic status quo in Catholic moral theology is followed by the positive suggestion that resources are at hand for remedying the situation. In the first place, there are the insights from a rich literature of African-American (Protestant) ethics, which include (1) an emphasis on the fundamental principle of "universal inclusion"; (2) a "passionate concern for justice" that entails actively listening to those made invisible by racism; (3) a recognition that differences in status as oppressor and oppressed require a "division" of ethical questions and tasks;

27. Preston Williams, a black Protestant ethicist from Harvard Divinity School, presented a paper in 1973 on "Religious and Social Aspects of Roman Catholic and Black American Relationships," *CTSA Proceedings* 28 (1973): 15–30.

28. *CTSA Proceedings* 29 (1974): 414–15, quoted by Massingale, "African American Experience," p. 11. The following year Nearon again addressed the CTSA, speaking on "The Situation of American Blacks," *CTSA Proceedings* 30 (1975): 177–202.

29. Massingale, "African American Experience," pp. 11–12. Massingale states that the 1982 meeting was the seminar's first, but this seminar was listed on programs for some years prior to its reorganization in 1982. In 1994 the CTSA redesigned its convention format, replacing former categories of ongoing seminars and workshops (which in recent years have included sessions on Black Catholic Theology and Hispanic/Latino Theologies) with the common designation "working groups."

and (4) a normative, utopian vision of eschatological hope.[30] Massingale also recognizes two "'windows' in Catholic moral reflection" already opening toward the possibility of influence by African-American experience, namely, the acknowledgment of social sin and the recent emphasis on solidarity with those who are poor. His criticism thus amounts to an invitation to moral theologians to draw out the implications of such positions and open themselves to a conversion that entails seeing "social reality from the perspective of the victims of injustice."[31]

This thoughtful, courageous, and hopeful essay certainly warrants reflection by those who have been members of the moral theology guild in recent decades. It has prompted me to probe for the causes of the lack of sustained attention in the academic literature of moral theology to matters of racial justice, and I find these to be complex. Most basically, there is the problem of racism itself, which operates even in well-meaning individuals who have consciously renounced bias but nevertheless occupy privileged positions as a result of long-entrenched social and economic systems. Nearon in 1970, and Massingale a quarter of a century later, have named a painful reality that must be changed: because racism is institutionalized, even an idealistic discipline like moral theology betrays the bias of the culture and reflects the sinful results of white privilege. A second factor is implied in Massingale's recourse to Protestant literature for most of his substantive suggestions. This causal factor derives from demographics; Catholics comprise only about 10 percent of African-American Christians, and this minority-within-a-minority situation has contributed to uncritical acceptance of a situation in which there are very few black Catholic theologians in general, with none specializing in moral theology until recently.[32] It would seem that having a "critical mass" of black moral theologians publishing in theological journals and planning the CTSA sessions would result in a rather prompt correction of the situation criticized

30. Ibid., pp. 14-24 passim. In developing this list Massingale draws especially on the thought of the following African-American Protestants: James Cone, Major J. Jones, Martin Luther King, Jr., Enoch H. Oglesby, Peter J. Paris, Theodore Walker, Jr., Cornel West, and Preston N. Williams.

31. Ibid., p. 27.

32. In *The Black Church in the African American Experience,* C. Eric Lincoln and Laurence H. Mamiya estimate that in 1989 there were 23.7 million black members of Christian churches in the United States, of whom two million were Roman Catholics. They note that "since 1985 black Roman Catholics have been among the fastest growing religious groups," due mainly to the influx of immigrants from Haiti and elsewhere and to some degree to the attraction of urban parochial schools (Durham, N.C.: Duke University Press, 1990), p. 407.

by Nearon and Massingale. But until the discipline's white practitioners become more proactively antiracist, is it likely that academically talented black Catholics—or, for that matter, Catholics of Asian, Hispanic, or Native American backgrounds—will have much incentive to enter the field?[33]

In a 1992 report to the CTSA Board of Directors, systematic theologian Jamie T. Phelps estimated the figure for U.S. black Catholics at 2.5 million and listed two ethicists among the thirteen black Catholic scholars then specializing in theology and related ecclesial disciplines; in 1996 there are four black Catholic ethicists teaching in this country.[34] It is understandable that Protestants, who number roughly 90 percent of African-American Christians, should have led the way in bringing wisdom gained from black experience to bear on the discipline of Christian ethics. At the same time it is lamentable that, despite the substantial number of black Catholics, so few

33. Massingale cites with appreciation several full-length studies by white Catholic theologians: John La Farge, *The Catholic Viewpoint on Race Relations* (Garden City, N.Y.: Hanover House, 1956); Joseph T. Leonard, *Theology and Race Relations* (Milwaukee: Bruce, 1963); Daniel C. Maguire, *A New American Justice* (Minneapolis: Winston, 1980), reissued as *A Case for Affirmative Action* (Dubuque: Shepherd, 1992); and Christopher F. Mooney, *Inequality and the American Conscience* (Mahwah, N.J.: Paulist, 1982). Also deserving mention is Barbara Hilkert Andolsen's *Daughters of Jefferson, Daughters of Bootblacks: Racism and American Feminism* (Macon, Ga.: Mercer University Press, 1986), which was the focus of a CTSA convention workshop in 1989. Massingale further observes that three publications of the U.S. bishops on race matters have not "received significant scholarly attention or pastoral implementation" (draft, p. 13). These texts are *Brothers and Sisters to Us* (1979), *The National Race Crisis* (1968), and *Discrimination and the Christian Conscience* (1958).

34. The ethicists named in Phelps's unpublished report on "Recruitment of CTSA Membership among African Americans" (June 12, 1992) are Msgr. Henry Charles of St. Louis University and Rev. Bryan Massingale of St. Francis Seminary, Milwaukee. Professor Toinette Eugene, listed by Phelps under "sociology of religion," now teaches social ethics at Garrett-Evangelical Theological Seminary, and Professor Sheila Briggs, a British citizen, teaches social ethics at the University of Southern California. A summary of Phelps's report, along with that of board member Orlando Espin concerning Hispanic theologians, was prepared by CTSA President Michael J. Buckley and published in the *CTSA Proceedings* 47 (1992): 189. In response to these reports the board established a committee to "identify African-American and other underrepresented ethnic/racial (Hispanic, Asian-American) Catholic graduate and doctoral students and faculty in theology and other ecclesial disciplines" as a "first step toward recruitment" as CTSA members. African-American Catholic religious scholars first met as the Black Catholic Theological Symposium (BCTS) in 1978 and have convened annually since 1991. Hispanics organized the Academy of Catholic Hispanic Theologians in the United States (ACHTUS) in 1988 and began publishing the *Journal of Hispanic/Latino Theology* in 1993. Papers from the first joint gathering of these two societies (June 1995) are published in *Journal of Hispanic/Latino Theology* 3/3 (February 1996): 3–58.

have been encouraged and supported in obtaining training for intellectual leadership in the church. Phelps sees this as the outcome of the "ambiguous history of the Catholic Church's relationship to African Americans," and she rightly decries the "resistance, insensitivity and marginalization [that] obstruct the identification and mentoring of black Catholic theologians within the United States."[35]

For Massingale's hope for a significant encounter of white moral theologians with African-American experience and wisdom to be realized, a third cause for the problem he identifies needs to be addressed. This has to do with the ecclesial context in which moral theology has operated in recent decades and with the understanding of our task that practitioners have brought to our work. Perhaps because such a solid consensus on the sinfulness of racism has existed among members of the Catholic hierarchy and theologians for some decades, the issue has not been considered intellectually problematic in the way that, say, *in vitro* fertilization and sterilization have been. Magisterial teaching clearly condemns racism, and most moral theologians support this teaching wholeheartedly. The need for scholarly reflection has been thought to lie more with questions still disputed within the tradition, especially those where official teaching appears problematic or unpersuasive. Insofar as the task is to clarify or contribute toward improving official moral teachings, matters of race seem to require less attention than certain other questions. However, if the task of moral theology is to awaken consciences as well as to help resolve doubts, then a more proactive agenda is required.

Perhaps an analogy with the problem of sexual violence may shed light on the failure of moral theologians to give sufficient attention to matters of race. In classical teaching, rape is among those actions judged "intrinsically evil" by the tradition, and contemporary experience and the intellectual advances of feminism both support and strengthen this basic condemnation of sexual violence. Thus, it may not seem surprising that there are only seven references to rape indexed for the two decades of "Notes in Moral Theology" surveyed by McCormick. Moreover, all of these references presume the evil of sexual violence and occur in discussions of other topics, whether practical (abortion) or theoretical (forms of moral reasoning involving teleology or proportionality). It is significant, I believe, that the first mention of rape in McCormick's surveys is found alongside the first mention of racism. Commenting on a 1965 paper on the controversial topic of "Responsible Parenthood" by Robert O. Johann, McCormick declares that because "one cannot love God without

35. Phelps, "Recruitment," typescript pp. 1–2.

loving the neighbor, . . . any exploitative conduct offensive to the dignity of the person is intrinsically evil (e.g., racial discrimination, economic exploitation, rape, etc.)."[36]

In view of the consensus that rape and racism are so clearly wrong, it is understandable that moral theologians may not have thought it necessary to belabor these undisputed matters, especially in an ecclesiastical context where various other judgments are hotly contested. However, when one deals with moral experience from the angle of vision of those who suffer from the injustice, a different sense of the responsibilities of the discipline emerges. Then the task is not only to decide which attitudes and acts are evil or permissible but also to *probe the systemic causes of the injustices people suffer* and to *suggest ways of thinking and acting that contribute to positive action in the direction of justice.* What such actions should involve is most interesting intellectually and most crucial morally. There is evidence that a number of moral theologians are about such work and that theoretical developments concerning character, justice, liberation, human rights, and the common good are indeed contributing to an expanded sense of the agenda for moral theology.[37] The title of a volume contributed by thinkers outside the guild of Christian ethics, *Transforming a Rape Culture,* suggests the proactive ambition that one hopes to see increasingly evident within it, with respect not only to rape and sexism but to other sinful dimensions of our culture as well—notably its racism, violence, consumerism, ecological irresponsibility, and preferential option for the rich.[38]

The second and third factors I have been discussing—ensuring sufficient representation of formerly excluded groups in the academy and expanding the scope of perceived responsibilities of moral theologians—are interwoven.

36. McCormick, *Notes on Moral Theology 1965 Through 1980,* p. 43.

37. Exemplary titles include David Hollenbach, *Justice, Peace, and Human Rights,* which includes a chapter on the "education of the heart for the pursuit of justice" (New York: Crossroad, 1988); Thomas F. Schindler, *Ethics: The Social Dimension,* which critiques individualism in Catholic morality (Wilmington, Del.: Michael Glazier, 1989); and Thomas L. Schubeck, *Liberation Ethics* (Minneapolis: Fortress, 1993).

38. The editors, Emilie Buchwald, Pamela R. Fletcher, and Martha Roth, begin by defining a rape culture as "a complex of beliefs that encourages male sexual aggression and supports violence against women" (p. vii). *Transforming a Rape Culture* (Minneapolis: Milkweed Editions, 1993) provides data, insights, and suggestions for change. Among its many contributors is one Catholic theologian, systematician Joan H. Timmerman, whose essay "Religion and Violence: The Persistence of Ambivalence" analyzes past complicity of the churches and points to encouraging signs and possibilities (pp. 201–11).

Here again the analogy between racism and sexual violence is instructive. Until women gained a purchase in the academic field of ethics, such matters as rape and domestic violence were not "interesting" to study. Now considerable attention is being paid to them, thanks to the involvement of women in the discipline, which itself has been facilitated by the proactive efforts of men like McCormick to include feminist concerns in the agenda and welcome female colleagues to the guild.[39] The main point of Massingale's critique is to inspire moral theologians to be proactive also where matters of racial justice are concerned. Similar invitations have repeatedly been issued to the entire theological profession by Hispanic-American theologians, who are conscious that although Hispanics comprise more than a third of the U.S. Catholic population they are not yet recognized by the Anglo majority as central to the church's identity in this country.[40] Indeed, commenting on the 1990 U.S. census figures that counted 22.4 million Hispanic Americans, biblical scholar Fernando F. Segovia estimated in 1992 that this group already comprised approximately 40 percent of the Catholic church in this country.[41] However,

39. Important contributions include Elisabeth Schüssler Fiorenza and Mary Shawn Copeland, eds., *Violence Against Women* (Maryknoll, N.Y.: Orbis, 1994); Pamela Cooper-White, *The Cry of Tamar: Violence Against Women and the Church's Response* (Minneapolis: Fortress, 1995); and Joanne Carlson Brown and Carole R. Bohn, eds., *Christianity, Patriarchy, and Abuse: A Feminist Critique* (New York: Pilgrim Press, 1989). An early episcopal response to the heightened concern over domestic violence is discussed in the above-mentioned chapter by Timmerman ("Religion and Violence," pp. 205–7); the episcopal document is *A Heritage of Violence? A Pastoral Reflection of Conjugal Violence* (trans. Antoinette Kinlough; Quebec: Social Affairs Committee, Assembly of Quebec Bishops, 1988). More recent episcopal responses include Bishop Kenneth Untener, "Domestic Violence," *Origins* 23 (October 28, 1993): 357–58; and Bishop Jorge Mejia, "The Roots of Violence Against Women," *Origins* 23 (November 4, 1993): 369–71. For instances of McCormick's proactive interest in justice for women, see *Notes on Moral Theology 1965–1980*, pp. 385–92; idem, *Corrective Vision*, p. 11; and, most recently, his co-edited volume (with Charles Curran and Margaret A. Farley), *Readings in Moral Theology No. 9: Feminist Ethics* (New York: Paulist, 1996).

40. See, for example, Marina A. Herrera, "Providence and Histories: One Hispanic's View," and Orlando O. Espin and Sixto J. Garcia, "'Lilies of the Field': A Hispanic Theology of Providence and Human Responsibility," *CTSA Proceedings* 44 (1989): 7–11 and 70–90; also Roberto S. Goizueta, "Theology as Intellectually Vital Inquiry: The Challenge of/to U.S. Hispanic Theologians," *CTSA Proceedings* 46 (1991): 58–69; Virgilio P. Elizondo, "Hispanic Theology and Popular Piety: From Interreligious Encounter to a New Ecumenism," *CTSA Proceedings* 48 (1993): 1–14; and Allan Figueroa Deck, "'A Pox on Both Your Houses': A View of Catholic Conservative-Liberal Polarities from the Hispanic Margin," in *Being Right: Conservative Catholics in America*, ed. Mary Jo Weaver and R. Scott Appleby (Bloomington: Indiana University Press, 1995), pp. 88–104.

41. Fernando F. Segovia, "Introduction" to a special issue on "Hispanic Americans in The-

despite eloquent protests against the continuing marginalization of Hispanic concerns, moral theology as such has yet to demonstrate a proactive interest in questions of particular import to Hispanic Catholics, such as immigration and education policies. If the concerns of moral theology were broader, perhaps among the many members of the Academy of Catholic Hispanic Theologians in the United States (ACHTUS) who describe their interests as "pastoral theology," "popular religion," or "liberation theology" more would be found who name "moral theology" as well. But as things stood in the 1995 ACHTUS Directory, of thirty-two active members, only two mentioned ethics, and neither has appeared on a program for a CTSA moral theology session.[42]

All in all, Massingale's article and the continuing inattention of moral theology to matters of racial and ethnic justice both testify to the high costs of our tradition's having delayed for so long the repair of the problematic situation described in the introduction to this volume. If up to now revisionists have been busy stitching those theoretical seams that allow for necessary changes in teachings concerning authority, women, and sexuality, it is time today to expand the agenda of moral theology much further in the direction of justice and liberation. Systematic theologian M. Shawn Copeland stated the agenda forcefully to the Catholic Theological Society of America in 1991:

> I believe theology in North America is called to put forward a critical mediation of the Christian gospel which takes into full account racism, sexism, class exploitation, and human objectification in a capitalist system of production as well as the psychological and affective realities which suffuse human living. North American theology must marshall . . . a critique of those values, orders, relations, institutions, meanings, and practices bent to the oppression of peoples of color, to the degradation and suppression of women, to global imperialism.[43]

---

ology and the Church," *Listening* 27 (Winter 1992): 5. According to the *1993 Catholic Almanac,* official figures for the U.S. Catholic population in 1992 were 55.3 million; the number of U.S. Hispanics who were baptized Catholic was estimated at about 80 percent of the 1990 U.S. census figures of 22.4 million Hispanics (Huntington, Ind.: Our Sunday Visitor, 1992), pp. 381, 488.

42. The scholars listed are Professors Ada María Isasi-Díaz of Drew University and Michael M. Mendiola of the Graduate Theological Union, Berkeley. Several associate members, including graduate students, also noted an interest in ethics. It is encouraging that at the 1994 CTSA convention the working group on Hispanic/Latino Theologies invited two prominent moral theologians, Lisa Sowle Cahill and David Hollenbach, to consider the topic of Isasi-Díaz's *En la Lucha* and María Pilar Aquino's *Our Cry for Life,* books I discuss later in this chapter.

43. M. Shawn Copeland, "Theology as Intellectually Vital Inquiry: A Black Theological Interrogation," *CTSA Proceedings* 46 (1991): 56–57.

Copeland went on to say that developing such a critique will require "radical conversion" on the part of North American theologians.

That even our converted selves will never do enough is not grounds for discouragement or inaction but rather for deepening our trust in God's mercy and supporting one another in the character traits required by our profession. Most especially we must cultivate two qualities, vision and courage. The first demands the willingness to scan the horizon for the most complete picture possible of how human systems, dispositions, and actions interact to cause good and harm. This involves, as we have seen in the preceding chapter, attending with the utmost care to the various "Rachels" whose cries disturb our complacency. Courage, the second requisite quality, entails the willingness to steer the ship of our labors into whatever currents and winds must be faced for the sake of increasing the proportion of good over evil.

CONSCIENCE AND THE COMMON GOOD

This language of proportionality is deliberate, intended to respect the fact that our ability to prevent evil and accomplish good is finite. Much that happens is beyond our control, and every attempted advance will be accompanied by side effects that reflect this finitude and require new corrections of course. Moreover, insofar as the vision of our common human good is concerned, we are never able to define this in a more than provisional manner because the full meaning of this transcendent ideal is wrapped up in the mystery of God. "[W]e are always 'on the way' toward an adequate understanding of what the ultimate human good truly is," moral theologian David Hollenbach reminds us, building on the insight from St. Thomas Aquinas that "'God's own goodness is the good of the whole universe.'"[44] This situation does not, however, absolve us of the obligation to seek the most adequate understanding possible; on the contrary, it mandates an ongoing effort to correct the biases of our individual limitations as well as our social locations. What the feminist-liberationist perspective stresses in this regard is that overcoming patriarchal interpretations of the common good requires the obedience of listening to women, especially those in situations of poverty and violence. This listening has been under way for some time, and it is helping to

---

44. David Hollenbach, "The Common Good in the Postmodern Epoch: What Role for Theology," in *Religion, Ethics, and the Common Good,* ed. Theresa Moser and James A. Donahue (Mystic, Conn.: Twenty-Third Publications, 1996), p. 20. Hollenbach quotes here from Aquinas's *Summa Theologiae,* IaIIae, Q.19 a.10.

shape more adequate visions of what God is enabling and requiring us to be and to do. To illustrate this point, I shall describe below some contributions by North American women theologians whose liberationist writings hold great promise for influencing positively the work done within the narrower field of moral theology.

M. Shawn Copeland, for example, has brought theological analysis to the situations of black women domestic workers in South Africa and the United States in a 1987 essay that shows how the biases of racism, sexism, and classism interact to undermine people's abilities to think and feel, thereby anesthetizing religion and injuring the common good. She calls for a "critical feminist theology" of global dimensions, "which refuses to rank or order oppression; which takes up the standpoint of the masses, the marginated and those beyond the margins; and which is committed to justice in the concrete." Overcoming the collusion of Christianity in the oppression of women and people of color, Copeland points out, requires the collaboration of theologians with other analysts within and beyond the tradition, especially those trained in critical understandings of economics, sociology, and politics.[45]

More recently Copeland has extended her analysis to challenge Christian feminist theologians of all backgrounds to go beyond the *rhetoric* of solidarity and commit themselves to the *critical practice* of solidarity. In a 1994 address commemorating the fiftieth anniversary of the first Catholic graduate program in theology open to women in this country (the School of Sacred Theology founded by Holy Cross Sister Mary Madeleva Wolff at Saint Mary's College in Indiana), Copeland argues that

> focus on solidarity not only problematizes the practice of theology for Celtic, Anglo, European-American feminist theologians, but also for indigenous North American and Asian American women theologians, for *mujerista* and womanist theologians. Focus on solidarity calls for an end to facile adoption of the rhetoric of solidarity by Celtic-, Anglo-, European-American feminists, while they ignore and, sometimes, consume the experiences and voices of the marginalized and oppressed, while, ever adroitly, dodging the penitential call to conversion—to authenticity in word and deed.[46]

45. M. Shawn Copeland, "The Interaction of Racism, Sexism and Classism in Women's Exploitation," in *Women, Work and Poverty,* ed. Elisabeth Schüssler Fiorenza and Anne E. Carr (Edinburgh: T & T Clark, 1987), pp. 25–26. See also Copeland's essay, "Reconsidering the Idea of the Common Good," in *Catholic Social Thought and the New World Order,* ed. Oliver F. Williams and John W. Houck (Notre Dame: University of Notre Dame Press, 1993), pp. 309–27.

46. M. Shawn Copeland, "Toward a Critical Christian Feminist Theology of Solidarity," in

Authentic solidarity, she observes, means recognizing that common problems do not automatically lead to sisterhood and that differences must be respected but not absolutized. Her suggestions for getting beyond "naive, 'politically correct,' cliched rhetoric of solidarity" to authentic Christian praxis are twofold. In the first place she calls for "active and attentive listening" to differentiated voices within and beyond one's own community. Such listening demands different virtues of those who are relatively more implicated in systems of oppression than of those who are less so. Thus she enjoins white women to practice humility, resolve, and relinquishment in an ongoing effort to balance attentive listening with appropriate speaking. She urges red, brown, yellow, and black women to forgo manipulative stances in favor of honesty, courage, and appropriate self-criticism. And she invites everyone to practice patience and restraint, "an ethics of respectful listening and an ethics of thinking before speaking," which is grounded theologically in the experience of God's liberating Word.[47]

In addition to this disciplined process of hearing and speaking, Copeland insists that a complex form of social analysis is also needed for the praxis of solidarity. This analysis involves critiquing one's own horizons, developing general descriptions of the factors at play in oppressive situations, probing the patterns that emerge from such descriptions, judging the incongruities thus uncovered in the light of the Gospel, and coming to specific decisions and commitments for action. The process is a continual one, and it is possible only in community and through the gift of God's Spirit.[48]

The implications of Copeland's critical perspective may be seen in a volume she co-edited in 1994 with New Testament scholar Elisabeth Schüssler Fiorenza, *Violence Against Women*. This book is a Christian theological and ethical analogue to the largely secular volume mentioned above, *Transforming a Rape Culture*. It gathers essays by women from Europe, Asia, and the Americas that explore the sociocultural factors, particularly gender construction and religious ideology, associated with violence against women in systems of patriarchal power, which in Western contexts Schüssler Fiorenza designates as "kyriarchal" because "ruling power is in the hands of elite propertied educated freeborn men."[49]

Women and Theology, ed. Mary Ann Hinsdale and Phyllis H. Kaminski (Maryknoll, N.Y.: Orbis, 1995), p. 3.

47. Ibid., pp. 25–26.

48. Ibid., pp. 28–29.

49. Elisabeth Schüssler Fiorenza, "Introduction," in her volume co-edited with M. Shawn Copeland, *Violence Against Women* (Maryknoll, N.Y.: Orbis, 1994), p. xxii.

In a concluding essay Copeland makes several proactive suggestions for change on the basis of her critical analysis of the material. First, the church must repent its historic misogyny as well as its ambivalence, complicity, and direct engagement in violence against women: "the blood of raped, battered, abused and murdered women summons the church to its own *kenosis*," or self-emptying in effective acts of penance that contribute to real change. Second, the church must develop a new model of pastoral care that values women's experience and replaces the "aesthetic of submission" associated with so much religious imagery and ritual in favor of an "aesthetic of liberation" that will inspire a "non-oppressive, non-sexist truly human and Christian future." Third, the church must adopt a renewed theological anthropology and challenge media and religious influences that reinforce unjust patterns in domestic relations, distort understandings of sexual desire and pleasure, and promote dualist or reductively "essentialist" views of women. Finally, the church must develop a pastoral ministry that heals the effects of clergy sexual misconduct against women and children, thereby restoring their bodies to "erotic and spiritual integrity" and the Body of Christ to "ontological and sacramental integrity."[50]

The collaborative and interdisciplinary approach exemplified in Copeland's work is also seen in the writings of another leading Catholic women's liberation theologian, the Cuban-born scholar Ada María Isasi-Díaz. With her Mexican-American colleague, Yolanda Tarango, Isasi-Díaz first developed a distinctively *mujerista* theology in their co-authored 1988 book, *Hispanic Women: Prophetic Voice in the Church*.[51] More recently Isasi-Díaz has elaborated this theology, which grows organically from a process of listening to women from a broad range of Latino cultural and economic backgrounds, in the 1993 study *En la Lucha: A Hispanic Women's Liberation Theology*.[52] Both works burst the bonds of the traditional theological subdisciplines, combining attention to matters of history, method, God-concepts, and ethics with ethnographic concern to respect the diverse blends of popular religiosity and institutional Catholicism found among Latinas of Mexican, Cuban, Puerto Rican, and other heritages. The words of one woman they interviewed, a mother of twelve who chose tubal ligation despite the objec-

---

50. M. Shawn Copeland, "Editorial Reflections," in *Violence Against Women*, pp. 121–22.

51. Ada María Isasi-Díaz and Yolanda Tarango, eds., *Hispanic Women: Prophetic Voice in the Church* (San Francisco: Harper & Row, 1988; reprint, Minneapolis: Fortress, 1992).

52. Isasi-Díaz, *En La Lucha: A Hispanic Women's Liberation Theology* (Minneapolis: Fortress, 1993).

tions of doctors, husband, and priest, cast light on the urgency of resolving the debate between classicist and revisionist moral theology in favor of the latter: "I would have had twenty-four children if I had listened to them."[53]

Furthermore, Isasi-Díaz's interpretation of the ongoing struggle for liberation sets the cultural debate about abortion legislation in a much fuller context than the polemics of "life" versus "choice": "The struggle for liberation is the struggle to be self-determining within the context of community and in view of the common good, and to have the material conditions needed to develop into the fulness of our capacity."[54] Her position seems compatible with that of a number of thoughtful Catholics who see merit in the values associated with both sides of the debate—women's moral agency and human life in all its stages—and who are unwilling to oppose and absolutize the abstractions "choice" and "life." This absolutization is theologically problematic because all values are relative to God, and it is morally problematic because of the effect it has on the common good. Exaggerated pro-life rhetoric not only betrays the intellectual heritage that has found reason to tolerate just war and to celebrate martyrdom; it has also fueled the lamentable violence at reproductive health clinics and contributed to a widespread social illness, which might be termed the Dylan Thomas syndrome: the vitalist obsession, in cases of terminal illness, to rage against the dying of the light by all sorts of expensive and disproportionate medical interventions. It also masks the realities of violence and death that shape the context in which so many women face the decision about whether or not to bring new life into a world that is not justly ordered to its support. Meanwhile exaggerated pro-choice rhetoric, also indefensible on moral and religious grounds, has been adopted by the gun and tobacco lobbies in this country to everyone's detriment. The subtleties of an argument such as Beverly Wildung Harrison delineates in *Our Right to Choose* tend to be lost on a culture that has understood liberty too often as independence from concern for the common good.[55]

Although neither Isasi-Díaz nor the prominent Mexican feminist theologian, María Pilar Aquino, has entered the abortion debate directly in their

53. Isasi-Díaz and Tarango, *Hispanic Women*, p. 53.

54. Isasi-Díaz, *En La Lucha*, p. xi.

55. According to Harrison, a Presbyterian ethicist, the legality of abortion is a necessary condition for women's exercise of moral responsibility. She writes: "Procreative choice is a morally right position because it creates conditions essential to the well-being of over half the human species, not because it allows any of us to live free of our social obligation to provide for the common welfare, especially that of less advantaged people." See Beverly Wildung Harrison, *Our Right to Choose: Toward a New Ethic of Abortion* (Boston: Beacon, 1983), p. 49.

major works, both imply that a compromise encompassing values from both sides is needed in the social order. Aquino has entitled her study of Latin American feminist theology *Our Cry for Life,* and she concludes it with an eloquent claim that in view of women's constant struggle against powerful forces of death, the central principles for Christian ethics must be "life, liberation, and human integrity." Of these, "life" is the chief criterion, and it entails "many particular tasks devoted to the eradication of structures and realities that deny the poor and oppressed the means of life and exclude women from their right and duty to be active protagonists."[56] Among these factors that inhibit life she recognizes capitalism as presently experienced in Latin America as preeminently a "project of death":

> Present-day capitalism is interested in maximizing profits at the expense of women . . . . In the social, cultural, and religious orders it enthrones and maintains the hierarchical order of masculine and feminine models, racial division, and control over women's sexuality, reproductive powers, and work.[57]

Acknowledging that socialist societies also fall short of the gospel insofar as they "dehumanize women and maintain male superiority," Aquino concludes that the ideal of God's reign mandates a vigilant "criticism of every system that makes life impossible for the majority and [of] all unequal relations that diminish human integrity."[58]

For the Brazilian theologian Ivone Gebara, the situation of violence against women in her country was so great that in 1993 she expressed opinions that led to her being silenced by the Vatican two years later. Essentially these opinions involve drawing out the implications of affirming the value and dignity of women's lives and consciences in a country where prostitution and rape, including marital rape, have been condoned since the colonial era but where abortion remains illegal and unregulated. With respect to child prostitution, for example, Brazil today ranks second only to Thailand, with 500,000 instances reported by the country's Ministry of Social Welfare in comparison to U.N. figures of 800,000 for Thailand.[59] The residual effects of centuries of slavery are especially evident in the northeast part of Brazil, the location of the city of Recife, where Gebara had lived in a favela among the poor for fif-

---

56. María Pilar Aquino, *Our Cry for Life: Feminist Theology from Latin America,* trans. Dinah Livingstone (Maryknoll, N.Y.: Orbis, 1993), p. 190.

57. Ibid., p. 188.

58. Ibid., p. 189.

59. Zilda Fernandes Ribeiro, "Prostitution and Rape in the Colonial Period," in *Violence Against Women,* ed. Schüssler Fiorenza and Copeland, p. 11.

teen years. In view of the fact that millions of illegal abortions occur annually in Brazil, and troubled by maternal mortality estimates as high as 10 percent, Gebara voiced to a journalist from the popular magazine *VEJA* her support for the legalization and regulation of abortion. She also said of a case involving a mentally ill mother of four who became pregnant again that "abortion is not necessarily a sin for a poor woman who is psychologically incapable of dealing with pregnancy."[60] The magazine published the interview under a headline Gebara did not approve, "Abortion Is Not a Sin," releasing the issue shortly after the promulgation of Pope John Paul II's encyclical *Veritatis Splendor* had enjoined bishops to protect the faithful from theological "dissent, in the form of carefully orchestrated protests and polemics carried on in the media" (#113). Dom José Cardoso Sobriho, the Archbishop of Recife, responded shortly after the magazine appeared by insisting that Gebara retract her statement or face expulsion from the religious congregation she had belonged to for nearly thirty years. Previously Gebara had taught for a decade at the theological institute founded by Recife's former archbishop, Dom Helder Câmara, and she continued to teach informally after Cardoso closed the seminary in 1989.

To clarify her position after the *VEJA* article, Gebara issued a statement that explained it as a response to a society that "condones the social abortion of its [grown] sons and daughters" by failing to "provide the conditions of adequate employment, health, housing, and schools." She argued:

> A society that continues to permit pregnancy testing as a requirement for hiring women is abortive. A society that remains silent about the responsibility of men and blames only women, disrespects their bodies and their history, and is exclusive and sexist is an abortive society.

It is in light of this reality as she has observed it that Gebara came to her judgment that Brazilian law should change:

---

60. Quoted here from David Molineaux, "Rome Moves to Silence Brazil's Gebara," *National Catholic Reporter,* May 26, 1995. On June 30, 1995, the newspaper published a follow-up article by Molineaux, "Brazil's Gebara Bows to Vatican For Now," as well as a letter Gebara had written explaining her decision to groups with which she could not keep speaking engagements. On August 25, 1995, *NCR* published a lengthy editorial, "Ivone Gebara Must Be Doing Something Right," which concluded: "By trying to silence Gebara, the curia is making her voice resound more powerfully among the People of God. The sanctions from the Vatican mean Gebara cannot engage in public speaking, teaching or publication. They do not mean the faithful cannot embrace her work."

For me as a Christian, to defend decriminalizing and regulating abortion does not mean disavowing the traditional teachings of the Gospel of Jesus and the church. Rather, it is a way to enter into them more deeply given the paradox of our human history, a way of actually decreasing violence against life. My position with regard to decriminalized and legalized abortion . . . is one of denouncing the evil, the institutionalized violence, the abuses, and the hypocrisy that envelop us. It is testimony for life; it is in defense of life.[61]

According to David Molineaux's account in the *National Catholic Reporter* for May 26, 1995, the case appeared to have been closed after Gebara met in 1994 with Dom Luciano Mendes de Almeida, president of the Brazilian hierarchy. However, her theological writings had been forwarded to the Congregation for the Doctrine of the Faith, and in June 1995 her religious superiors notified Gebara that she would be obliged to observe two years of silence and to return to Europe (in 1973 she had been awarded the doctorate in philosophy by the Catholic University of Louvain) for further study in traditional theology.

Ivone Gebara's case combines features of the U.S. cases discussed in chapters 4 and 5 of this volume. Like Charles Curran, Gebara has been censured for expressing dissenting opinions on questions of morality and law in the secular press, and, like the Vatican 24, she has been disciplined because of her status as a member of a women's religious congregation and because the moral and legal matter at issue is abortion. This case is unique, however, in that it represents the first time a female theologian has been publicly silenced in such a direct fashion since women entered the profession after the Second Vatican Council. Moreover, the mandate for remedial theological education also seems to be unique, and one may hazard that gender is a factor in this aspect of Rome's treatment of Gebara.

These several thinkers—Copeland, Schüssler Fiorenza, Isasi-Díaz, Tarango, Aquino, and Gebara—represent North and South American expressions of the liberation theology that has developed around the world since the 1960s. Although their liberationist writings reflect a much wider set of issues than those typically dealt with in moral theology, they have influenced the subdiscipline a great deal. Indeed, such writings constitute an important resource for correcting the biases that otherwise can result in a sort of "gourmet ethics," a

61. Quoted here from *Conscience* (Summer 1994): 3. Additional information concerning the case is provided by editor Maggie Hume in "Defending Lives: Brazilian Theologian Ivone Gebara" (pp. 2–3). See also Ivone Gebara, "The Abortion Debate in Brazil," *Journal of Feminist Studies in Religion* 11/2 (Fall 1995): 129–35.

preoccupation with individualistic moral righteousness, especially among those whose affluence allows them to worry about choices that are beyond the realm of possibility for most human beings. Also inspiring moral theology to sharper visions of the common good have been the writings of those concerned with environmental issues. Another North American Catholic feminist, Rosemary Radford Ruether, has taken leadership in this area. In 1992 she published *Gaia and God: An Ecofeminist Theology of Earth-Healing,* and four years later she edited a collection of ecofeminist essays, *Women Healing Earth: Third-World Women on Ecology, Feminism and Religion.*[62]

CONTEMPORARY REVISIONIST CONTRIBUTIONS

There are many instances where instead of burying the talent of our moral tradition under fearful defenses of classicist positions, Catholic scholars have been willing to invest it on the open market of contemporary reality, including the reality of women's struggles, which patriarchy would prefer remained invisible. Such literature by revisionist moral theologians is marked by its vision and courage as well as its efforts to seek as wide a consensus as possible on matters of social well-being instead of waging crusades against those who differ from their positions.

In the aftermath of the controversies over the Curran case and the threatened expulsion of the Vatican 24, for example, Catholic ethicists Patricia Beattie Jung and Thomas A. Shannon edited the volume *Abortion and Catholicism: The American Debate.* This anthology gathers writings of twenty-five thinkers ranging from Cardinal Joseph Ratzinger to Rosemary Radford Ruether. In their introduction, the editors voice the belief that "only

---

62. Rosemary Radford Ruether, *Gaia and God: An Ecofeminist Theology of Earth Healing* (San Francisco: HarperSanFrancisco, 1992) and *Women Healing Earth: Third-World Women on Ecology, Feminism and Religion* (Maryknoll, N.Y.: Orbis, 1996). There has been an explosion of interest in ecology in recent years, and the burgeoning literature suggests that ecofeminists and others share a conviction about the urgency of making care for the planet a central task of ethics. See, for example, Carol J. Adams, ed., *Ecofeminism and the Sacred* (New York: Continuum, 1993); Leonardo Boff, *Ecology and Liberation: A New Paradigm,* trans. John Cumming (Maryknoll, N.Y.: Orbis, 1995); David G. Hallman, ed., *Ecotheology: Voices from South and North* (Maryknoll, N.Y.: Orbis, 1994); and James M. Gustafson, *A Sense of the Divine: The Natural Environment from a Theocentric Perspective* (Cleveland, Oh.: Pilgrim Press, 1994). In this recent work Gustafson adds an ecological dimension to his earlier statement of the ethical task: "Humans are to seek to discern what God is enabling and requiring them to be and to do as participants in the patterns and processes of interdependence of life in the world" (p. 148).

open, honest, and respectful dialogue will bring the Catholic community to some resolution of this problem."[63] Such trust in the value of reflecting on the abortion issue from various angles had earlier been seen in the lay-edited journal *Commonweal*, whose editorial policy over the years has favored the "consistent ethic of life" without limiting articles to one-sided rehearsals of official Catholic positions. In 1981, for example, an issue devoted to the abortion question included one essay advocating the toleration of abortion for "therapeutic" indications only and another proposing that Catholic liberals should promote legislation that would prohibit abortions after eight weeks of fetal development.[64]

One sees in more recent Catholic literature the fruitfulness of an open debate on these questions. On the one side, the Catholics for a Free Choice publication *Conscience* has invited critical reflection on a number of matters, including the ambiguities of the organization's own name.[65] On the other, the Jesuit periodical *America*, once guilty of a theologically questionable editorial headline—"Life, not choice, is absolute"—has restored some balance by publishing essays that recognize the necessity of legal compromise in this country on the issues of abortion and euthanasia.[66] Two of these pieces are particularly successful in illustrating how revisionist moral theology can pro-

63. Patricia Beattie Jung and Thomas A. Shannon, eds., *Abortion and Catholicism: The American Debate* (New York: Crossroad, 1988), p. 6.

64. These articles in *Commonweal* for November 20, 1981, are by Raymond Tatalovich and Byron W. Daynes ("The Trauma of Abortion Politics," pp. 644–49) and Peter Steinfels ("The Search for an Alternative," pp. 660–64). *Commonweal* has continued to offer substantial essays from diverse perspectives in subsequent years, including the following: Joan C. Callahan, "The Fetus and Fundamental Rights" (April 11, 1986): 203–9; Sidney Callahan, "Abortion and the Sexual Agenda" (April 25, 1986): 232–38; Daniel C. Maguire and James Tunstead Burtchaell, "The Catholic Legacy and Abortion: A Debate" (November 20, 1987): 657–80; and Madelein Gray, "Giving Up the Gift" (February 25, 1994): 13–15. The phrase "consistent ethic of life" is associated with Cardinal Joseph Bernardin, who as chair of the U.S. Bishops' pro-life activities committee declared in 1983 that concerns about abortion should be understood as related to such matters as warfare, genetics, and capital punishment. In a more recent articulation of his position, "The Abortion Controversy: Seeking a Common Ground" (*Catholic International* [May 19, 1993]: 215–21), Bernardin observed that the consistent ethic requires promoting the basic human rights of women and children, which entails "working for economic justice." At that time Bernardin also called upon all participants in the public debate about abortion "to speak and act in an honest, mutually respectful manner that can seek the truth and find a common ground" (p. 221).

65. Rosemary Radford Ruether, "Reflections on the Word 'Free' in Free Choice," *Conscience* 15 (Summer 1994): 2–3.

66. *America* 153 (October 19, 1985): 229.

vide a way for Catholic values, including respect for religious freedom as well as respect for life, to be articulated to good effect in the public forum. These articles are Lisa Sowle Cahill's "Abortion, Sex and Gender: The Church's Public Voice," and James F. Bresnahan's "The Catholic Art of Dying."[67] Both articles reflect the egalitarian-feminist propensity to seek *influence* over the wider social context rather than the impossible level of *control* associated with patriarchal ambitions. They also express the tendency of Catholic social thought to analyze issues from a communitarian perspective, bringing the debates about policy issues beyond the impasse of opposing individual rights into a context of interdependency and community.

Cahill, a moral theologian who in a recent book explores war and peace in the Catholic tradition, argues in the *America* essay:

> Instead of medieval crusade preaching, Catholic discussions of abortion, sex and gender should take their keynote from our great tradition of social encyclicals, with their optimistic confidence that reasonable public discourse is possible and can lead to greater consensus and social cooperation on justice issues.

Regarding herself as a "moderate" on issues of sexuality and abortion, one who affirms the "intrinsic relation of sexuality and parenthood" as well as the value of gestating life, Cahill registers deep discomfort at the behavior of "certain self-defined champions of Catholic orthodoxy who seem to be arming true believers for a battle aimed at total obliteration of the enemy, rather than building consensus about a more humane common life."[68] She argues that current church teaching and practice on women and sexuality are impeding its efforts to discourage abortion, and she declares that "unless the pro-life position can come to terms with the legitimacy of women's need to be integral moral agents in the sexual sphere, and to enjoy social equality, it will never be a convincing alternative to the legal right to choose abortion."[69] Furthermore, she points out that the complexity of the processes of human fertilization and embryonic development, including the fact that up to 60 percent of fertilized ova are spontaneously expelled from the uterus, require accepting the possibility that morally serious persons can have honest differences about the status of the fetus. She also finds it important to recognize that "while the

---

67. Lisa Sowle Cahill, "Abortion, Sex and Gender: The Church's Public Voice," *America* (May 22, 1993): 6–11; and James F. Bresnahan, "The Catholic Art of Dying," *America* (November 4, 1995): 12–16.

68. Cahill, "Abortion," p. 7. This essay was prepared shortly before the publication of her *Love Your Enemies: Discipleship, Pacifism, and Just War Theory* (Minneapolis: Fortress, 1994).

69. Cahill, "Abortion," p. 9.

basic value of life should be unquestioned, there will be unavoidable differences in the way cultures institutionalize protection of life." Although she is by no means identified with the pro-choice movement, Cahill believes common ground exists for working toward a shared objective: "social measures that will reduce abortion, even if not outlawing it entirely."[70] She challenges church leaders to be much more active in addressing the root causes of abortion by promoting improvements in women's self-concepts and opportunities so that they will have equal access to the spiritual and material benefits that comprise the common good.

On the related issue of active euthanasia, the Jesuit ethicist James Bresnahan voices a similar trust that the merits of Catholic values will speak for themselves to the wider culture if they are not muffled by attempts at all-controlling legislation. He is more explicit than Cahill in naming religious freedom as a factor in his willingness to tolerate some compromise at the level of public policy, but like her he reasons that the common good is better served by seeking to build consensus than by attempting to impose absolutes on a pluralistic society. He recommends a position of "Catholic medical pacificism" in cases where intervention beyond palliative care would pose excessive burdens to a terminally ill patient, drawing a clear line against direct efforts to hasten death.

Bresnahan recognizes, however, that morally serious persons may conscientiously differ from this ideal, for instance those committed to the stoicism of the Hemlock Society. They believe that in certain circumstances it is virtuous to end one's life, thereby asserting as much control as possible over the complications of death and sparing others the hardships associated with one's prolonged dying. Bresnahan argues that those who are convinced that inflicted death is moral under certain medical circumstances should not be coerced to act against their beliefs, but at the same time he fears that to legalize active euthanasia in medical settings could lead to widespread abuses, especially the tendency to favor inflicted death as a "quicker and cheaper response to dying than hospice care." Bresnahan concludes that Catholics may need to allow those who believe in inflicted death to have a separate sector of care outside ordinary medical facilities, meanwhile "insisting on more legal constraints against the abuses we fear than some proponents of inflicted death appear to find convenient." He also recommends that Catholics intensify the practice of a "new corporal work of mercy," that of caring so well for the dying that other Americans will be less inclined to support the widespread

70. Ibid., p. 11.

practice of inflicted death than were the Oregon voters who passed a referendum in 1994 (currently under judicial review) that approved medical assistance in inflicting death when a dying person asks for this.[71]

As important as it remains for Catholic values and principles to influence our state and national debates on matters of social well-being, it is also crucial that moral theologians give increasing attention to ways of enlarging the focus of Catholics' moral interests to include international and planetary ones. The papal social encyclical tradition has led the way in many of these matters, together with such documents as the *Pastoral Constitution on the Church in the Modern World* (*Gaudium et Spes*) of the Second Vatican Council and *Justice in the World* of the 1971 Synod of Bishops.[72] A recent instance of moral theology that is exemplary in this regard is a volume edited by Kenneth R. Overberg, *AIDS, Ethics & Religion: Embracing a World of Suffering.* This work opens with essays describing the geography of AIDS suffering, including specific treatments of Asia, Africa, the U.S.A., and Latin America, as well as general discussions of the pandemic's scope.[73] Likewise, moral theologian James E. Hug makes an important contribution to the discussion of health-care reform in his 1993 essay "Health Care: A Planetary View." Hug challenges Americans, who comprise 4.75 percent of the world's population and consume 41 percent of its health resources, to open their eyes to "the hardships of our brothers and sisters in the rest of the human community." He cites statistics contrasting life expectancy in Niger (thirty-eight years) and Japan (seventy-nine years) and notes that eleven million children worldwide and seven million adults die unnecessarily each year.[74]

71. Bresnahan, "Catholic Art," p. 16.

72. An international perspective has always characterized modern Catholic social teaching; sustained attention to environmental concerns is relatively recent. The *Catechism of the Catholic Church* insists that human "dominion" is not absolute but rather is "limited by concern for the quality of life of [the] neighbor, including generations to come," and it "requires religious respect for the integrity of creation" (#2415). Pope John Paul II is the first pontiff to bring environmental concerns explicitly into social teaching, notably in his 1991 encyclical *Centesimus Annus* ##37–38. For instances of episcopal teaching on ecology, see Anthony M. Pilla, "Reverence and Responsibility: Pastoral Letter on the Environment," and Michael D. Pfeifer, "The Earth Is Our Home: Pastoral Message on Ecology and Environment," in *Catholic International* (February 1–14, 1991): 116–22 and 122–26; and National Conference of Catholic Bishops, "Renewing the Earth: An Invitation to Reflection and Action on the Environment in Light of Catholic Social Teaching," *Origins* 21 (December 12, 1991): 425–32.

73. Kenneth R. Overberg, ed., *AIDS, Ethics & Religion: Embracing a World of Suffering* (Maryknoll, N.Y.: Orbis, 1994).

74. James E. Hug, "Health Care: A Planetary View," *America* (December 11, 1993): 8–12.

When I survey the situation of Catholic moral theology more than three decades after the Second Vatican Council, I find considerable room for growth toward the conciliar ideal of inspiring believers to "bring forth fruit in charity for the life of the world" (*Optatem Totius* #16). At the same time I also see reason to celebrate the growth and fruitfulness that have already been achieved. Without denying the tensions between Catholics who labor in different capacities and from different angles of vision, I believe it is useful now to build on an increasingly shared recognition, namely, that collaboration with all women and men of good will is needed to create the future of justice that our earth and its inhabitants require.

FOR THE LIFE OF THE WORLD

In 1974 the then Archbishop of Olinda-Recife in northeast Brazil, Dom Helder Câmara, published a small book on spirituality and social justice called *The Desert Is Fertile*.[75] This title suggests an image for understanding the Catholic moral tradition today, one that draws on the biblical association of water with wisdom. Our moral tradition is a complex one that may be likened to a braided river, flowing with life-giving wisdom in strands that weave across one another, influencing and being influenced by each other in an ongoing process. All of the channels draw from the wellsprings of scripture and tradition, and often they flow together, although at times there are divergences on account of distinctive experiences or approaches to knowledge. The main channel of this braided stream is that of magisterial wisdom, which continues to proclaim with great power such truths as the unique dignity of each person, the communitarian character of human existence, the value of reason, the possibility of forgiveness, and the mandate to begin ethics with a preferential concern for the poor. Over the centuries it has been clogged with patriarchal silt and sediment, and in our day the life-giving waters have carved out new channels, including some that have figured prominently in this book, especially Catholic feminist forms of liberation theology and revisionist moral theology. All the channels have limitations, but they do carry wisdom, the extent of which will best be known by the fruitfulness made possible when the wisdom touches situations that would otherwise be barren.

To transform our world's desert of injustice, violence, and ecological irre-

---

75. Helder Câmara, *The Desert Is Fertile,* trans. Dinah Livingstone (Maryknoll, N.Y.: Orbis, 1974).

sponsibility, surely many streams of wisdom are required beyond the Catholic one. Fortunately the planet is blessed with a number of religious and ethical traditions, great and small, each of which contributes wisdom that can inspire people to live more justly and lovingly on this planet. In fact, in 1993 representatives of many of these traditions gathered in Chicago to commemorate the centenary of the Parliament of World's Religions. There they affirmed a "Declaration Toward a Global Ethic" based on values and insights held in common, including the following four principles:

1. Commitment to a culture of nonviolence and respect for life.
2. Commitment to a culture of solidarity and a just economic order.
3. Commitment to a culture of tolerance and a life of truthfulness.
4. Commitment to a culture of equal rights and partnership between men and women.[76]

Signatories to this 1993 declaration included representatives of many faith traditions: Bahai, Brahma Kumaris, Buddhism, Christianity, Hinduism, Jainism, Judaism, Islam, Neo-pagans, Sikhs, Taoists, Theosophists, Zoroastrians, and several indigenous religions (including Akuapi, Yoruba, and Native American) as well as a few inter-religious organizations.

Catholics contributed much to this declaration, and our moral tradition has a great deal of wisdom to bring to the task its signatories identified as common to all religions today, namely, to convert the world's peoples to "a common global ethic, to better mutual understanding, as well as to socially-beneficial, peace-fostering, and Earth-friendly ways of life."[77]

The hope of the archbishop who trusted in God's power to render the desert fertile must inspire Catholics today to clear the impediments of patriarchy from the river of moral wisdom that is our heritage. Although the seminary Dom Helder Câmara founded has been closed and one of its leading teachers exiled, the commitment to truth, love, and justice remains alive. This positive energy is the gift of God's Spirit, working mysteriously in our ambiguous lives and history to renew the face of the earth.

76. Hans Küng and Karl-Josef Kuschel, eds., *A Global Ethic: The Declaration of the Parliament of the World's Religions* (New York: Continuum, 1993), pp. 24–36.
77. Ibid., p. 36.

Selected Bibliography

Adams, Carol J., ed. *Ecofeminism and the Sacred*. New York: Continuum, 1993.

Andolsen, Barbara Hilkert. *Daughters of Jefferson, Daughters of Bootblacks: Racism and American Feminism*. Macon, Ga.: Mercer University Press, 1986.

———. *Good Work at the Video Display Terminal: An Ethical Analysis of the Effects of Office Automation on Clerical Workers*. Knoxville: University of Tennessee Press, 1989.

———, ed. "Professional Resources: Selected Topics in Feminist and Womanist Ethics." *The Annual of the Society of Christian Ethics* (1994): 257–305.

Andolsen, Barbara Hilkert, Christine Gudorf, and Mary Pellauer, eds. *Women's Consciousness, Women's Conscience: A Reader in Feminist Ethics*. Minneapolis: Seabury, 1985.

Aquino, María Pilar. *Our Cry for Life: Feminist Theology from Latin America*. Trans. Dinah Livingstone. Maryknoll, NY: Orbis, 1993.

Boyle, John P. *Church Teaching Authority: Historical and Theological Studies*. Notre Dame, Ind.: University of Notre Dame Press, 1995.

———. *The Sterilization Controversy: A New Crisis for the Catholic Hospital?* New York: Paulist, 1977.

Brown, Joanne Carlson, and Carole R. Bohn, eds. *Christianity, Patriarchy, and Abuse: A Feminist Critique*. New York: Pilgrim Press, 1989.

Buchwald, Emilie, Pamela R. Fletcher, and Martha Roth, eds. *Transforming a Rape Culture*. Minneapolis: Milkweed Editions, 1993.

Butler, Sara, ed. *CTSA Research Report: Women in Church and Society*. Bronx, N.Y.: Catholic Theological Society of America, 1978.

Cahill, Lisa Sowle. "Abortion, Sex and Gender: The Church's Public Voice." *America* (May 22, 1993): 6–11.

———. "Feminist Ethics." *Theological Studies* 51 (March 1990): 49–64.

———. "Feminist Ethics and the Challenges of Cultures." *CTSA Proceedings* 48 (1993): 65–83.

———. *Love Your Enemies: Discipleship, Pacifism, and Just War Theory.* Minneapolis: Fortress, 1994.

———. *Women and Sexuality.* New York: Paulist, 1992.

Cahill, Lisa Sowle, and Margaret A. Farley, eds. *Embodiment, Morality, and Medicine.* Norwell, Mass.: Kluwer Academic Publishers, 1995.

Callahan, Sidney. *In Good Conscience: Reason and Emotion in Moral Decision Making.* San Francisco: HarperSanFrancisco, 1991.

Carmody, Denise Lardner. *Virtuous Woman: Reflections on Christian Feminist Ethics.* Maryknoll, N.Y.: Orbis, 1992.

Carr, Anne E. *Transforming Grace: Christian Tradition and Women's Experience.* San Francisco: Harper & Row, 1988.

Condit, Celeste Michelle. *Decoding Abortion Rhetoric: Communicating Social Change.* Urbana: University of Illinois Press, 1990.

Conn, Joann Wolski. *Spirituality and Personal Maturity.* New York: Paulist, 1989.

Conn, Walter E. *Conscience: Development and Self-Transcendence.* Birmingham, Ala.: Religious Education Press, 1981.

Cooper-White, Pamela. *The Cry of Tamar: Violence Against Women and the Church's Response.* Minneapolis: Fortress, 1995.

Copeland, M. Shawn. "Reconsidering the Idea of the Common Good." In *Catholic Social Thought and the New World Order,* ed. Oliver F. Williams and John W. Houck, 309–27. Notre Dame, Ind.: University of Notre Dame Press, 1993.

———. "Theology as Intellectually Vital Inquiry: A Black Theological Interrogation." *CTSA Proceedings* 46 (1991): 56–57.

Coriden, James, ed. *Sexism and Church Law: Equal Rights and Affirmative Action.* New York: Paulist, 1977.

Curran, Charles E. *Catholic Higher Education, Theology, and Academic Freedom.* Notre Dame, Ind.: University of Notre Dame Press, 1990.

———. *Faithful Dissent.* Kansas City: Sheed & Ward, 1986.

Curran, Charles E., Margaret A. Farley, and Richard A. McCormick, eds. *Readings in Moral Theology No. 9: Feminist Ethics.* New York: Paulist, 1996.

Daly, Lois K., ed. *Feminist Theological Ethics: A Reader.* Louisville: Westminster John Knox Press, 1994.

Farley, Margaret A. "New Patterns of Relationship: Beginnings of a Moral Revolution," *Theological Studies* 36 (1975): 627–46.

———. *Personal Commitments: Beginning, Keeping, Changing.* San Francisco: Harper & Row, 1986.

———. "Power and Powerlessness: A Case in Point." *CTSA Proceedings* 37 (1982): 116–19.

Ferraro, Barbara, and Patricia Hussey (with Jane O'Reilly). *No Turning Back: Two Nuns' Battle with the Vatican over Women's Right to Choose.* New York: Poseidon Press, 1990.

Fortune, Marie. *Sexual Violence: The Unmentionable Sin.* New York: Pilgrim Press, 1983.

Fuentes, Carlos. *The Good Conscience.* Trans. Sam Hileman. New York: Noonday, 1961.

Gallagher, John P. *Time Past, Time Future: An Historical Study of Catholic Moral Theology.* New York: Paulist, 1990.

Gardiner, Anne Marie, ed. *Women and Catholic Priesthood.* New York: Paulist, 1976.

Gilligan, Carol. *In a Different Voice: Psychological Theory and Women's Development.* Cambridge, Mass.: Harvard University Press, 1982.

Graff, Ann O'Hara, ed. *In the Embrace of God: Feminist Approaches to Theological Anthropology.* Maryknoll, N.Y.: Orbis, 1995.

Gudorf, Christine E. *Body, Sex, and Pleasure: Reconstructing Christian Sexual Ethics.* Cleveland, Oh.: Pilgrim, 1994.

———. *Victimization: Examining Christian Complicity.* Philadelphia: Trinity Press International, 1992.

Guindon, André. *The Sexual Creators: An Ethical Proposal for Concerned Christians.* Lanham, Md.: University Press of America, 1986.

———. *The Sexual Language: An Essay in Moral Theology.* Ottawa: University of Ottawa Press, 1976.

Häring, Bernard. *My Witness for the Church.* Trans. Leonard Swidler. New York: Paulist, 1992.

Harrison, Beverly W. *Making the Connections: Essays in Feminist Social Ethics.* Edited by Carol S. Robb. Boston: Beacon, 1985.

———. *Our Right to Choose: Toward a New Ethic of Abortion.* Boston: Beacon, 1983.

Hayes, Diana L. *Hagar's Daughters: Womanist Ways of Being in the World.* New York: Paulist, 1995.

Heyward, Carter. *Our Passion for Justice.* New York: Pilgrim Press, 1984.

Hinsdale, Mary Ann, and Phyllis H. Kaminski, eds. *Women and Theology.* Maryknoll, N.Y.: Orbis, 1995.

Hinze, Christine Firer. "Bridge Discourse on Wage Justice: Roman Catholic and Feminist Perspectives on the Family Living Wage." *The Annual of the Society of Christian Ethics* (1991): 133–50.

Hunt, Mary E. *Fierce Tenderness: A Feminist Theology of Friendship.* New York: Crossroad, 1991.

Isasi-Díaz, Ada María. *En La Lucha: A Hispanic Women's Liberation Theology.* Minneapolis: Fortress, 1993.

———. *Mujerista Theology: A Theology for the Twenty-First Century.* Maryknoll, N.Y.: Orbis, forthcoming.

Isasi-Díaz, Ada María, and Yolanda Tarango. *Hispanic Women: Prophetic Voice in the Church.* San Francisco: Harper & Row, 1988. Rpt. Minneapolis: Fortress, 1992.

Johnson, Elizabeth. *She Who Is.* New York: Crossroad, 1992.

———. *Women, Earth, and Creator Spirit.* New York: Paulist, 1993.

Journal of Feminist Studies in Religion 9 (1993). Special issue on feminist ethics in honor of Beverly Wildung Harrison.

Jung, Patricia Beattie. "Give Her Justice." *America* 150 (April 14, 1984): 276–78.

Jung, Patricia Beattie, and Ralph F. Smith. *Heterosexism: An Ethical Challenge.* Albany: State University of New York Press, 1993.

Jung, Patricia Beattie, and Thomas A. Shannon, eds. *Abortion and Catholicism: The American Debate.* New York: Crossroad, 1988.

Kaiser, Robert Blair. *The Politics of Sex and Religion.* Kansas City, Mo.: Leaven Press, 1985.

Keane, Philip S. *Christian Ethics and Imagination: A Theological Inquiry.* New York: Paulist, 1984.

King, Ursula, ed. *Feminist Theology from the Third World: A Reader.* Maryknoll, N.Y.: Orbis, 1994.

Kolbenschlag, Madonna, ed. *Authority, Community and Conflict.* Kansas City, Mo.: Sheed & Ward, 1986.

———. *Kiss Sleeping Beauty Goodbye: Breaking the Spell of Feminine Myths and Models.* 1979. Rpt. New York: Bantam Books, 1981.

Küng, Hans, and Karl-Josef Kuschel, eds. *A Global Ethic: The Declaration of the Parliament of the World's Religions.* New York: Continuum, 1993.

LaCugna, Catherine, ed. *Freeing Theology: The Essentials of Theology in Feminist Perspective.* San Francisco: HarperSanFrancisco, 1993.

Lebacqz, Karen. "Love Your Enemy: Sex, Power, and Christian Ethics." *The Annual of the Society of Christian Ethics* (1990): 3–23.

Lerner, Gerda. *The Creation of Feminist Consciousness.* New York: Oxford University Press, 1993.

———. *The Creation of Patriarchy.* New York: Oxford University Press, 1986.

Lugones, María C. "On the Logic of Pluralist Feminism." In *Feminist Ethics,* ed. Claudia Card, 35–44. Lawrence: University Press of Kansas, 1991.

Maguire, Daniel C. *A Case for Affirmative Action.* Dubuque, Ia.: Shepherd, 1992.

———. *The Moral Choice.* Garden City, N.Y.: Doubleday, 1978.

Mahoney, John. *The Making of Moral Theology: A Study of the Roman Catholic Tradition.* Oxford: Clarendon Press, 1987.

May, William W., ed. *Vatican Authority and American Catholic Dissent: The Curran Case and Its Consequences.* New York: Crossroad, 1987.

McCormick, Richard A. *Corrective Vision: Explorations in Moral Theology.* Kansas City, Mo.: Sheed & Ward, 1994.

———. *The Critical Calling: Reflections on Moral Dilemmas Since Vatican II.* Washington, D.C.: Georgetown University Press, 1989.

Mieth, Dietmar, and Jacques Pohier, eds. *Changing Values and Virtues.* Edinburgh: T & T Clark, 1987.

Miles, Margaret R. *Practicing Christianity: Critical Perspectives for an Embodied Spirituality.* New York: Crossroad, 1988.

Milhaven, Annie Lally, ed. *The Inside Stories: 13 Valiant Women Challenging the Church.* Mystic, Conn.: Twenty-Third Publications, 1987.

Mooney, Christopher F. *Inequality and the American Conscience.* Mahwah, N.J.: Paulist, 1982.

Moser, Antonio, and Bernardino Leers. *Moral Theology: Dead Ends and Alternatives.* Trans. Paul Burns. Maryknoll, N.Y.: Orbis, 1990.

Moser, Theresa, and James A. Donahue, eds. *Ethics and the Common Good.* Mystic, Conn.: Twenty-Third Publications, 1996.

Murdoch, Iris. *The Sovereignty of Good.* New York: Schocken Books, 1971.

———. "Vision and Choice in Morality." In *Christian Ethics and Contemporary Philosophy,* ed. Ian Ramsey, 195–218. New York: Macmillan, 1966.

National Conference of Catholic Bishops. *Brothers and Sisters to Us.* Washington, D.C.: United States Catholic Conference, 1979.

———. *The Challenge of Peace: God's Promise and Our Response.* Washington, D.C.: United States Catholic Conference, 1983.

———. "Confronting a Culture of Violence." *Origins* 24 (December 1, 1994): 422–30.

———. "Doctrinal Responsibilities: Approaches to Promoting Cooperation and Resolving Misunderstandings Between Bishops and Theologians." *Origins* 19 (June 29, 1989): 97–110.

———. *The Hispanic Presence: Challenge and Commitment.* Washington, D.C.: United States Catholic Conference, 1983.

Neal, Marie Augusta. *The Just Demands of the Poor.* New York: Paulist, 1987.

Nugent, Robert, ed. *A Challenge to Love.* New York: Crossroad, 1983.

Nugent, Robert, and Jeannine Gramick. *Building Bridges: Gay and Lesbian Reality and the Catholic Church.* Mystic, Conn.: Twenty-Third Publications, 1992.

Nussbaum, Martha C. *The Fragility of Goodness: Luck and Ethics in Greek Tragedy and Philosophy.* Cambridge: Cambridge University Press, 1986.

O'Brien, William J., ed. *Jesuit Education and the Cultivation of Virtue.* Washington, D.C.: Georgetown University Press, 1990.

O'Connell, Timothy. *Principles for a Catholic Morality.* New York: Seabury, 1978.

O'Connor, June E. *The Moral Vision of Dorothy Day: A Feminist Perspective.* New York: Crossroad, 1991.

Overberg, Kenneth R., ed. *AIDS, Ethics & Religion: Embracing a World of Suffering.* Maryknoll, N.Y.: Orbis, 1994.

Patrick, Anne E. "Authority, Women, and Church: Reconsidering the Relationship." In *Empowering Authority,* ed. Patrick J. Howell and Gary Chamberlain, 31–49. Kansas City: Sheed & Ward, 1990.

———. "Inculturation, Catholicity, and Social Justice." *CTSA Proceedings* 45 (1990): 41–55.

Peter-Raoul, Mar, Linda Rennie Forcey, and Robert Frederick Hunter, Jr., eds. *Yearning to Breathe Free: Liberation Theologies in the U.S.* Maryknoll, N.Y.: Orbis, 1990.

Phelps, Jamie T., ed., *Black and Catholic: The Challenge and Gift of Black Folk: Contributions of African American Experience and World View to Catholic Theology.* Milwaukee: Marquette University Press, forthcoming.

———. "Women and Power in the Church: A Black-Catholic Perspective." *CTSA Proceedings* 37 (1982): 119–23.

Pohier, Jacques, and Dietmar Mieth, eds. *Christian Ethics: Uniformity, Universality, Pluralism.* New York: Seabury, 1981.

Porter, Jean. "Moral Reasoning, Authority, and Community in *Veritatis splendor.*" *The Annual of the Society of Christian Ethics* (1995): 201–19.

———. *The Recovery of Virtue: The Relevance of Aquinas for Christian Ethics.* Louisville: Westminster John Knox, 1990.

Quiñonez, Lora Ann, and Mary Daniel Turner. *The Transformation of American Catholic Sisters.* Philadelphia: Temple University Press, 1992.

Raiche, Annabelle, and Ann Marie Biermaier. *They Came to Teach.* St. Cloud, Minn.: North Star Press, 1994.

Raming, Ida. *The Exclusion of Women from the Priesthood: Divine Law or Sex Discrimination? A Historical Investigation of the Juridical and Doctrinal Foundations of the Code of Canon Law, Canon 968, Section 1.* Trans. Norman R. Adams. Metuchen, N.J.: Scarecrow Press, 1976.

Ricoeur, Paul. *The Symbolism of Evil.* Boston: Beacon, 1967.

Ross, W. D. *The Right and the Good.* Oxford: Clarendon Press, 1930.

Ruether, Rosemary Radford. *Gaia and God: An Ecofeminist Theology of Earth Healing.* San Francisco: HarperSanFrancisco, 1992.

———. *Sexism and God-Talk: Toward a Feminist Theology.* Boston: Beacon, 1983.

———, ed. *Women Healing Earth: Third-World Women on Ecology, Feminism and Religion.* Maryknoll, N.Y.: Orbis, 1996.

Saiving, Valerie [Goldstein]. "The Human Situation: A Feminine View." *Journal of Religion* 40 (April 1960): 100–112.

Sands, Kathleen M. *Escape from Paradise: Evil and Tragedy in Feminist Theology.* Minneapolis: Fortress, 1994.

———. "Uses of the Thea(o)logian: Sex and Theodicy in Religious Feminism." *Journal of Feminist Studies in Religion* 8/1 (Spring 1992): 7–33.

Sapiro, Virginia. *The Political Integration of Women: Roles, Socialization, and Politics.* Urbana: University of Illinois Press, 1983.

Schüssler Fiorenza, Elisabeth, and Anne E. Carr, eds. *Women, Work and Poverty.* Edinburgh: T & T Clark, 1987.

Schüssler Fiorenza, Elisabeth, and M. Shawn Copeland, eds. *Violence Against Women.* Maryknoll, N.Y.: Orbis, 1994.

Secker, Susan L. "Human Experience and Women's Experience: Resources for Catholic Ethics." *The Annual of the Society of Christian Ethics* (1991): 133–50.

Segers, Mary C., ed. *Church Polity and American Politics: Issues in Contemporary American Catholicism.* New York: Garland, 1990.

Soelle, Dorothee. *Beyond Mere Obedience.* Trans. Laurence W. Denef. New York: Pilgrim Press, 1982.

Spelman, Elizabeth V. *Inessential Woman: Problems of Exclusion in Feminist Thought.* Boston: Beacon, 1988.

Timmerman, Joan. *The Mardi Gras Syndrome: Rethinking Christian Sexuality.* New York: Crossroad, 1984.

———. *Sexuality and Spiritual Growth.* New York: Crossroad, 1992.

Townes, Emily M., ed. *A Troubling in My Soul: Womanist Perspectives on Evil and Suffering.* Maryknoll, N.Y.: Orbis, 1993.

Tracy, David. *Plurality and Ambiguity: Hermeneutics, Religion, Hope.* San Francisco: Harper & Row, 1987.

Untener, Kenneth. "Domestic Violence." *Origins* 23 (October 28, 1993): 357–58.

———. "*Humanae Vitae:* What Has It Done to Us?" *Commonweal* (June 18, 1994): 12–14.

Ware, Ann Patrick. "A Case Study in Oppression: A Theological and Personal Analysis." Chicago: National Coalition of American Nuns, 1993.

———, ed. *Naming Our Truth: Stories of Loretto Women.* Inverness, Calif.: Chardon Press, 1995.

Warnock, G. J. *Morality and Language.* Totowa, N.J.: Barnes & Noble Books, 1983.

Warnock, Mary. *Ethics Since 1900.* 3rd ed. Oxford: Oxford University Press, 1978.

Weaver, Mary Jo. *Springs of Water in a Dry Land: Spiritual Survival for Catholic Women Today.* Boston: Beacon, 1993.

Welch, Sharon D. *A Feminist Ethic of Risk.* Minneapolis: Fortress, 1990.

Yeager, D. M. "On Making the Tree Good: An Apology for a Dispositional Ethics." *Journal of Religious Ethics* 10/1 (Spring 1982): 103–20.

Index